M000250840

Grade 4 Teacher's Guide

EVERY DAY
COUNTS®
CALENDAR MATH

Janet G. Gillespie

Patsy F. Kanter

GReaT SouRCe®
EDUCATION GROUP
A Houghton Mifflin Company
New Ways to Know®

ACKNOWLEDGMENTS

We offer special thanks to

- **our mentors:** the late Mary Baratta-Lorton, Marilyn Burns, Andy Clark, Jay Greenwood, Constance Kamii, Ruby Payne, Kathy Richardson, Allyn Snider, and the late Robert Wirtz for inspiring and guiding our work in the classroom through their workshops and writing.

- **our families:** Tim, Nathan, and Josh Gillespie; and David, Julie, and Nathan Kanter for making our lives count every day and without whose support none of this could have been written.

- **our contributing authors:** Andy Clark, Karen Hardin, and Esta Elizondo for their vision and expertise.

- **our parents:** Nat and Louise Friedler and Ragnar and Anna Giske for being our first teachers and for believing in us and valuing our work as teachers.

- **the Great Source team:** Evelyn Curley, Betsy Donaghey, Rick Duthe, Kathy Kellman, Susan Rogalski, and Richard Spencer for making this edition of *Every Day Counts*® *Calendar Math* a reality.

CREDITS

Cover Design: Kristen Davis, Great Source
Cover Art: Amy Vangsgard & Kristen Davis
Design: Taurins Design
Electronic Art: Taurins Design

Copyright © 2005 by Great Source Education Group, a division of Houghton Mifflin Company. All rights reserved.

Permission is hereby granted to the teacher who has purchased the *Every Day Counts*® *Calendar Math* Grade 4 kit (ISBN 0-669-51451-9) to reprint or photocopy in a quantity for a single classroom the Planner (page 11), the Assessment section (pages 141–161), and the Teaching Resources in this work that carry a copyright notice, provided each copy made shows the copyright notice. Such copies may not be sold and further distribution is expressly prohibited. Except as authorized above, prior written permission must be obtained from Great Source Education Group to reproduce or transmit this work or portions thereof in any other form or by any other electronic or mechanical means, including any information storage or retrieval system, unless expressly permitted by federal copyright law. Address inquiries to Permissions, Great Source Education Group, 181 Ballardvale Street, Wilmington, MA 01887.

Great Source®, *Every Day Counts*®, and *New Ways to Know*® are registered trademarks of Houghton Mifflin Company.

Printed in China

International Standard Book Number-10: 0-669-51452-7

International Standard Book Number-13: 978-0-669-51452-0

8 9 10 11 1639 13 12 11 10 09

4500205701

TABLE OF CONTENTS

Letter from the Authors 4

Welcome to Every Day Counts Calendar Math 5

Getting Started 8

Customizing Your Plans 10

Scope and Sequence 12

August/September 16

October 30

November 46

December 60

January 74

February 90

March 104

April 118

May/June 132

Bibliography 140

Assessment 141

Teaching Resources 162

Index 187

Dear Fellow Teachers,

We are so glad that you have chosen *Every Day Counts® Calendar Math* for your classroom. For our new users, welcome and for our veteran users, thanks for your continued confidence in and support for *Every Day Counts Calendar Math*.

Every Day Counts Calendar Math is built on our many years of classroom experience teaching mathematics. An interactive K–6 supplemental mathematics program, *Every Day Counts Calendar Math* is designed to capitalize on daily discussions to foster children's mathematical confidence and competence. The program is based on our observations from our years of teaching and is supported by research that shows:

1. Children need to learn mathematics incrementally, giving them the opportunity to develop understandings over time.

2. Visual models help children visualize and verbalize number and geometric relationships.

3. Classroom discussion fosters the growth of language acquisition and development of reasoning. It also allows children to discover that there are many strategies for solving problems.

4. Over time, children can learn to think algebraically. Early exposure to this type of thinking will lead them to a successful future in mathematics.

5. Observing and listening to children is essential to ongoing assessment that can guide instruction.

This edition of *Every Day Counts Calendar Math* has new features to reduce your workload, and new elements to increase the level of success for your students. The Teacher's Guide is organized to aid instruction: **Concepts and Skills** tell the focus of each lesson, **Author Notes** explain the thinking behind the elements, **Materials** and **Setup** list preparation tips, and **Daily Routine** outlines the update procedure. As always **Discussion** offers questions and sample dialogues to help guide your lessons, and **Helpful Hints** further enrich the lessons. New to this edition are **Ongoing Assessment** questions that reveal individual children's knowledge and help you to meet different students' instructional needs. Ongoing Assessment also appears in a separate booklet in the kit for easy use during Calendar time.

The kit contains the usual materials needed to get started—counting tape paper, a Calendar, Calendar Pieces for each month, month strips, yesterday, today, and tomorrow markers for grades K–2, demo coins, play money for grades 3–5, and plastic pockets. New to this kit are some background posters to arrange the bulletin board with ease, Counting Tape Pieces to count the days in school, manipulatives, paper clips to get the calendars ready for immediate use, and storage bags.

We have learned much from our teaching colleagues and appreciate their support, suggestions and the opportunities to teach together. Most of all we offer our thanks to our main teachers—the children throughout the country with whom we've had the privilege to work, and who have taught us so much. Best wishes to you as you teach math this year and in years to come.

Collegially,

Janet Gillespie *Patsy F. Kanter*

© Great Source. Copying is prohibited.

WELCOME TO EDC CALENDAR MATH

Every Day Counts® Calendar Math appeals to the natural way children learn math—building on concepts a little at a time, every day. Simple to use, the Teacher's Guide and kit contain a full year of activities with suggestions for discussions that will have your students excited about "talking math."

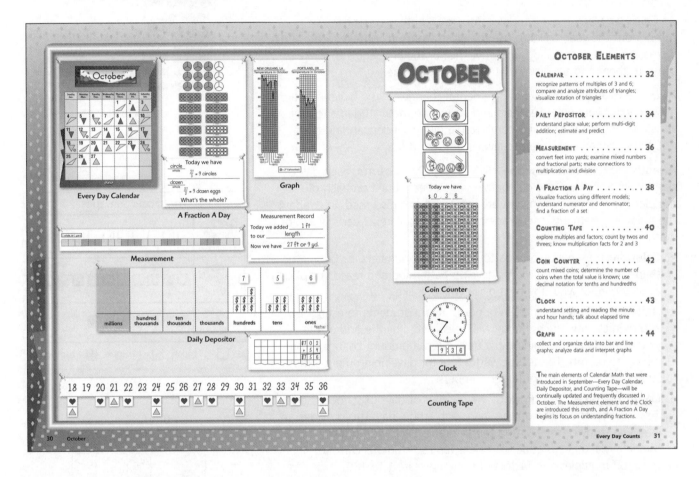

A lot of math in a little time. In just 10–15 minutes a day, *Every Day Counts* provides supplemental math instruction that revolves around a simple interactive bulletin board with a variety of elements, or components. As children build the bulletin board, they also build mathematical understanding and confidence. Great progress is made in small incremental steps.

Children learn from their discoveries. Students' observations and thinking are the driving force behind *Every Day Counts.* Different monthly elements provide a continuous learning experience in which students examine mathematical relationships central to the curriculum for their grade level. This daily, visual, hands-on exposure to critical math concepts complements the natural way children learn—building on concepts a little at a time, every day, to help them develop mathematical competence and confidence.

"The EDC board was a hit with my kids because it was interactive and it was not from a book. It was almost difficult to convince them that it was math! It dovetailed into so many areas that the book covers anyway, it was either a great introduction or a great review for many concepts."

Linda Hoerling-Glenn

Teacher, Tacoma, WA

© Great Source. Copying is prohibited.

Classroom discussion: the heart of *Every Day Counts*. With the discussion questions that are provided for a variety of levels, children use mathematical language to explain their thinking in the common "folk language" of math such as "I had 5 marbles and I got 3 more, and now I have 8." Asking students to share the various ways they arrived at answers helps them see that

- There are many ways to work with numbers
- There is more than one way to approach a problem
- The same way of working out a problem may be explained in several different ways.

As Calendar Math conversations continue and grow in depth throughout the year, children use the math words in context with increasing confidence and familiarity. The vocabulary begins to make sense to them and becomes part of their knowledge.

Help for struggling learners. Incremental changes in the bulletin board allow English Language Learners and struggling math students to build skills and understanding at a comfortable rate. If understanding does not come immediately, there is always another day.

A mathematical kaleidoscope. With *Every Day Counts*, each day is slightly different from the day before. As students build on each of the elements, new relationships are examined and discussed. In Grade 4 the following elements encourage students to explore a year's worth of math concepts and skills:

- **Calendar** presents unique patterns of colors, numbers, or geometric shapes each month. Students develop patterning and reasoning skills as they predict what the next piece will look like.

- **Daily Depositor** provides an opportunity for students to estimate and predict how much money will be collected by the end of the year as the rule determining the daily deposit amount changes from month to month. This is a powerful tool for developing mental math strategies for addition of larger numbers.

- **Counting Tape** keeps track of the number of days of school as one new number is written on the Tape each school day. This provides an intensive study of multiples in fourth grade. Each month, new Multiple Markers are attached to the Tape so students can see common multiples and factors of numbers from 1 to 180.

- **Coin Counter** gives students practice with counting mixed coins, determining change from purchases of one or more of an item, and understanding decimal notation by seeing pennies and dimes as hundredths and tenths of dollars.

- **Graph** offers a variety of activities, opinion polls, and probability experiments for students to gather, display, and interpret a variety of data in many different contexts.

- **A Fraction A Day** introduces students to fractions, mixed numbers, equivalent fractions, and simplifying using a variety of models. Students use fractions to describe parts of wholes and parts of sets.

- **Measurement** helps students experience the language of estimation, comparing, and measuring using customary and metric units of length, capacity, and weight.

- **Clock** gives students daily practice reading and setting the hands on the clock, understanding A.M. and P.M., and moving ahead and back.

Daily Depositor

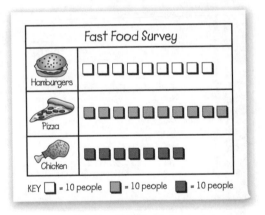

Graph

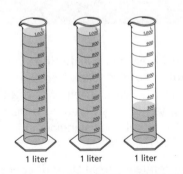

1 liter   1 liter   1 liter

Measurement Record

Today we added ___100 mL___

to our ___container___ .

Now we have ___2.3 L, or___
___$2\frac{3}{10}$ L, or 2,300 mL.___

Measurement

© Great Source. Copying is prohibited.

A Comprehensive Teacher's Guide. The Teacher's Guide for each grade level of *Every Day Counts* is organized by month and by elements. Each month begins with a picture of what the bulletin board might look like toward the middle of the month. A brief overview of suggested elements and activities for the month follows. As each element is introduced, you will find:

- **Concepts & Skills** for that activity

- A list of **Materials** for the activities, all either in the kit or readily available like paper clips

- The **Daily Routine**, which provides an easy-to-follow explanation of how to present this month's activities

- **Discussions** with suggestions for discussion and assessment as well as sample dialogues

- **Helpful Hints** to share ideas such as games, literature, or extensions of the month's activities. Many of these hints originated with teachers using *Calendar Math* in their classrooms.

Key math **vocabulary** terms are highlighted where they are first introduced and are also defined and illustrated in the Teacher Resource section.

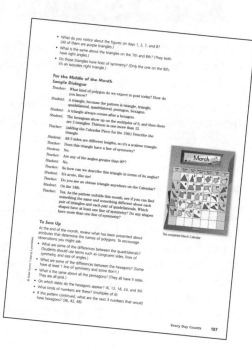

ONGOING ASSESSMENT TOOLS

- The **Ongoing Assessment** booklet provides an organized list of suggested assessment questions for use with each month's activities. These questions may also be used as a quick reference guide to instruction on days when time is limited.

- Each month **Ongoing Assessment** questions for each element are provided in the Teacher's Guide to help you gain insight into children's developing mathematical thinking.

- The teacher's everyday role is that of observer, listener, recorder, and questioner. Through daily observations and listening to children's discussions, assessment is ongoing.

- **Assessment copy masters** in the Teacher's Guide provide an easy way to capture progress at significant points of the year. A pretest for the beginning of the year allows you to assess children's prior knowledge. Two interim tests for use at the first and second quarters and a post test for the end of the year help you to gauge growth of understanding.

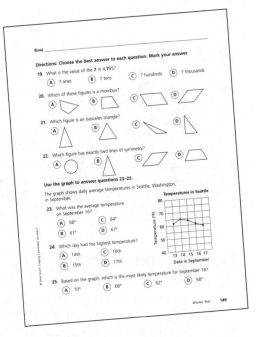

Every Day Counts® Calendar Math **is supported by research and practice.** Research shows that continuous exposure to critical math concepts allows children to develop an understanding of important mathematical concepts over time and to learn at an individual pace. Experience from classroom practice demonstrates that young children actively, incrementally construct mathematical knowledge. Understanding is solidified through reflection on real-life data, group discussion, and cooperative problem solving. The topics and challenges at each grade are aligned with NCTM standards and build on what students learn in class with activities that engage students, allowing them to explore, make and test conjectures, and apply their mathematics. Students using *Every Day Counts® Calendar Math* have been shown to develop higher-level thinking skills, enjoy math more, see its application in the real world, and score higher on standardized tests.

© Great Source. Copying is prohibited.

There is little preparation for *Every Day Counts Calendar Math*. Once the materials are prepared and organized, your prep work for the year is minimal.

The following materials will be very useful in organizing and preparing the materials in your kit: a roll of masking tape, a craft knife, a box of bulletin board push pins, and a stapler.

PREPARING THE CALENDAR

Use a "slit and clip" method to attach the Calendar Pieces to the Calendar. To prepare the Calendar use a craft knife to make a half-inch cut at the top of each space on the Calendar. You'll find a hairline rule at the top of each space to show you where to make the slit. Insert a small paper clip in each slit. Each Calendar Piece will slide beneath a clip. To secure the paper clips, put strips of masking tape over the paper clips on the back of the Calendar. This method allows you to place the Calendar on a wall or other surface that doesn't accept push pins.

Calendar

PREPARING THE DAILY DEPOSITOR

Place the Depositor poster on a flat surface with the green section on your left. Fold up the bottom section along the indicated fold line so you can read the place value names. Secure the fold and create the money pockets with a staple at each indicated location. Attach the Depositor to the bulletin board with several push pins.

millions	hundred thousands	ten thousands	thousands	hundreds	tens	ones
Every Day Counts* Daily Depositor						GREAT SOURCE EDUCATION GROUP

Daily Depositor

PREPARING THE COUNTING TAPE

Use the roll of adding machine tape in the kit to create the Counting Tape. Cut a piece of adding machine tape 4–5 feet long and attach it to the wall above your bulletin board. Write the daily numbers directly on the Tape throughout the school year. To make the Counting Tape continuous, add additional sections of adding machine tape as needed throughout the year. In Grade 4, cardstock Multiple Markers are attached to the Tape all year, so be sure it is posted securely.

© Great Source. Copying is prohibited.

ORGANIZING THE CARDSTOCK

You have a set of cardstock Calendar Pieces for the Calendar that are organized and labeled by month. Carefully punch out a set (three sheets) for each month. Put each month's pieces in the resealable plastic bags and label them with the name of the month. You can also store the 8 different cardstock Multiple Markers for the Counting Tape in envelopes or plastic bags.

CHOOSING AMONG THE POSSIBILITIES

Flip to the beginning of each month in this Teacher's Guide and scan through the range of elements that make up *Every Day Counts* at your grade level. The first year you might want to start small and limit the number of elements you share with the class. Your preparation can be minimized, and your primary focus can be facilitating class discussions. Begin with the year-long elements—the Calendar, Daily Depositor, and Counting Tape. You might also choose an element that provides experience with a topic students have had difficulty with in the past. As the year goes by and you become familiar with the program, you may choose to add new elements to further enrich your discussions.

September Calendar Pieces

ARRANGING THE EDC BULLETIN BOARD DISPLAY

Choose a place in your room where you can create a bulletin board that is easily accessible to you and your students. Many teachers who use *Every Day Counts* Counts do not hang everything in one location. Sometimes graphs are placed across the room or the Counting Tape is hung under the chalkboard. Some teachers choose an area where children can gather together on the floor to hold daily class meetings to make updates to the bulletin board.

PLANNING CLASS TIME

We recommend that the EDC discussion last for only 10–15 minutes each day. In order to stay within this time period all displays are updated, but only 1–2 elements are discussed. A quick update of the Counting Tape in Grade 3 might flow like this:

Teacher: Yesterday we had been in school 47 days. How many days have we been in school as of today?

Class: 48.

Teacher: Will today's square be pink or yellow?

Class: Yellow, because 48 is an even number.

This simple update takes less than 30 seconds. If the Counting Tape is to be discussed, an extended series of questions might be asked, such as:

Multiple Markers

- What day will it be in three days?

- How did you figure out that answer?

- Talk to us about a pattern you see on the Counting Tape.

If a special occasion means you will not have time for any EDC discussion, at least commit to keeping the display updated so the elements are always current.

© Great Source. Copying is prohibited.

CUSTOMIZING YOUR PLANS

Every classroom runs on a different schedule. You may have special events, field trips, or snow days that change your daily routine. To help you keep track of the concepts you want to cover with *Every Day Counts Calendar Math,* we have provided a simple planner copy master that you can use to organize your plans.

EDC Weekly Planner

	MONDAY Date: Nov 9 Day in School: 45	TUESDAY Date: Nov 10 Day in School: 46	WEDNESDAY Date: Nov 11 Day in School: 47	THURSDAY Date: Nov 12 Day in School: 48	FRIDAY Date: Nov 13 Day in School: 49 new Quart Drawing
Materials to Prepare				Counting Tape 48—multiple of 2, 3, and 4	Meas. cups, pints 3 quarts = 6 pints
Element to Discuss	Fraction A Day	Depositor— add 10 x $10			
Concepts to Focus on	$\frac{1}{4}$ dozen = 3 $\frac{9}{4}$ dozen = 27 = $2\frac{1}{4}$ dozen	add money for today and tomorrow		2 types of trapezoids on Calendar	purchases less than 49¢
Students to Observe	Ali – right angles Bobby – rectangles and squares			Kendra, Tim – multiples of 4 Pat – time after the half-hour	
Special Days			Veterans Day Holiday		

© Great Source. Copying is permitted; see page ii.

Every Day Counts

11

10   Customizing Your Plans

© Great Source. Copying is prohibited.

EDC WEEKLY PLANNER

	MONDAY Date: _____ Day in School: _____	TUESDAY Date: _____ Day in School: _____	WEDNESDAY Date: _____ Day in School: _____	THURSDAY Date: _____ Day in School: _____	FRIDAY Date: _____ Day in School: _____
Materials to Prepare					
Element to Discuss					
Concepts to Focus on					
Students to Observe					
Special Days					

© Great Source. Copying is permitted; see page ii.

Numbers & Operations	Aug/Sept	Oct	Nov	Dec	Jan	Feb	Mar	April	May/June
Whole Numbers									
place value	CC, CT, D	C, CC, D	C, CC, D	C, CL, CT, D	D, CC, CT, D	CT, D, H			D
represent/compare	CC, CT, D	C, CC, D	C, CC, D	C, CT, D	C, CC, CT, D	CT, D	CT, G		D
greater numbers	D	D	D	D	D	D	D	D	D
expanded form	D	D	D			D	D		
even/odd numbers	C, CT	C, D		D	D				
rounding	D		D	D		D	D		
factors	CT	CT	C, CT	CT	CT	CT	CT	CT	CT
multiples	C, CT	C, CL, CT	C, CT, D	CL, CT	C, CT, D	CT	C, CT, D	CT	CT
prime, composite, & triangular numbers						CT		C	CT
consecutive numbers				D	D				
estimation and/or mental math strategies	D	CL, D, M	CC, CL, M	D, CC, CT, M	CT, D, M	CC, D, H	D, M	C, D	CT, D
Decimals									
place value	CC, D	CC	CC	CC, F, M	CC	CC	M		
represent/compare	CC	CC	CC	M			M		
equivalencies				M		G	M		
Fractions									
as parts of a whole		F, M	F, M	CL, E, F, M	CC, F, M	G, H	M		
as parts of sets		F	F, M	F			M	F	
on number lines		M	F	F					
as divisions of whole numbers		F, M		M	M				
compare using models		F, M		M	M				
mixed numbers		F, M	F, M	F, M	F, M	CC	M	F	
simplest form		F, M	F, M	F	F, M		M	F	
fractions models		F, M	M	F	F, M		M	F	
compare/order decimals, fractions, & percents		F, M	F	CL, F	CC, F, M	G	M	F	
Addition									
fluency with whole numbers	CC, D	CL, D	CC, D	CC, D	CC, CT, D	D	CL, D, G	C, CL, D, F	D
add w/ fractions			M	F, M	F	F, M			
add w/ decimals					M				
add w/ mixed numbers			F						

© Great Source. Copying is prohibited.

KEY

C = CALENDAR   CC = COIN COUNTER   CL = CLOCK
CT = COUNTING TAPE   D = DAILY DEPOSITOR   E = ENDING THE YEAR   F = A FRACTION A DAY
G = GRAPH   H = ONE HUNDREDTH DAY CELEBRATION   M = MEASUREMENT

Numbers & Operations (Continued)	Aug/Sept	Oct	Nov	Dec	Jan	Feb	Mar	April	May/June
Subtraction									
fluency with whole numbers		CC	CC, D			D	CC, D, G		D
subtract w/ fractions				F					
subtract w/ decimals				CC		CC			
Multiplication									
multiply whole numbers	C, CT	CT	CT, D	C, CC, CT, D	CT, D	CC, CT, D, H	C, CT	CT, D	D
multiply w/ fractions		M, F		F					
Division									
divide w/ whole numbers	CT	CT, M	CT, F	CT	CT	H			
divide w/ fractions			M		F	F			
Properties									
commutative property	C, CT	CT	CT	E	CT	CT, H			
associative property	CT	CT		E		CT, H	CT	C	
distributive property	CT	CT		E, CC, D	CT	CC, H	CT		
identity property	CT	CT	C	E		H			
inverse operations	CT	CT, M	F	E, CT		H			

Algebra (Patterns and Functions)	Aug/Sept	Oct	Nov	Dec	Jan	Feb	Mar	April	May/June
describe/extend/predict visual, numeric, or geometric patterns	C, CC, CT, D	C, CC, CT, D, M	C, CC, CT, D, F, M	C, CT, D	C, CC	C, CC	C, CT, G	C, CT, D	C, CT
represent and analyze patterns w/ words, tables, or graphs	CT	CT	CT, D, F	CT, D	C, CC	C	C, CT	C	C
represent relations & functions w/ words, tables, or graphs		C			C		C		
expressions		CT	D, F	CT					
equations	CT, D	CT, D	CT, D, F	CT, E, M	D	CT, H	C, CT	C, CT	
order of operations	CT	CT		E	C		CT	C	
identify, describe constant or varying rates of change						C		C	C
use algebraic thinking to solve problems		D	C	CT	C, CC, D	C	C, CT, G	C	

Geometry	Aug/Sept	Oct	Nov	Dec	Jan	Feb	Mar	April	May/June
lines and angles			C	C		C	C		
geometric vocabulary	C	C	C	C	M	C	C		
transformations: slides, flips, turns	C	C	C			C			
congruence & similarity		C	C			M	C		
explore symmetry		C	C				C		

KEY

C = CALENDAR CC = COIN COUNTER CL = CLOCK
CT = COUNTING TAPE D = DAILY DEPOSITOR E = ENDING THE YEAR F = A FRACTION A DAY
G = GRAPH H = ONE HUNDREDTH DAY CELEBRATION M = MEASUREMENT

© Great Source. Copying is prohibited.

Geometry (Continued)	Aug/Sept	Oct	Nov	Dec	Jan	Feb	Mar	April	May/June
describe geometric relationships	C	C	C	C	C, CT	C, M	C, CT	C	C
explore perimeter, area, volume						M	C	M	
2-Dimensional Shapes (Plane Shapes)									
identify, compare, analyze attributes	C	C	C, CT		C, CT	M	C, G	C, CT, M	C, CT
classify according to properties	C	C	C		C		C	C, M	C
circles and related concepts					C				C
3-Dimensional Shapes (Solids)									
identify, compare, analyze attributes					C, M				
classify according to properties					C				

Measurement	Aug/Sept	Oct	Nov	Dec	Jan	Feb	Mar	April	May/June
length		M		M			G		
area						M		M	
perimeter						M		M	
weight					M				
capacity			M				M		
angle size						C			
choose appropriate tool and unit		M		M	M	C, M	M		
customary measures		M	M		M	M		M	
metric measures				M			M		
Celsius and Fahrenheit temperature and systems		G							
count/use money	CC, D	CC, D	CC, D	CC, D, F	CC, D	CC, D	CC, D	D	
time		CL	CL	CL		CL	CL	CL	

Data Analysis/Probability	Aug/Sept	Oct	Nov	Dec	Jan	Feb	Mar	April	May/June
Collect/Analyze/ Interpret Data									
design investigations					G				
collect/organize data	CT, D	C, D, G	G	CT	C, CC, G, M	D, G	CT, G		D, G
surveys					G				
experiments	G								
tables	CT	C, D	D	CT	C, CC	D, G			D, G
interpret graphs	G	G			G		G		
picture graphs					G				

© Great Source. Copying is prohibited.

KEY

C = CALENDAR   CC = COIN COUNTER   CL = CLOCK

CT = COUNTING TAPE   D = DAILY DEPOSITOR   E = ENDING THE YEAR   F = A FRACTION A DAY

G = GRAPH   H = ONE HUNDREDTH DAY CELEBRATION   M = MEASUREMENT

Data Analysis/Probability (Continued)	Aug/Sept	Oct	Nov	Dec	Jan	Feb	Mar	April	May/June
bar graphs	G	G							
line graphs		G							
stem-and-leaf plot		G							
explore mean, median, mode, and range							G		
develop inferences and predictions	G	D, G	D, F	CT, M	CT, D, G, M	M	CT, D, G		G
justify conclusions	G	D, G	D, F	CT	CT, D, M		CT, D, G		G
Probability									
explore outcomes expressed as likely, unlikely, equally likely, & impossible	G				G	G			
test predictions	G				G	G			
theoretical probability					G	G			

Problem Solving	Aug/Sept	Oct	Nov	Dec	Jan	Feb	Mar	April	May/June
apply a variety of appropriate strategies to solve problems (i.e. guess and check, make a list)	CC, D	D, F, G, M	CC, F, M	C, CC, CT, D, E	CC, CT, D, F, M	CC, CT, G, H, M	C, CC, CT, D, G, M	CT, F, M	D
monitor and reflect on the process of mathematical problem solving	CC, D, G	D, F, G, M	CC, F, M	CC, CT, D, E, M	CC, CT, D, F, M	CC, CT, G, H, M	C, CC,	CT, F, M CT, D, G	D
choose appropriate computation methods (pencil/paper, estimate, calculator, mental math)	D	CL, D, F, G, M	CC, D, F, M	CC, CT, D, E	CC, CT, D, F, M	CC, CT, H, M	D, CC, CT, D, G, M	CT, F, M	D

Reasoning & Proof	Aug/Sept	Oct	Nov	Dec	Jan	Feb	Mar	April	May/June
recognize reasoning and proof as fundamental aspects of mathematics	C, CC, CT, D, G	C, CL, CT, D, F, G, M	C, CC, CT, D, F, M	C, CC, CT, D, E, M	C, CC, CT, D, F, M	CC, CT, H, M	C, CC, CT, D, G, M	C, CT, F	C, D, G
select and use various types of reasoning and methods of proof	C, CC, CT, D, G	C, CL, CT, D, F, G, M	C, CC, CT, D, F, M	CC, CT, D, E, M	C, CC, CT, D, F, M	CC, CT, H, M	C, CC, CT, D, G, M	C, CT, F	C, D, G

Communication, Connections & Representation	Aut/Sept	Oct	Nov	Dec	Jan	Feb	Mar	April	May/June
communicate mathematical thinking	C, CC, CT, D, G	C, CL, CT, D, F, G, M	C, CC, CT, D, F, M	C, CT, D, E, M	C, CC, CT, D, F, M	CC, CT, H, M	C, CC, CT, D, G, M	CT, F	D, G
recognize and use connections among mathematical ideas	C, CC, CT, D, G	C, CT, D, F, G, M	C, CC, CT, D, F, M	C, CC, CT, D, E, M	C, CC, CT, D, F, MC	C, CT, H, M	C, CC, CT, D, G, M	CT, F	D, G
use representations to model and interpret mathematical phenomena	C, CC, CT, D, G	C, CL, CT, D, F, G, M	C, CC, CT, D, F, M	C, CC, CT, D, M	C, CC, CT, D, F, M	CC, CT, H, M	C, CC, CT, D, G, M	CT, F	D, G

© Great Source. Copying is prohibited.

KEY

C = CALENDAR   CC = COIN COUNTER   CL = CLOCK
CT = COUNTING TAPE   D = DAILY DEPOSITOR   E = ENDING THE YEAR   F = A FRACTION A DAY
G = GRAPH   H = ONE HUNDREDTH DAY CELEBRATION   M = MEASUREMENT

Every Day Calendar

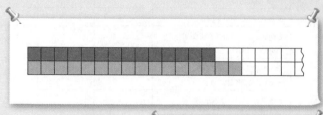

Graph

Predictions

- I predict that we will have the same number.
- I predict we will have half red and half blue.
- I predict we will have about 30 reds and 30 blues.

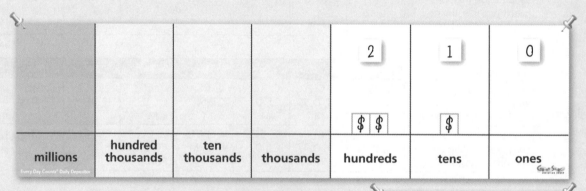

millions	hundred thousands	ten thousands	thousands	hundreds	tens	ones

Daily Depositor

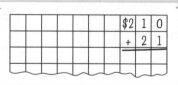

1 2 3 4 5 6 7 8 9

Counting Tape

SEPTEMBER

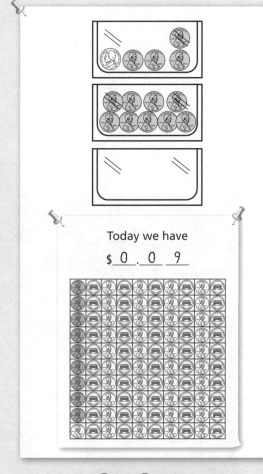

Today we have

$ _0_ . _0_ _9_

Coin Counter

AUGUST/SEPTEMBER ELEMENTS

CALENDAR **18**

analyze and predict patterns; recognize patterns of multiples of 2 and 5; compare and analyze attributes of two-dimensional shapes

DAILY DEPOSITOR **21**

use mental math; perform multi-digit addition; understand place value

COUNTING TAPE **23**

examine multiples of 2; observe counting patterns for even and odd numbers; explore multiplication and division

COIN COUNTER **26**

count mixed coins; create coin combinations for a given amount; use decimal notation for tenths and hundredths

GRAPH **28**

collect and organize data into a bar graph; predict and test the probability of outcomes of simple experiments

Getting started in fourth grade requires only a few elements of Every Day Counts Calendar Math. The number of elements used at the beginning of the school year is minimized in order to provide adequate time to establish a classroom procedure and to model desired classroom behavior. To begin, you will need the Every Day Calendar, the Daily Depositor, and the Counting Tape. The Coin Counter and Graph activities can be added later in the month.

The Calendar Pieces provided for August are identical to the pieces in September except that the colors have been changed. If your school year begins in August, attach the August Month Strip and Calendar Pieces, and catch up to the date of the first day of school. For example, if your school year begins on August 16th, put up all the Calendar Pieces from the 1st to the 16th of August. Make use of Calendar time in August to preview some of the math concepts that will be presented and discussed in September.

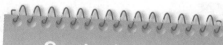

CALENDAR

Concepts & Skills

- Analyze and predict patterns
- Recognize patterns of multiples of 2 and 5
- Compare and analyze attributes of two-dimensional shapes
- Visualize rotation of two-dimensional shapes
- Reason logically

Materials for the Year

Every Day Calendar, Month Strip, and Calendar Pieces for the current month

Author Notes

"The Every Day Calendar uses numbered Calendar Pieces to create patterns. During Calendar discussions, early guesses may change to more reasoned theories as more information is revealed. This process calls upon students to share their reasoning, thereby solidifying their mathematical thinking. Summation activities help students communicate and clarify what they see on the Calendar. Describing patterns and developing the ability to generalize is the beginning of algebraic thinking.

The September Calendar pattern allows students to make predictions, to understand multiples of 2 and 5, and to examine common multiples. In addition, the Calendar Pieces explore attributes of the rectangle and the square. By seeing rectangles that are rotated every time they appear, students begin to understand that the properties of a figure are not changed when the orientation is changed."

Setup

- Display the Calendar with the September Month Strip attached.
- Post the Calendar Pieces from the first of the month. For example, put the first 4 pieces on the Calendar if you start school on September 4th.

Daily Routine

- Each day of the month, attach the Calendar Piece for that day. On Monday, add Calendar Pieces for Saturday and Sunday.
- Ask students to describe any patterns they see.
- Frequently, ask students to predict what will appear next or at some future date in the pattern. Allow time for students to share how they came up with their predictions.

Ongoing Assessment

1. What are the next two numbers in the pattern 5, 15, 25, 35?
2. Name two multiples of both 2 and 5 that are greater than 10.
3. Write one characteristic of a square that is not necessarily true of a rectangle.

The September Calendar Pieces use red squares and blue rectangles to create an ABAB pattern. The rectangle is rotated every time it appears, and is in a horizontal position on all multiples of 4. A yellow dot marks all multiples of 5.

© Great Source. Copying is prohibited.

DISCUSSION

For the Beginning of the Month

Ask students to tell what patterns they are beginning to see. Here are some possible responses:

- All the blue rectangles are even numbers.
- All the odd numbers are red squares.
- The pattern alternates red square, blue rectangle.
- 5 and 10 have dots on them.
- The rectangle is turned every time it appears.
- The pattern going up and down is also red, blue, red, blue.
- The diagonals are all the same color.

For the Middle of the Month

Geometry Some questions to emphasize concepts of rectangles, squares, congruence, and rotation include:

- What 2 shapes do you see on the Calendar? (squares, rectangles)
- What kind of corners does a rectangle have? (right angles or 90°)
- Describe the sides of the rectangle. (The opposite sides seem to be equal in length and parallel.)
- What does it mean that opposite sides are parallel? (If the sides were extended they would never meet.)
- What is the same about a square and rectangle? (Both have 4 corners, 4 right angles, and opposite sides equal and parallel. Both are closed figures and have straight sides.)
- What is different? (In a square all the sides are equal, but not always in the rectangle.) Students may say that a rectangle has long and short sides. Explain that this is not true of all rectangles. To be a rectangle, the shape must only have four right angles. This is very difficult for some students.
- Is a square a rectangle? Why? (Yes. Since a square is a quadrilateral with 4 right angles and opposite sides equal and parallel, it is a rectangle. A square is a special kind of rectangle in which all the sides are equal in length.)
- Why do the rectangles on the Calendar look different? (Some are standing up and some are lying down.)
- How are they the same? (It looks like they are the same shape and size.) Emphasize that if they are the same size and shape, we say the 2 shapes are congruent.
- How can you tell if they are congruent? (by measuring them)
- When a shape is turned it is called a rotation. How much are the rectangles turned each time they appear? (It looks like 90°.)

It is important to be able to describe shapes by attributes. We will return to these ideas and terms many times this year so all students can become familiar with them and use them to describe shapes.

© Great Source. Copying is prohibited.

For the End of the Month

Sample Dialogue

Teacher: What do we call the numbers 2, 4, 6, 8, 10, 12, and so on?

Student: They are even numbers.

Student: You can split them into 2 even groups.

Teacher: The math word we use to describe that is multiple . It means a number that is the product of that number and another number. It can be divided into even groups of that number without leaving any extras. Is 15 a multiple of 2?

Student: No, it can't be divided into 2 equal parts.

Teacher: Can someone describe a different pattern?

Student: I notice a pattern for the numbers 2, 6, 10, and 14. What is the same about the pieces?

Student: They are all blue rectangles standing up.

Teacher: What is the last blue rectangle that is standing up?

Student: 30.

Teacher: If the pattern continued, what would be the next number with a blue rectangle standing up?

Student: 34 because that is 4 more than 30.

Teacher: I notice something special about the pieces 10 and 20.

Student: They are blue rectangles with yellow dots.

Teacher: What would the next one be?

Student: 30.

Teacher: Do you see any other patterns?

> Sample vocabulary words are also defined and illustrated on TR23 and TR24. Encourage students to practice using these terms in class discussions.

What patterns do you see?

To Sum Up

Have students talk and/or write about their observations and findings. Create a chart with these observations. Some teachers like to label the patterns discovered with the student's name, thereby creating an environment in which all students are considered mathematicians making discoveries and observations.

HELPFUL HINTS

- Sometimes students discover patterns we have not seen. This is a wonderful opportunity to change roles with students and be on the discovery end of mathematics.

- Keep the Calendar Pieces in an envelope near the Calendar. Then a student can attach the next piece on days when time is short.

- Some teachers have students review multiplication facts that have been presented on the Calendar. One way to do this is to make a copy of the Multiplication Facts Progress Record (TR1) for each student. Have students color the facts for 2 blue when they know them fluently. They can color the facts for 5 yellow when they know those. Encourage students to use facts they know to figure out facts they are less fluent with. For example, if I know 5 × 5 is 25 because 5 nickels is 25 cents, then 6 × 5 is easy because it is just 5 more.

Calendar Observations

- All blue rectangles are even numbers.

- All red squares are odd numbers.

- The pattern alternates red square, blue rectangle.

- Multiples of 5 have yellow dots.

- The rectangle is turned every time it appears.

© Great Source. Copying is prohibited.

DAILY DEPOSITOR

Concepts & Skills

- Use mental math
- Perform multi-digit addition
- Understand place value
- Estimate and predict

Materials for the Year

Daily Depositor poster, Play Money cardstock or copies of TR2, Inch Squared Paper (TR3), large clear pocket, calculator

Author Notes

"The Daily Depositor is a place value mat that will help students sharpen their mental math skills, develop estimation strategies, and study place value in a problem-solving framework. From the first day it is used, it should be accompanied by predicting whether the Depositor will accumulate one million dollars by the end of the school year. It is important to encourage students to be independent thinkers and good risk takers. A non-threatening classroom environment will help students make predictions that may not be correct, but from which learning takes place. It is by this trial-and-error method, or by patterning, or by any other problem-solving strategy chosen that students become stronger mathematicians.

Students estimate how much money will be collected in September if they are given the number of dollars equal to the date for every day of the month. The amount of money added each day changes monthly throughout the year."

Setup

- Post the Daily Depositor poster on the board.
- To use the Inch Squared Paper as a recording sheet, put it in the large clear pocket and post it near the Depositor.

Daily Routine

- Each day in September, add a dollar amount equal to the date to the Depositor. Be sure to add money for weekend days and any other days students are not in school.
- If you cannot begin on September 1st, be sure to catch up to the current date whenever you do begin.
- When trades are necessary, let students tell you what should be traded and where the new bill should be placed.
- When the money has been added and any trades are complete, write the addition on the recording sheet. Ask a student to check it with a calculator.

© Great Source. Copying is prohibited.

Ongoing Assessment

1. What is 37 + 6? Explain how you solved the problem.
2. What is the sum of 40 + 6 + 200?
3. Which number has more tens, 548 or 465?

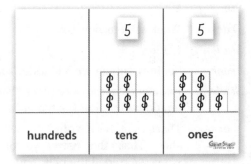

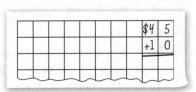

"Will we have one million dollars by the end of the school year?"

DISCUSSION

For the Beginning of the Month

Explain that $1 will be added to the Depositor on the first day of September, $2 on the second, and $3 on the third. The amount accumulates, so there will be a total of $6 by September 3rd. Be sure students know that money will be collected for the weekend days. Then explain that the amount to be added will increase from month to month.

Ask students if they think there will be one million dollars in the Depositor by the end of the year. Encourage students to think first about how much money will be deposited in September, adding $1 times the date. Students can register their predictions by a show of hands or by writing their estimates on paper.

Sample Dialogue

Teacher: Today is the 6th of September. How much money do we have today?

Student: A ten and 5 ones is $15.

Teacher: How much money will we add today?

Student: $6.

Teacher: What will our new total be?

Student: $21.

Teacher: So, how should we add today's amount?

Student: Put 6 ones in the ones place. Then trade 10 of them for a ten-dollar bill. Put the ten in the tens place.

Teacher: That's right. Let's write $15 + $6 = $21 on our recording sheet. That's the answer we got when we added mentally, when we traded the bills, and when we wrote it down. Is that the same answer you get on the calculator?

Student: Yes.

Teacher: Good, because no matter how we do it, we always have to get the same answer. If our answers are not the same, we need to check to see which one is correct. All our answers, the mental, the written, the money total, and the calculator, must be the same.

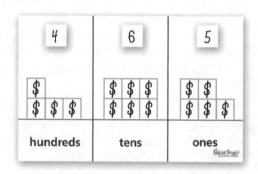

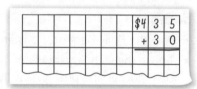

Number Sense Use these questions to encourage discussion:

• 21 can be shown with 2 tens and 1 one. How else can we show 21? (1 ten, 11 ones)

• 342 can be shown with 3 hundreds, 4 tens, and 2 ones. How else can we show 342? (2 hundreds, 14 tens, 2 ones)

• What is 53 rounded to the nearest ten? (50)

• What is 439 rounded to the nearest hundred? (400)

For the End of the Month

The actual amount in the Depositor on the last day of September should be $465. Remove the bills and record the monthly total from the Depositor in plain view. This will give students the opportunity to see the relationship between the amounts collected in September and October.

© Great Source. Copying is prohibited.

HELPFUL HINT

- Management of the Depositor, because it requires daily attention, may best be accomplished by having a math helper or two. This allows classroom discussion to be focused on the quantity being collected, along with the mental math, multi-digit addition, and estimation involved.

Daily Depositor				
Month	Days in the Month	Total for the Month	Cumulative Total	Daily Deposit Amount
September	30	$465		$1 times date
October	31			
November	30			
December	31			
January	31			
February	28 or 29			
March	31			
April	30			
May	31			

Number & Operations   Algebra   Geometry   Measurement   Data & Probability
Problem Solving   Reasoning   Communication   Connections   Representation

COUNTING TAPE

Concepts & Skills

- Explore the concept of multiples
- Examine multiples of 2
- Observe counting patterns for even and odd numbers
- Explore multiplication and division with and without remainders

Materials for the Year

Adding machine tape, copies of Hundred Chart (TR4) and Equation Chart (TR5) for each student, dark broad-tip felt pen, small counters, tape. In September you will also need Heart Multiple Markers cardstock or copies of TR6, a copy of Multiplication Facts Progress Record (TR1) and a manila folder for each student, stapler, glue stick

Ongoing Assessment

1. How can you prove that the number in a set of objects is an odd number?

2. What is 8 groups of 2, or 8 times 2?

3. How many hearts appear on the Tape by Day 15? How many twos are in 15?

Author Notes

"The Counting Tape is a paper strip for keeping track of the

"So far, there are 8 multiples of 2."

number of days in school. Each school day a new number is added. A major focus of this unfolding number line in fourth grade is a review of the relationship between multiplication and division, and multiples and factors. In September, students consider if the day's number is a multiple of 2. Using counters to show whether the number can be divided into equal groups of 2 with no remainders gives students an awareness of 2 as a factor and an understanding of even and odd numbers.

Different months feature different multiple patterns. To highlight the relationship between the numbers on the Tape and the multiple pattern, Multiple Markers visually associated with the multiples (red hearts for 2s, green triangles for 3s, and so on) are attached to the Tape. At the end of the month, students record their findings on a Hundred Chart, discuss the evolving patterns, and note their progress in mastery of computation on a Multiplication Facts Progress Record."

© Great Source. Copying is prohibited.

Setup

- Post a length of adding machine tape where it will be easily accessible for students.

Daily Routine

- On the first day of school, write the number *1* on the left end of the posted adding machine tape to begin the number line. Continue to add numbers each day students are in school. If it is impossible to begin on the first day of school, make sure to catch up by going back and recording from day 1.

- At the end of the first full week of school, ask students which numbers on the Tape are multiples of 2. Invite a student helper to use a number of counters equal to the Counting Tape number to see if that number can be divided into equal groups of 2 without any leftovers.

- When students identify a number as even, or as a multiple of 2, use tape to attach a Heart Multiple Marker below the number. This continues for the rest of the school year.

- Discuss two or three times a week.

"4 can be divided equally into groups of 2. We put a heart on 4."

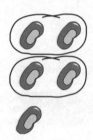

"5 cannot be divided equally into groups of 2."

DISCUSSION

For the Beginning of the Month

Explain that the Counting Tape is used to record the number of days in school. It will also be used to explore multiplication and division, including multiples and factors.

The following questions will help explain the meaning of the term multiple.

- Can you put 2 counters into equal groups of 2 with no leftovers? (yes) So 2 is a multiple of 2 and gets a heart on the Counting Tape.

- How about 3? Can the counters be put into equal groups of 2 with no leftovers? (no) So 3 is not a multiple of 2.

- How about 4? Can the counters be put into equal groups of 2 with no leftovers? (yes) How many groups of 2 can you make? (2) Is 4 a multiple of 2? (yes)

Keep using the language of "equal groups with no leftovers" when you discuss the Counting Tape. These discussions will help students to understand multiples as the year progresses.

For the Middle of the Month
Sample Dialogue

Teacher: Today we have been in school for 9 days. Who can help us find out if 9 is a multiple of 2 using the counters?

Student: I have 9 counters. I put them into groups of 2.

Teacher: How many groups did you get?

Student: 4 with one leftover.

Teacher: Great! Now, can you tell us if 9 will have a heart?

Is the Number Even?

2	🫘🫘	YES!
3	🫘🫘🫘	NO! (1 left over)
4	🫘🫘🫘🫘	YES!
5	🫘🫘🫘🫘🫘	NO! (1 left over)

© Great Source. Copying is prohibited.

Student: No, it won't. It has leftovers.

Teacher: That is right; 9 is not a multiple of 2 because we cannot make equal groups of 2 without leftovers. Can you tell us a story to go along with what you have done?

Student: There were 9 socks in my drawer, 4 pairs and one left.

Teacher: What number sentence goes along with that story?

Student: $9 \div 2 = 4$ with a remainder of 1.

Teacher: Yes. We read this 9 divided into groups of 2 is 4 groups of 2, remainder 1.

Choose questions like these with different numbers to provide practice with a variety of concepts and language.

Multiplication and division:

- What number has the 5th heart? The 7th heart?
- Can you name some multiples of 2?
- Is 9 a multiple of 2? What about 8? How do you know?
- Where is the 6th multiple of 2?

For the End of the Month

Work with the class so that each student can make his or her own Multiplication Book. As new multiples are introduced from month to month, it will be important to maintain the Multiplication Book throughout the year. This becomes a very useful math tool for fourth grade.

- First, give each student a manila folder to serve as the book's cover.

- Next, give each student 1 copy of a Hundred Chart (TR4). Have students shade each multiple of 2 that has appeared so far on the Counting Tape with a red crayon. Invite discussion of any patterns students notice. Staple this page to the inside right of the manila folder. Pages showing multiples of other numbers will be added in future months.

- Then, give each student a copy of the Multiplication Facts Progress Record (TR1). This will serve as the outside front cover of the Multiplication Book. As students demonstrate mastery, they can color red the times 2 facts they know well and leave blank the ones they still need to work on. This should be attached to the front cover of the manila folder with a glue stick.

- Finally, give each student a copy of the Equation Chart (TR5) and some counters. Staple the Equation Chart to the inside left of the manila folder. As students use the counters to determine whether the current number on the Counting Tape can be divided into equal groups of 2, they fill in the Equation Chart to reflect what they discover. They begin by recording the day's number (the total number of counters for the day), the number of equal groups of 2 they formed, and the remainder. Then students write a daily equation that reflects what they did with the counters. As the month progresses, students look for patterns that develop in each category. Pages showing equations for other multiples will be added in future months. This procedure was developed by Esta Elizondo, a teacher in the Houston area.

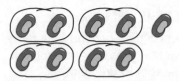

"9 divided into equal groups of 2 is 4 groups of 2 with 1 leftover. It's not a multiple of 2."

1 group of 2 = 1 x 2 = 2	6 groups of 2 = 6 x 2 = 12
2 groups of 2 = 2 x 2 = 4	7 groups of 2 = 7 x 2 = 14
3 groups of 2 = 3 x 2 = 6	8 groups of 2 = 8 x 2 = 16
4 groups of 2 = 4 x 2 = 8	9 groups of 2 = 9 x 2 = 18
5 groups of 2 = 5 x 2 = 10	10 groups of 2 = 10 x 2 = 20

1	2	3	4	5	6	7	8	9	10
11	12	13	14	15	16	17	18	19	20
21	22	23	24	25	26	27	28	29	30
31	32	33	34	35	36	37	38	39	40
41	42	43	44	45	46	47	48	49	50
51	52	53	54	55	56	57	58	59	60
61	62	63	64	65	66	67	68	69	70
71	72	73	74	75	76	77	78	79	80
81	82	83	84	85	86	87	88	89	90
91	92	93	94	95	96	97	98	99	100

Pattern of multiples of 2

Day	Groups	Remainder	Equation
1	0	1	(0 x 2) + 1 = 1
2	1	0	1 x 2 = 2
3	1	1	(1 x 2) + 1 = 3
4	2	0	2 x 2 = 4
5	2	1	(2 x 2) + 1 = 5
6	3	0	2 x 3 = 6
7	3	1	(2 x 3) + 1 = 7
8	4	0	2 x 4 = 8
9	4	1	(2 x 4) + 1 = 9
10	5	0	2 x 5 = 10

The Equation Chart shows a pattern in every column.

© Great Source. Copying is prohibited.

HELPFUL HINTS

- Attach the Counting Tape to the wall so that students can see it and work on it easily. Allow room for markers to be added below the hearts in future months.
- Using Circular Array Paper (TR7) to create Array Flash Cards for times 2 facts can help students who need to practice these facts. These models can also be used to illustrate the commutative property and to introduce the meaning of factors as the number of equal groups and the number within each group.

front   back

6 x 2
2 x 6

12

6 rows of 2 is 12. 12 divided into groups of 2 makes 6 groups.

Number & Operations	Algebra	Geometry	Measurement	Data & Probability
Problem Solving	Reasoning	Communication	Connections	Representation

COIN COUNTER

Concepts & Skills

- Count mixed coins
- Determine coin combinations for a given value
- See pennies and dimes as hundredths and tenths of a dollar
- Use decimal notation for tenths and hundredths
- Understand that ten hundredths is equal to one tenth

Ongoing Assessment

1. What are the fewest coins possible to make 17¢?
2. A penny is what fraction of a dollar?
3. A dime is what fraction of a dollar?

Materials for the Year

Three 3" × 6" clear pockets; real coins, or Play Money: Coins cardstock or a copy of TR8; 100 Penny Grid cardstock or a copy of TR9

Author Notes

"One of the challenges students face in learning to count mixed coins is the change in the counting pattern as they move from one kind of coin to another. Using the Coin Counter on a regular basis provides students with visual and mental practice. The Coin Counter also helps students understand decimal notation and is used to encourage mental math when students determine the fewest coins for a given amount."

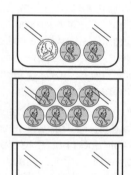

Setup

- Post three 3" × 6" clear pockets one above the other on the board.
- Cut the Coins cardstock on the indicated lines.

Daily Routine

- Each day, have students show the number of days in school by displaying that value with the fewest possible coins in the top pocket of the Coin Counter.
- Display other possible combinations for the same amount in the bottom 2 pockets.
- Shade the same number of pennies on the 100 Penny Grid. This is a visual representation of the pennies as a fractional part of one dollar. Record this amount using decimal notation.

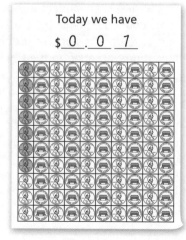

Today we have

$ 0 . 0 7

"7 cents is 7 hundredths of a dollar."

© Great Source. Copying is prohibited.

DISCUSSION

For the Seventh Day of School

When introducing the Coin Counter, explain that the purpose is to practice counting coins, to develop mental math skills, and to learn about decimals.

Sample Dialogue

Teacher: Today is school day 7 and we want to show 7 cents in the Coin Counter. What coins should we use?

Student: One nickel and 2 pennies.

Student: Seven pennies.

Teacher: Which combination uses the fewest coins?

Student: One nickel and 2 pennies.

Teacher: Yes. That only uses 3 coins. Let's agree to always show the fewest coins for the day's amount in the top pocket. What is another way to show 7 cents?

Student: Seven pennies.

Teacher: Yes, Let's color in 7 pennies in the first column of our 100 Penny Grid and record the amount using the dollar sign and decimal point. How many pennies are in a whole dollar?

Student: One hundred.

Teacher: Yes, and that's why we call a penny one cent. The prefix *centi* means one out of one hundred, or one hundredth. So what fraction of a dollar have we colored in?

Student: Seven hundredths.

Teacher: Yes, and we write it $0.07. The first zero says we don't have enough for one dollar yet. The 0 to the right of the decimal point says we don't have enough for a dime either. The 7 tells us we have 7 cents, or 7 hundredths of a dollar.

For Later in the Month

On day 10, the Coin Counter should look like the picture at the right. Point out that 10 cents is one tenth of a dollar. When we record the day's amount as $0.10 we can read it, "Ten cents are ten hundredths of a dollar." However, we can also say, "One dime and zero extra cents is the same as one tenth of a dollar and no extra hundredths."

On day 11, we can read $0.11, "Eleven cents is 1 dime and 1 cent, or one tenth plus one hundredth of a dollar." On the 100 Penny Grid, point out that one completely colored in column represents one tenth of the entire grid. This is another way for students to see that 10 cents is one tenth of a dollar.

For the rest of the month, talk frequently about dimes and pennies as tenths and hundredths of a dollar. Have students interpret decimal notation in a variety of ways.

© Great Source. Copying is prohibited.

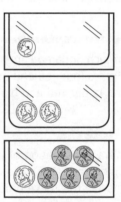

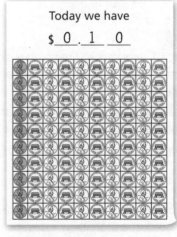

Today we have

$ _0_ . _1_ _0_

"10¢ is the same as 1 dime and no extra cents. That's one tenth of a dollar and zero extra hundredths."

HELPFUL HINTS

- There is no substitute for the use of real coins. Telling students you trust them to take care of your coins so that the coins can be used all year long may help the class to meet your expectations. Limiting the supply to 15 of each coin and keeping them in marked clear containers or resealable bags also seems to help prevent loss.

- Encourage students to count the money orally since some students learn best by listening, and verbal reinforcement is very helpful.

Number & Operations	Algebra	Geometry	Measurement	Data & Probability
Problem Solving	Reasoning	Communication	Connections	Representation

GRAPH

Concepts & Skills

- Collect and organize data into a bar graph
- Analyze data and interpret graphs
- Predict probability and test the predictions
- Express the likelihood of an occurrence

Materials for September

2 copies of Inch Squared Paper (TR3), 2 unnumbered September Calendar Pieces (one red and one blue), paper bag, one piece of construction paper, red and blue crayons, scissors, tape

Author Notes

"This month's investigation of probability gives students the opportunity to make predictions about the likelihood of outcomes. Hands-on experiments like this make probability concepts come alive for students in a meaningful way."

Setup

- Place 1 unnumbered red square and 1 unnumbered blue rectangle from the September Calendar Pieces in a small paper bag. The Calendar Pieces should not have yellow dots on them.

- Use Inch Squared Paper (TR3) to make the bar graph. Cut and tape together 2-inch widths to make a 60" × 2" strip.

- Label a piece of construction paper *Predictions* and post it nearby.

Daily Routine

- Show students the 2 Calendar Pieces. Inform students that they will be used in a probability experiment.

- Students will draw a piece from the bag at random. Each draw will be recorded on the bar graph. Then the piece will be replaced in the bag. This procedure is repeated a total of 15 times every week this month, for a total of 60 draws.

- Have students begin drawing one piece at a time. Use a red and a blue crayon to record the result of each draw on the bar graph. One row will show red pieces; the other will show blue ones. Color in one square for each piece drawn.

Ongoing Assessment

1. Look at the Graph. How many reds are there? How many blues?

2. Why do you think there are about as many reds as blues?

3. If you did this experiment again with 1 yellow piece and 1 green piece, do you think the results would be the same?

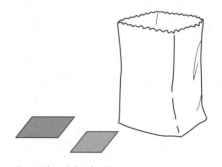

September Calendar Pieces

© Great Source. Copying is prohibited.

- Discuss the results of the draws each week. Allow students to revise their predictions based on what they see as the experiment proceeds.

DISCUSSION

For the Beginning of the Month
Sample Dialogue

Teacher: I have 2 Calendar Pieces. They are 1 red square and 1 blue rectangle. I will put them in a bag and draw 1 piece at a time, replacing it in the bag each time. One day each week we will draw 15 times and record what we draw. How could we record our collected data?

Student: We could use tally marks.

Student: We could color in squares on graph paper.

Teacher: Let's color in squares on graph paper. We'll use red for the square and blue for the rectangle. Which color do you think will be drawn the most? Let's record your predictions on this *Predictions* poster.

Student: I predict we will have the same number of reds as blues.

Student: I predict we will have half red and half blue.

Teacher: During September, we will draw and replace 15 times each week, for a total of 60 draws.

Predictions

- I predict that we will have the same number of reds as blues.
- I predict we will have half red and half blue.
- I predict we will have about 30 reds and 30 blues.

A Predictions poster

For the Middle of the Month

To encourage comparing:

- How many draws do we have so far?
- What is the difference between the number of red and blue draws?

To encourage probability and outcomes:

- What color has been drawn the most so far?
- Is it likely at the end of our experiment that red will be drawn more often? Will blue be drawn more often? Will red and blue be drawn the same number of times? Explain your thinking.
- What do you think will happen after 15 more draws?

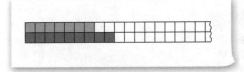

"There are about as many reds as blues."

For the End of the Month

Some of the following questions will be helpful in discussing the bar graph.

- By coloring a square for each draw, what did we make? (a bar graph)
- How many total draws did we record? (60)
- How many were red and how many were blue?
- How do the results of the experiment compare with our predictions?
- If we did the experiment again, do you think the results would be the same or different? Why?

HELPFUL HINT

- If you want students to experience more probability experiments in the classroom, use two different-colored tiles in a bag. Students draw and replace 60 times, keep track of the draws, and record the data.

© Great Source. Copying is prohibited.

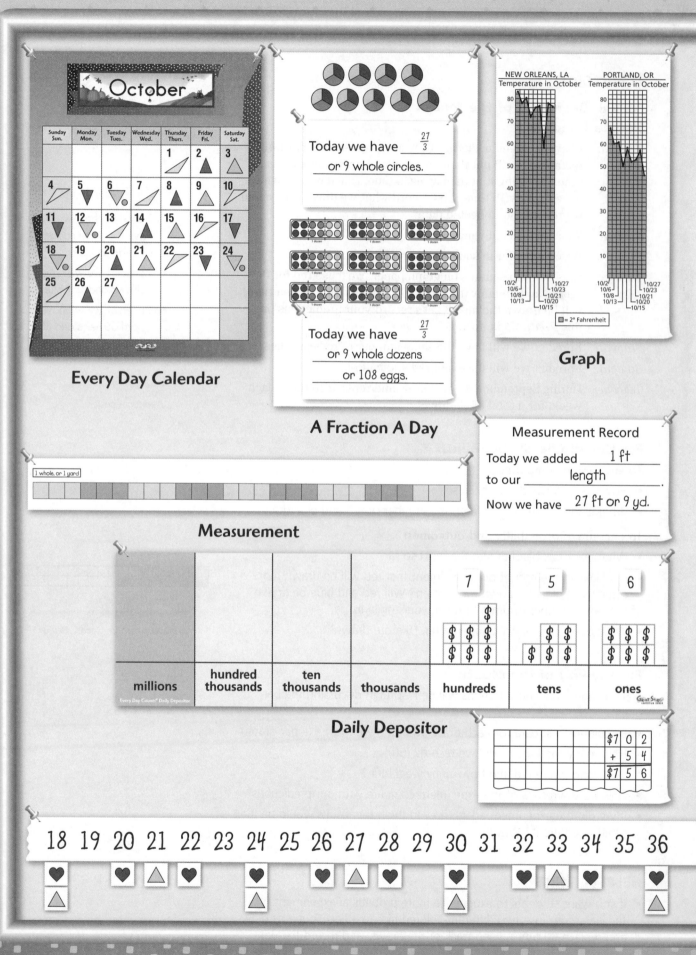

Every Day Calendar

October

Sunday Sun.	Monday Mon.	Tuesday Tues.	Wednesday Wed.	Thursday Thurs.	Friday Fri.	Saturday Sat.
				1	2	3
4	5	6	7	8	9	10
11	12	13	14	15	16	17
18	19	20	21	22	23	24
25	26	27				

A Fraction A Day

Today we have $\frac{27}{3}$ or 9 whole circles.

_____

Today we have $\frac{27}{3}$ or 9 whole dozens or 108 eggs.

Graph

NEW ORLEANS, LA Temperature in October	PORTLAND, OR Temperature in October

10/2 10/6 10/8 10/13 10/15 10/20 10/21 10/23 10/27

■ = 2° Fahrenheit

Measurement

1 whole, or 1 yard

Measurement Record

Today we added _____ 1 ft _____

to our _____ length _____.

Now we have _____ 27 ft or 9 yd. _____

_____

Daily Depositor

millions	hundred thousands	ten thousands	thousands	hundreds	tens	ones
				7	5	6

Every Day Counts® Daily Depositor

					$7	0	2
				+		5	4
				$7	5	6

18 19 20 21 22 23 24 25 26 27 28 29 30 31 32 33 34 35 36

Coin Counter

Clock

Counting Tape

OCTOBER ELEMENTS

CALENDAR **32**
recognize patterns of multiples of 3 and 6; compare and analyze attributes of triangles; visualize rotation of triangles

DAILY DEPOSITOR **34**
understand place value; perform multi-digit addition; estimate and predict

MEASUREMENT **36**
convert feet into yards; examine mixed numbers and fractional parts; make connections to multiplication and division

A FRACTION A DAY **38**
visualize fractions using different models; understand numerator and denominator; find a fraction of a set

COUNTING TAPE **40**
explore multiples and factors; count by twos and threes; know multiplication facts for 2 and 3

COIN COUNTER **42**
count mixed coins; determine the number of coins when the total value is known; use decimal notation for tenths and hundredths

CLOCK **43**
understand setting and reading the minute and hour hands; talk about elapsed time

GRAPH **44**
collect and organize data into bar and line graphs; analyze data and interpret graphs

The main elements of Calendar Math that were introduced in September—Every Day Calendar, Daily Depositor, and Counting Tape—will be continually updated and frequently discussed in October. The Measurement element and the Clock are introduced this month, and A Fraction A Day begins its focus on understanding fractions.

CALENDAR

Concepts & Skills

- Recognize patterns of multiples of 3 and 6
- Compare and analyze attributes of triangles
- Visualize rotation of triangles
- Recognize lines of symmetry

DISCUSSION

For the Beginning of the Month

Explain that a new pattern will be emerging on the Calendar this month. After about one week, ask students to describe any patterns or observations. Some responses might be:

- The pattern is yellow, red, green, yellow, red, green.
- Multiples of 3 are always green triangles.
- Every other green triangle has a dot on it.
- The shapes repeat but turn.

Geometry Here are some questions you can ask about the classification and rotation of triangles.

- What is a triangle? (a polygon with 3 straight sides)
- What is the same about the yellow triangles and the red triangles? What is different? (They both have 3 sides and 3 angles. In the red triangles, 2 sides are the same length; in the yellow triangles, no sides are the same length.)

Write the word *scalene* on the board and explain that it means that no 2 sides of a triangle are the same length. Write *isosceles* and explain that it means 2 sides are of equal length. Then ask:

- What word describes 2 line segments that are the same length? (congruent)
- Describe the sides of the green triangle. (They are all equal length or congruent.) Write the word *equilateral* to describe the triangle.
- Can any of these triangles be folded so that the two sides match up? (yes, the isosceles and equilateral triangles)

Draw the isosceles triangle with a line of symmetry and explain that a mirror placed on the line would make it look like the same triangle was being reflected. If possible, actually do this with a mirror. Half the triangle is reflected in the mirror.

- How many lines of symmetry can you find on the equilateral triangles? (3) Describe them. (They are lines from each corner or vertex to the middle of the opposite side.)

For the Middle of the Month
Sample Dialogue

Teacher: Today is Thursday, October 22nd. What piece do you suppose will go on the Calendar today?

© Great Source. Copying is prohibited.

Ongoing Assessment

1. Name two multiples of 3 between 20 and 30.
2. Draw an obtuse isosceles triangle. Draw dotted lines to show any lines of symmetry.
3. Draw an equilateral triangle. Then draw what the same equilateral triangle will look like if it is rotated 90°.

The October Calendar Pieces feature three kinds of triangles: scalene, isosceles, and equilateral. They are used in a repeating ABC color pattern of yellow, red, and green. In every repetition, the triangle is rotated 180°. Every 6th triangle has a dot on it.

Student: A yellow triangle, because yesterday has a green triangle and green is always followed by yellow.

Student: A yellow scalene triangle because the pattern is scalene, isosceles, equilateral and the 21st was equilateral.

Student: If you look at the Thursdays on the Calendar, the pattern is yellow, red, green, so the next one must be yellow.

Teacher: When will the next green equilateral triangle show up?

Student: On the 24th.

Teacher: Why?

Student: Because every multiple of 3 is a green triangle.

Teacher: Let's say all the multiples of 3 that appear on the Calendar in October. (The class recites the multiples of 3 up to 30 as the teacher points to the pieces.) What do you notice about the triangles on the dates 6, 12, and 18?

Student: They are all green triangles with a dot on them.

Student: They all have a corner, or vertex, pointing down.

Teacher: Is it still an equilateral triangle?

Student: Yes, I think so. It's still a triangle with 3 equal sides.

Student: It is just rotated, like we did last month with the rectangles.

For the End of the Month

Algebra Some questions to support concepts about representing patterns in a table and using patterns to make predictions:

- The first equilateral triangle appears on the 3rd, and the 2nd on the 6th. When does the 4th one appear? (the 12th)

- How can you figure it out without looking at the Calendar? (You can multiply 3 times 4, or count by threes.)

- On what date will the 10th equilateral triangle appear? How do you know? (the 30th, or 10 × 3)

- If the pattern continued when would the 20th one appear? (60, or 20 × 3)

Draw the table at the right on the board. Complete it with student help. Then ask the following questions:

- If the table continued, what date would be on the 100th green triangle? (300)

- What is a rule for finding any date on a green equilateral triangle? (Multiply that number by 3.)

To Sum Up

Have students talk and/or write about their observations and findings. Create a chart with these observations.

Some patterns that may be noticed include:

- 3, 6, 9, 12, 15, 18, 21, 24, 27, and 30 are all green triangles.

- The green triangles on even multiples of 3 are pointing down and have dots.

- The even multiples of 3 are also multiples of 6.

- The same kind of triangle appears on all the diagonals going down to the left.

Number of Green Triangle	Date
1	3
2	6
3	9
4	
5	
6	

Draw this table on the board.

© Great Source. Copying is prohibited.

- The pattern for the yellow scalene triangles is 1, 4, 7, 10, 13, 16, or beginning with 1, add 3 each time.
- The pattern for the red isosceles triangles is 2, 5, 8, 11, 14, 17, or beginning with 2, add 3 each time.

HELPFUL HINT

- Remember that learning geometry concepts is more than memorizing the vocabulary. The more experience students have actually manipulating triangles, the better their understanding will be. Lines of symmetry, for example, are difficult for some students to visualize. Folding a triangle or putting a mirror on it leads to long-term insight.

Number & Operations   Algebra   Geometry   Measurement   Data & Probability
Problem Solving   Reasoning   Communication   Connections   Representation

DAILY DEPOSITOR

Concepts & Skills

- Double numbers
- Use mental math
- Perform multi-digit addition
- Understand place value
- Estimate and predict

Setup

- Be sure the September Depositor total is in plain view. Empty the Depositor of play money and start fresh on the first day of October.

Daily Routine

- Each day in October, add a dollar amount equal to twice the date.
- Record the addition and the total every day.

DISCUSSION

For the Beginning of the Month

Explain how the daily deposit amount will be determined throughout the month. Here are some sample questions.

- How much money will we deposit on October 1st? ($2) How much on the second of October? ($4) How much will we deposit on the fifth of October? ($10)
- How much will we collect this month? (Encourage students to make predictions.)
- How much money do you think we will have altogether at the end of October when we add October's amount to what we deposited in September? (Allow for a wide range of estimates.)

Ongoing Assessment

1. What is 9 doubled? What is 19 doubled? Explain your mental math strategy.
2. What is the value of the 4 in 849?
3. What is 4 tens more than 278?

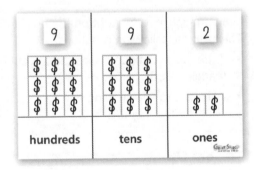

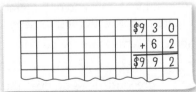

The Depositor at the end of October

© Great Source. Copying is prohibited.

For the Middle of the Month

Help students use subtraction to solve problems by posing pretend expenditures once a week. Allow students to offer different ways to solve the problems and record one solution. After discussion, return the bills to the Depositor.

Sample Dialogue

Number	Double that Number	Answer
5	5 + 5	10
15	15 + 15	30
6	6 + 6	12
16	16 + 16	32
7	7 + 7	14
17	17 + 17	34
8	8 + 8	16
18	18 + 18	36

Teacher: Today is the 16th of October. How much money should we deposit today?

Student: Thirty-two dollars.

Teacher: How did you get your answer?

Student: I know that 6 plus 6 is 12, and 10 plus 10 is 20, so 12 plus 20 is 32.

Teacher: How much money did we deposit yesterday?

Student: Thirty dollars.

Teacher: Good, so 15 doubled is 30, and 16 doubled is 32. What do you think we will get tomorrow when we double 17?

Student: Thirty-four dollars.

Helping students to see that patterns are connected to computation helps prevent teaching these two important math topics in isolation. Also, examination of patterns in computation can arouse curiosity about other patterns and helps students see that math makes sense.

For the End of the Month

At the end of the month, add the $992 deposited in October to the $465 deposited in September and display the new cumulative total of $1,457. Ask questions like the following:

Patterns and algebraic thinking:

- How much money did we deposit through October 30th? ($930)

- We deposited $465 in September and $930 for the same number of days in October. How are the numbers 465 and 930 related? (930 is twice as much as 465.) Why do you think this relationship works? (We deposited twice as much each day during October as we did in September, so the total for the first thirty days of October should be twice as much as the thirty days of September.)

Daily Depositor				
Month	Days in the Month	Total for the Month	Cumulative Total	Daily Deposit Amount
September	30	$465		$1 times date
October	31	$992	$1,457	$2 times date
November	30			
December	31			
January	31			
February	28 or 29			
March	31			
April	30			
May	31			

- What is the total amount of money we have deposited in October? ($992) How many days are in October? (31) Why is the total for October $62 more than twice the amount from September? (Because $62 is twice the date on October 31st. If there were exactly 31 days in September, our October amount would be exactly twice as much.)

Place value and number sense:

- How many hundreds did we collect this month? (9) How many tens? (9) How many ones? (2) How much more will we need to deposit to get to $1,000? (8 ones)

- How can we write this month's total in expanded notation? (900 + 90 + 2, or 9 hundreds + 9 tens + 2 ones)

Estimating and predicting:

- How much money have we deposited altogether? ($1,457) Do you think we will have one million dollars by the end of December?

© Great Source. Copying is prohibited.

HELPFUL HINTS

- Demonstrate to the students that doubling always yields an even number for an answer. Questions such as "Why is the amount to be deposited each day always an even number?" or "Why do we get an even number when we add two odd numbers?" or "What is the result when we add an even and an odd number?" can involve students in a thoughtful discussion about the additive properties of odd and even numbers.

- Some teachers find it helpful to keep a cumulative daily total when working with the Depositor. To do this, use several copies of Inch Squared Paper (TR3) displayed on the side of the bulletin board. Record the date, the amount added, and the new total each day.

		$8	7	0
October 30		+ $6	0	
		$9	3	0
October 31		+	6	2
		$9	9	2

Use Inch Squared Paper to keep a daily cumulative total.

<table>
<tr><td>Number & Operations</td><td>Algebra</td><td>Geometry</td><td>Measurement</td><td>Data & Probability</td></tr>
<tr><td>Problem Solving</td><td>Reasoning</td><td>Communication</td><td>Connections</td><td>Representation</td></tr>
</table>

MEASUREMENT

Concepts & Skills

- Convert feet into yards
- Examine mixed numbers and fractional parts
- Make connections to multiplication and division

Materials for October

Thirty-one 12" × 3" strips of colored paper (16 red and 15 blue); a 36" strip of adding machine tape; Measurement Record cardstock or a copy of TR10 in a large clear pocket; watercolor marker; 3 rulers; one yardstick

Author Notes

"Including Measurement as an element in Calendar Math exposes students to measurement activities regularly, rather than in a single unit. The emphasis in October is to have students think about the relationship between feet and yards, and to have a referent in the classroom."

Setup

- Make 31 foot-long strips of colored paper, 16 red and 15 blue. These can be made from adding machine tape and colored, or from colored construction paper cut into 12" × 3" strips. Each strip should be labeled *1 ft ($\frac{1}{3}$ yd)*.
- Cut a yard-long strip of adding machine tape. Label it *1 whole, or 1 yard*. Post this strip horizontally on the wall.

Daily Routine

- Post one red 12-inch strip on the wall each day. Begin posting below the yard strip.
- After 3 days, change to posting blue strips. Continue alternating color every 3 days.
- Record the length in yards and feet and as a mixed number each day.

Ongoing Assessment

1. How many feet are in one yard?
2. How many yards do we have today? How many feet is that?
3. How can we write today's total amount as a mixed number?

© Great Source. Copying is prohibited.

DISCUSSION

For the Beginning of the Month

Show students the yard-long and foot-long strips that have been cut and point out the place where they will be displayed. Explain that each day of the month a foot-long strip will be added. Demonstrate that 3 feet equal 1 yard by placing 3 rulers on top of a yardstick. Ask students where these units of measure are used in real life.

Sample Dialogue

Teacher: (pointing to the place where the display will begin) Each day this month we will add a foot-long strip here, under the yard strip. How many feet are in one yard?

Student: 3.

Teacher: If the yard is the whole, what part of the whole is each foot?

Student: $\frac{1}{3}$ of a yard.

Teacher: We'll start with 3 red strips and then change to 3 blue strips. That will make it easy to see how many yards we have altogether. Can we estimate where the strips will reach by the end of the month?

For the Eleventh Day of the Month

The following questions should help stimulate discussion about mixed numbers and fractions. Adapt them for use on any day of the month.

- How many feet do we have today? (11) How many yards is that? (3 yards) How many extra feet? (2)

- How can we write the leftover amount as a fraction? ($\frac{2}{3}$, because 2 out of the 3 feet needed to make another yard are left over.)

- How many thirds do we have altogether? ($\frac{11}{3}$) When this is written as a whole number and a fraction, we have $3\frac{2}{3}$ yards. That is called a mixed number because it is a whole number and a fraction mixed together. If you look at the board, do you see $3\frac{2}{3}$ yards displayed?

For the End of the Month

Summarize all the facts that have been observed.

- Review that the whole is a yard.

- Review how many feet equal a yard.

- Review a foot as $\frac{1}{3}$ of a yard.

- Examine how many feet have been displayed and ask how many yards in all.

- Compare the actual length with the estimates made earlier.

HELPFUL HINT

- Have students cut the strips and post them all month.

1 whole, or 1 yard		
1 ft ($\frac{1}{3}$ yd)	1 ft ($\frac{1}{3}$ yd)	1 ft ($\frac{1}{3}$ yd)

Measurement Record

Today we added _____ 1 ft _____

to our _____ length _____.

Now we have _____ 1 yd or 3 ft. _____

1 whole, or 1 yard

Measurement Record

Today we added _____ 1 ft _____

to our _____ length _____.

Now we have _____ 11 ft. or $3\frac{2}{3}$ yd. _____

© Great Source. Copying is prohibited.

A FRACTION A DAY

Concepts & Skills

- Visualize fractions
- Understand numerator and denominator
- Write improper fractions as mixed numbers
- Find a fraction of a set
- Add fractions

Materials for October

11 circles from TR11, 11 egg carton Dozens from TR12, Fraction Record (TR13), markers or crayons in 3 bright colors and black

Author Notes

A Fraction a Day helps students develop number sense for fractions and mixed numbers, as well as see equivalencies, compare fractions, and add fractions. Fractions are represented using different visual models to help students develop flexibility in thinking about fractions. Set models such as a dozen eggs, linear models such a giant inch, and area models such as pizza (or circles) are used as students explore fraction concepts.

Setup

- Cut out 11 circles and post one on the board, leaving space for the other 10.
- Cut out 11 egg cartons Dozens. Post one, leaving space for 10 more.
- Post the Fraction Record.

Daily Routine

- **The first day,** tell the class that you will draw 3 equal parts of a pizza (or circle).Use the black marker to draw thirds on one circle. (Connect the 4, 8, and 12 o'clock points on the rim to the center point.)
- Shade in one third of the circle each day, including weekends and holidays. **Use alternating colors to keep the thirds distinct.**
- As each circle is filled, post a new one next to it, and continue to shade one third each day.
- Also shade one third of the egg carton Dozen (4 eggs) each day. Use three colors and dotted lines to keep the thirds distinct.
- Each day record the amount displayed as both a fraction and (after day 3) as a mixed number.

DISCUSSION

To Get Started

Make sure that students understand that the denominator tells how many equal parts a whole has been divided into. Draw a line segment,

Ongoing Assessment

1. A whole pizza is cut into thirds. How many equal parts are there?

2. If you have two whole pizzas, how many thirds are there in all?

3. When we talk about a dozen eggs, what is the whole? How many eggs are in $\frac{1}{3}$ of a dozen?

Use a black marker to mark thirds.

2 out of 3 equal parts is $\frac{2}{3}$.

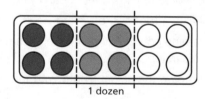

1 dozen

A dozen eggs divided into 3 equal parts.

© Great Source. Copying is prohibited.

and label it "1 whole." Draw another identical line segment underneath that and divide the line in half with a mark in the center. Repeat this exercise to create thirds, fourths, sixths, and eighths.

Point to each line segment one at a time and ask:

- What is the whole? (1 line)
- Into how many equal parts is the whole divided? (2, 3, 4, 6, 8)
- How do we say and write each part? (1 out of 2 equal pieces or $\frac{1}{2}$, 1 out of 3 equal pieces or $\frac{1}{3}$, 1 out of 4 equal pieces or $\frac{1}{4}$, and so on)
- What do you notice about the size of the sections as the number of sections increases? (They get smaller.)
- What pattern do you notice about the numbers in the denominator as more sections are shown on the line segments? (The numbers in the denominator are larger, telling us that the whole has been cut into more pieces.)

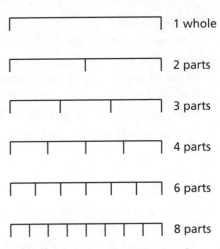

"What do you notice about the size of the sections as the number of sections increases?"

For the Beginning of the Month

As soon as possible in October, introduce A Fraction a Day. Begin with the area model of a circle and then introduce the set model of a dozen eggs.

Sample Dialogue

Teacher: Into how many equal parts has the circle been divided?

Student: It has been divided into three equal parts.

Teacher: What do we call one part?

Student: One third?

Teacher: Yes, and how do we write one third?

Student: First write a 1, then draw a line under it, then write 3.

Teacher: Yes, when I write one third as a fraction, the 3 below the bar is called the denominator. It tells us that the circle has been cut into three equal parts. If I color one third for October 1st and one third for the 2nd, how many parts will be shaded?

Student: 2

Teacher: Yes, and I can write $\frac{2}{3}$ for the two shaded parts out of the three equal parts. The 2 above the bar is called the numerator and it tells us how many parts we are referring to. On our Fraction Record, we write that we have $\frac{2}{3}$ of a circle, meaning we have 2 out of 3 equal parts.

Today we have _____ $\frac{2}{3}$ of a circle. _____

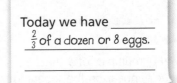

1 dozen

Today we have _____ $\frac{2}{3}$ of a dozen or 8 eggs. _____

For the Middle of the Month

The following sample questions can be adapted for use on any day.

Fractions of a set:

- Into how many equal parts is the whole dozen divided this month? (3)
- If I color one third for the first of October, how many eggs is that? (4) So 4 eggs is one third of a dozen? (Yes)
- What is another way to say $\frac{2}{3}$? (Two out of three equal parts.)
- How many eggs are two thirds of a dozen? (8)

© Great Source. Copying is prohibited.

Mixed numbers:

- If the whole is the circle, how many thirds make the whole? (3)
- How many whole circles will we have when we have seven thirds? (2 whole circles with $\frac{1}{3}$ left over.) How do you know? (3 thirds and 3 thirds is 2 wholes, and 1 more third makes 7 thirds)
- How can we write $\frac{7}{3}$ as a mixed number? (2 and $\frac{1}{3}$ or $2\frac{1}{3}$)
- How many whole circles will we have on the 18th day? (6)

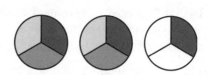

Today we have $\frac{7}{3}$

or 2 wholes and $\frac{1}{3}$

or $2\frac{1}{3}$ circles.

"Seven thirds ($\frac{7}{3}$) is the same as two wholes and one third."

•HELPFUL HINT

- *Fraction Kits* Many teachers make copies of Circles from TR11 and have students label, color, and cut out their own set of thirds. Students use the kits to act out story problems involving adding and subtracting fractions and converting between improper and mixed fractions.

Number & Operations   Algebra   Geometry   Measurement   Data & Probability
Problem Solving   Reasoning   Communication   Connections   Representation

COUNTING TAPE

Concepts & Skills

- Explore multiples and factors
- Know multiplication facts for 2 and 3
- Investigate multiplication and division with and without remainders

Ongoing Assessment

1. Count by threes from 3 to 30.
2. On what number will we hang our 7th triangle? Our 9th?
3. What number can you think of that can be put into groups of two and also into groups of three with no leftovers?

Materials for October

Triangle Multiple Markers cardstock, copies of Circular Array Paper (TR7), Hundred Chart (TR4), and Equation Chart (TR5)

Daily Routine

- Continue to mark multiples of 2 with Heart Multiple Markers. Begin marking multiples of 3 with green Triangle Multiple Markers.

DISCUSSION

12 13 14 15 16 17 18 19 20 21 22 23 24 25

For the Beginning of the Month

Identify multiples of 3 that already appear on the Tape and mark each with a green triangle. Note numbers that have both a heart and a triangle marker. Ask, "What does this tell us about 6, 12, and 18?" Introduce the term common multiple.

"12, 18, and 24 are multiples of both 2 and 3."

Count by threes up to the present day with the class. State the number of groups of 3 and any remainder. Use counters to demonstrate multiples of 3. As students arrange the counters into groups of 3 with and without remainders, have them fill in the Equation Chart for 3s, shown at the right. This will be stapled into their Multiplication Books at the end of the month. Point out the patterns on the chart. Continue until all the multiples of 3 through the current day have been discussed.

Day	Groups	Remainder	Equation
1	0	1	$(0 \times 3) + 1 = 1$
2	0	2	$(0 \times 3) + 2 = 2$
3	1	0	$1 \times 3 = 3$
4	1	1	$(1 \times 3) + 1 = 4$
5	1	2	$(1 \times 3) + 2 = 5$
6	2	0	$2 \times 3 = 6$
7	2	1	$(2 \times 3) + 1 = 7$
8	2	2	$(2 \times 3) + 2 = 8$
9	3	0	$3 \times 3 = 9$
10	3	1	$(3 \times 3) + 1 = 10$

© Great Source. Copying is prohibited.

To encourage thinking about multiples of 3 as quantities that can be broken up into groups of 3, try telling some multiplication story problems. For example, "There are 7 sections in the parking lot with 3 cars in each section. How many cars are there?" To help students with division, include some division story problems. For example, "I need 24 glue sticks. They come in boxes of 3. How many boxes should I buy?"

For the Middle of the Month

The following questions can be used to introduce the concept of common multiples.

- What patterns do you see on the Tape? (Every other number has a heart. Every third number has a triangle. Every other multiple of 3 is also a multiple of 2.)
- What do 6, 12, and 18 have in common? (They all have a heart and a triangle. They break up into groups of both 2 and 3. They are common multiples of 2 and 3.)
- What is the next number after 18 that is a common multiple of both 2 and 3? (24)

For the End of the Month

- Give each student a copy of the Hundred Chart (TR4) and the Equation Chart (TR5), if you haven't used them earlier in the month. Students shade green the multiples of 3 up to 30 on the Hundred Chart, and record the equations for groups of 3 on the Equation Chart. Encourage students to use counters to discover the patterns of remainders for groups of 3. Ask what patterns they notice on the Hundred Chart for the multiples of 3. Have students write the multiplication facts for 3 above the Hundred Chart. Both of these charts are added to the Multiplication Books.

- When students show they have recall of the multiplication facts for 3 when presented to them in random order, they can color those facts green on the Multiplication Facts Progress Record attached to the cover of their Multiplication Books.

- Using Circular Array Paper (TR7) to create Array Flash Cards for facts from 3 × 3 to 9 × 3 can help students who need to practice those facts. These models can also be used to illustrate the commutative property and to show that the factors of a number include the number of equal groups and the number within each group. If any students still need help with the multiplication facts for 2, they can make Array Flash Cards for these specific facts and add them to their collection for practice.

HELPFUL HINT

- Another way to help students understand multiples is to make lists of things that come in 3s, 4s, 5s, 6s, and so on. This is an activity that parents can get involved in and which you can refer to each month as a new multiple is introduced.

© Great Source. Copying is prohibited.

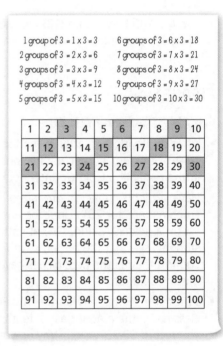

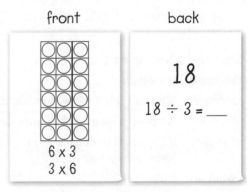

"6 rows of 3 is 18 and 18 divided into groups of 3 makes 6 groups."

COIN COUNTER

Concepts & Skills

- Count mixed coins
- Determine the number of coins when the total value is known
- Make change
- See pennies and dimes as hundredths and tenths of a dollar
- Use decimal notation for tenths and hundredths

Daily Routine

- Continue to display the combination with the fewest coins in the top pocket.
- Use the 100 Penny Grid (TR9) to see and talk about the day's amount as tenths and hundredths of a dollar.

DISCUSSION

For the Twenty-fifth Day

- After displaying a quarter in the top pocket, invite the class to begin a list of the remaining combinations. Select 2 combinations to display in the remaining Coin Counter pockets.

- Have students create an organized list showing all the possible coin combinations for 25¢. Limit the number of pennies to 5. Display the list on a poster. Asking, "What patterns do you see?" can help students see that the patterns within an organized list can help confirm that all the possibilities have been found or point out a missing solution.

- When the 25th penny on the 100 Penny Grid is colored in, have the class name the amount as "2 tenths and 5 hundredths of a dollar" as you record $0.25. Ask," Why do you think a coin worth 25 cents is called a quarter?" Challenge students to think of other uses of the term *quarter*, as in quarter of a game, quarter of an hour, quarter of an orange, quart of milk, and so on.

For the Middle of the Month
Sample Dialogue

Teacher: Who can tell me how to make 29¢ using the fewest coins?

Student: We need a quarter. A quarter and 4 pennies is just 5 coins.

Teacher: If you used the quarter to buy an eraser for 12¢, what would your change be?

Student: 13¢.

Teacher: How did you get your answer?

Student: I know 12 and 12 is 24, and 25 cents is just one more, so it's 13.

Student: I start with 12 and add 10 to get 22 and 3 more is 13.

Student: I did 25 take away 12 in my head and got 13.

Teacher: Great! That's 3 different ways to get the same answer.

Ongoing Assessment

1. If you use a quarter to buy a pencil for 12¢, what will your change be?

2. How many tenths of a dollar are in today's amount?

3. If you have 5 coins that make 30¢, what are the coins?

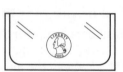

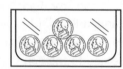

Today we have
$ _0_ . _2_ _5_
(one quarter of a dollar)

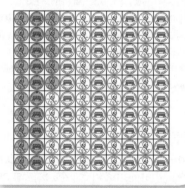

25 cents is one quarter or one fourth of a dollar.

© Great Source. Copying is prohibited.

CLOCK

Concepts & Skills

- Count by fives and tens
- Read and set the hour and minute hands
- Talk about elapsed time

Materials for the Year

Clock cardstock or a copy of TR14 in a large clear pocket, a pair of Clock Hands cardstock attached with a paper fastener on the outside of the clear pocket, marker

Author Notes

"Incorporating the Clock into Calendar Math allows students to be exposed to the topic all year long. This increases the depth of coverage and allows for absorption throughout the year rather than during just one unit."

Daily Routine

- Set the hour hand on the Clock to 9 this month.
- Use the number of the day in school, shown on the Counting Tape, to determine where to set the minute hand.

DISCUSSION

For the Beginning of the Month

Introduce the Clock activity as early in October as possible. Explain how the time will be set each day and determine what time the Clock should show. For example, if it is the 18th day of school, the Clock should show 9:18.

- If the time to be shown on the Clock is 9:18, approximately where will the minute hand be? Where will the hour hand be?
- If the time to be shown is 7 minutes later than the time right now, how would you set the minute hand?
- If you cannot see the Clock well from where you are standing in a room, but you can distinguish approximately where the minute hand is, how can you use the numbers on the outside of the Clock to estimate time?

For the End of the Month
Sample Dialogue

Teacher: Today we have been in school 36 days. What time will the Clock show today?

Student: 9:36, or 24 minutes before 10.

Teacher: About where is the minute hand situated?

Student: The minute hand comes between the 7 and 8. **MORE ▶**

Ongoing Assessment

1. What time will it be 5 minutes after 9:17?
2. What time is it now? What time was it 5 minutes ago?
3. What is another name for 2:32?

In October, set the hour hand to 9 and the minute hand to the number of the day in school. Add a minute a day.

Today the Clock shows 9:36, or 24 minutes before 10.

© Great Source. Copying is prohibited.

Teacher: How can we check to see if this answer is correct?

Student: We can count by fives around the Clock.

Student: We can count the minutes from 9:30 and see where 6 minutes more would be.

Student: We could count backward from 10:00 for 24 minutes.

Teacher: You have found many different ways to explain the placement of the minute hand on the Clock.

HELPFUL HINT

- Frequently, students should be asked about the placement of the hands on the Clock and asked to estimate the time rather than tell the actual time.

Number & Operations	Algebra	Geometry	Measurement	Data & Probability
Problem Solving	Reasoning	Communication	Connections	Representation

GRAPH

Concepts & Skills

- Collect and organize data into bar and line graphs
- Analyze data and interpret graphs
- Make predictions using graphs

Materials for October

3 copies of Centimeter Squared Paper cardstock or TR15; crayons or markers in 2 colors; newspaper or computer access to daily temperatures, scissors, tape

Author Notes

"Graphing is a way to represent data. By graphing with students, we allow them to collect and organize data, to analyze information, to interpret data, and to make predictions. These are very important skills."

Setup

- Cut and tape the Centimeter Squared Paper to create 2 graphs, each about 10 cm by 50 cm. Add labels identifying your locale and the other city where you want to record the temperature.
- Add a key below the graphs showing that each square centimeter represents 2 degrees Fahrenheit.
- Assign 10 dates in October to a few students who will be responsible for bringing temperature information for both cities. They can get the data from the newspaper or the computer. For example, if a student is reporting information on the 15th, be sure the information is the high temperature from the day before in both locales.

Daily Routine

- Record the temperatures by coloring the appropriate number of squares in columns for both cities. Use a different color for each city.

Ongoing Assessment

1. Which city has the highest temperature today?
2. What is the difference in the temperature of the two cities?
3. Are there any days when the temperatures were the same in both cities?

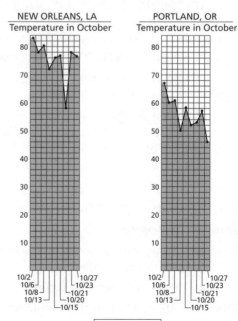

NEW ORLEANS, LA
Temperature in October

PORTLAND, OR
Temperature in October

■ = 2° Fahrenheit

© Great Source. Copying is prohibited.

DISCUSSION

For the Beginning of the Month

Explain that students will be gathering information about temperatures in their city and one other city. Assign students dates to bring information to class.

Sample Dialogue

Teacher: Today we'll graph the temperatures in our city and in another city. What were yesterday's high temperatures?

Student: The high in New Orleans was 83°F. In Portland, it was 67°F.

Teacher: Notice that each square on our graph equals 2°F. How many squares will we color to show 83 degrees?

Student: We'll need 41 whole squares and half of another.

Teacher: Great. Let's color that in red. How many squares do we need to color to represent 67 degrees?

Student: We need 33 and half of another.

Teacher: Yes. Let's color that in blue. What was the difference between the temperatures in New Orleans and in Portland yesterday? What are some quick ways we can count up from 67 degrees to 83 degrees?

For the Middle of the Month

Here are some questions to help students make inferences.

- What can you tell from these graphs?
- Has there been any pattern of temperatures in New Orleans this month? In Portland?
- How many days has the temperature in New Orleans been warmer than that in Portland?
- What has been the highest temperature in Portland? In New Orleans?
- Is this the highest temperature New Orleans experienced this month? (Maybe, we don't know since we only have a sample.)

For the End of the Month

At the end of the month, convert the Graph from a bar graph into a modified line graph. Draw a circle at the top of each column as shown at the right. Connect each circle to the ones before and after to form a line graph. Do the same on both graphs. Ask some questions to compare the use of different kinds of graphs.

- What can you tell from a line graph that is not as easy to see from a bar graph?
- Which graph tells you more at a glance? Why?
- If you had to make another graph, which one would you use to reflect the information you gathered?

HELPFUL HINTS

- Record the temperatures on self-sticks notes so they can easily be reordered from least to greatest. Have students find the range of temperatures by comparing the lowest and highest temperature.
- At the end of the month, the class can present the same data using a stem-and-leaf plot, as shown at the right.

October Temperatures
in New Orleans

5	8
6	
7	2 6 6 7 8 8
8	0 3

Key: 5 | 8 means 58°F

A stem-and-leaf plot

© Great Source. Copying is prohibited.

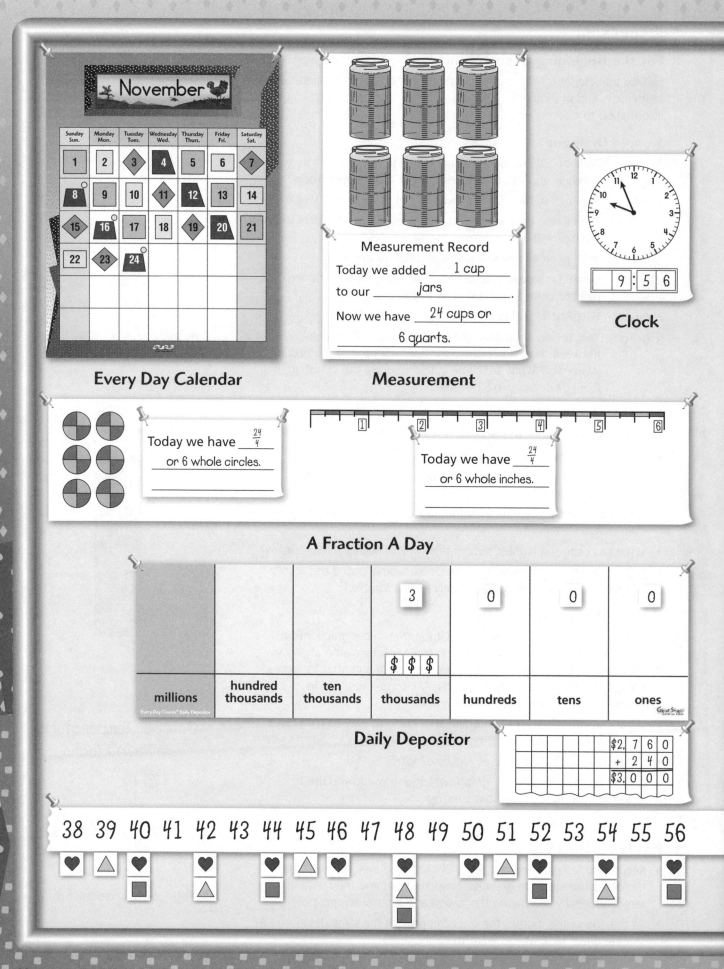

November

Sunday Sun.	Monday Mon.	Tuesday Tues.	Wednesday Wed.	Thursday Thurs.	Friday Fri.	Saturday Sat.
1	2	3	4	5	6	7
8	9	10	11	12	13	14
15	16	17	18	19	20	21
22	23	24				

Every Day Calendar

Measurement Record

Today we added ___1 cup___

to our ___jars___.

Now we have ___24 cups or___

___6 quarts.___

Measurement

Clock

9 : 5 6

Today we have $\frac{24}{4}$

or 6 whole circles.

Today we have $\frac{24}{4}$

or 6 whole inches.

| 1 | 2 | 3 | 4 | 5 | 6 |

A Fraction A Day

			3	0	0	0
			$ $ $			
millions	hundred thousands	ten thousands	thousands	hundreds	tens	ones

Every Day Counts® Daily Depositor

Daily Depositor

		$2,	7	6	0
	+		2	4	0
		$3,	0	0	0

38 39 40 41 42 43 44 45 46 47 48 49 50 51 52 53 54 55 56

NOVEMBER

Shopping Record

Purchase(s)

JUICE DRINK 47¢

Today's Amount $ 0.56

Show Your Work Here

Total Cost $ 0.47

Amount Left $ 0.09

Today we have

$ 0 . 5 6

Coin Counter

Counting Tape

NOVEMBER ELEMENTS

CALENDAR **48**

recognize patterns in multiples of 4 and 8; compare and analyze attributes of quadrilaterals; visualize rotation of quadrilaterals; recognize lines of symmetry

DAILY DEPOSITOR **50**

understand place value; multiply by ten; perform multi-digit addition; use mental math

MEASUREMENT **52**

convert cups to quarts; examine mixed numbers and fractional parts

A FRACTION A DAY **54**

visualize fractions; write improper fractions as mixed numbers; see equivalence between fourths and halves

COUNTING TAPE **56**

explore multiples and factors; continue patterns of multiples of 2, 3, and 4

COIN COUNTER **57**

count mixed coins; solve word problems using mental addition and subtraction; determine the least number of coins for a given amount

CLOCK **59**

read and set the minute and hour hands; understand passage of time up to an hour

In November, there is a strong focus on multiples of 4, 4 as a factor, and fourths. Square Multiple Markers are added to the Counting Tape. The Every Day Calendar focuses on quadrilaterals and number patterns. Measurement focuses on cups and quarts, and the Coin Counter features pretend shopping problems. The Daily Depositor adds an amount equal to ten times the date all month.

Number & Operations   Algebra   Geometry   Measurement   Data & Probability
Problem Solving   Reasoning   Communication   Connections   Representation

CALENDAR

Concepts & Skills

- Analyze and predict patterns
- Recognize patterns of multiples of 4 and 8
- Compare and analyze attributes of quadrilaterals
- Visualize rotation of quadrilaterals
- Recognize lines of symmetry
- Reason logically

Daily Routine

- Each day, attach the Calendar Piece for that day. On Mondays, attach pieces for the weekend days.

Ongoing Assessment

1. What is the first multiple of 4 greater than 30?

2. Compare a trapezoid and a rhombus. How are they alike? How are they different?

3. What are the next 3 numbers in the pattern that begins 3, 7, 11, 15?

DISCUSSION

For the Beginning of the Month

As in earlier months, encourage students to share their early observations about the patterns they see.

- Every 4th shape seems to be a trapezoid.
- The pattern repeats every 4 days.
- The diagonals going down to the right repeat the same shape.

Sample Dialogue

Teacher: What do you notice about the Calendar shapes this month?

Student: They all have 4 sides.

Teacher: Does anyone remember what we call polygons with 4 sides?

Student: Quadrilaterals .

Teacher: What are the names of these particular quadrilaterals?

Student: The first one is a square and the second one is a rectangle.

Teacher: Yes, and what about the next one?

Student: It looks like a diamond.

Teacher: Yes it does. We call it a rhombus. What is the name of the last shape?

Student: It looks something like a red pattern block. I think it's called a trapezoid .

Teacher: Yes, this is a trapezoid. How is it different from the other 3 shapes?

Student: The others have parallel opposite sides and it looks like some of the sides are the same length. But the trapezoid doesn't look like that.

Teacher: Are any sides parallel in the trapezoid?

Student: Yes, the top and the bottom.

Teacher: What if I turned it? Then which sides are parallel?

The November Calendar Pieces create an ABCD pattern using quadrilaterals in the order square, rectangle, rhombus, and trapezoid. The multiples of 8 are all isosceles trapezoids. The square, rectangle, and rhombus are rotated 90° each time they appear. There are two different trapezoids in the pattern. They are not rotated so that students can more easily compare them. Also, the square does not seem to be rotated because it appears the same when rotated 90°.

© Great Source. Copying is prohibited.

Student: The left and right sides.

Teacher: So however I turn it, the trapezoid has 1 pair of parallel sides, but the other shapes have 2 pairs of parallel sides. Let's make a list of the attributes of these 4 quadrilaterals.

For the Middle of the Month

The following questions might prompt more algebraic thinking.

- Today is the 18th of November. What shape will be on the Calendar Piece today? (upright rectangle)
- What shape will appear 1 week from today? (square)
- When will the next isosceles trapezoid appear? (on the 24th, a multiple of 8)
- What is the number pattern for the trapezoids? (the multiples of 4)
- Describe the dates for the squares in terms of the dates for the trapezoids. (The squares are 1 more than a multiple of 4. Since 0×4 is 0, the first square is on the 1st.)
- What do you notice about the pattern moving diagonally down to the right? (The shape is the same and the number increases by 8.)
- Why does the shape pattern repeat itself on that diagonal? (Every 4 days the pattern repeats, so it will repeat again every 8 days.)
- Which shapes look the same when they are turned 90° and which look different? (The rectangle and rhombus are congruent but look different when turned. The square looks the same.)

To Sum Up
Sample Dialogue

Teacher: In what ways are a rhombus and a square alike?

Student: Both are four-sided polygons with equal sides.

Teacher: How are they different?

Student: The square has right angles but the rhombus doesn't.

Teacher: A rhombus is a quadrilateral with all sides equal and opposite sides parallel. Is a square a rhombus?

Student: Yes, because all its sides are equal and parallel.

Teacher: Does it matter how the rhombus is turned? Is it still a rhombus?

Student: It looks different, but it's still a rhombus.

Teacher: Does a rhombus have a line of symmetry?

Student: Yes, it has 2. They go from one corner to the opposite corner.

Teacher: Does the trapezoid have a line of symmetry?

Student: Some of them do.

Teacher: Which ones?

Student: The ones that are on the multiples of 8. It goes from one parallel side to the other in the middle of the shape. But trapezoids like the one on the 4th don't have a line of symmetry.

Teacher: Yes. The trapezoid on the 4th has right angles, but the one on the 8th doesn't. So we can't say that either a line of symmetry or a right angle is an attribute of a trapezoid.

Calendar Shapes
- quadrilateral: a closed figure with 4 sides
- rectangle: a quadrilateral with 2 pairs of parallel sides and 4 right angles
- square: a rectangle with all 4 sides equal
- rhombus: a quadrilateral with 4 equal sides
- trapezoid: a quadrilateral with one pair of parallel sides

The completed November Calendar

© Great Source. Copying is prohibited.

HELPFUL HINT

- Continue to use the Calendar to practice and reinforce the multiplication facts. This month students should see that the facts for 8 are just double the facts for 4.

DAILY DEPOSITOR

Concepts & Skills

- Multiply by ten
- Use mental math
- Perform multi-digit addition
- Understand place value
- Estimate and predict

Ongoing Assessment

1. What is 12 × 10? 23 × 10? 55 × 10?

2. What is three hundred more than 2,820?

3. How would you write 3,689 in expanded notation?

Author Notes

"In November, the amount deposited each day and the daily total will both have a zero in the ones place. This gives students both a model for and practice with the fact that multiplying any number by 10 will always yield a zero in the ones place. This is wonderful preparation for double-digit multiplication, since it provides a strong background for mentally computing an answer to a problem such as 12 × 7."

Setup

- Be sure the totals for September ($465) and October ($992) are in plain view. The cumulative total ($1,457) should also be visible. Empty the Depositor of play money and start fresh on the first day of November.

Daily Routine

- Each day in November, add a dollar amount equal to 10 times the date.
- Record the addition and the total every day.

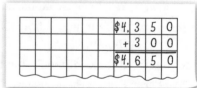

DISCUSSION

For the Beginning of the Month

Explain the rule that will determine how much money will be deposited each day during the month. Here are some sample questions to initiate the discussion.

- How much money will we deposit on November 1st? ($10) How much will we deposit on November 2nd? ($20) How much on the 8th of November? ($80)

- How much money do you predict we will collect this month?

- How much do you predict we will have in the Depositor altogether at the end of November? How did you make your predictions?

© Great Source. Copying is prohibited.

Help students to use subtraction to solve problems by posing a pretend expenditure once a week. After discussion, return the bills to the Depositor.

For the Eighth Day of the Month
Sample Dialogue

Teacher: Before we add today's amount, let's do some mental math. We have $280, but we need $325 for a field trip. How much more money do we need?

Student: $45.

Teacher: That's right. How did you get your answer?

Student: I added $20 to $280 to get $300. Then I added $25 more.

Teacher: So you used addition. Did anyone use mental subtraction?

Student: Yes. I subtracted $25 from $325. Then I subtracted $20 more to get to $280. The total difference was $45.

For the Eighteenth Day of the Month
Sample Dialogue

Teacher: How much money did we have this morning?

Student: $1,530.

Teacher: Today is the 18th. How much will we add today?

Student: $180.

Teacher: How did you get your answer?

Student: I added a zero at the end of 18.

Teacher: Why?

Student: Because I've noticed that every time we multiply by 10 we get a number with a zero at the end.

Teacher: Can we say that every date we have multiplied by 10 always gives us a result with a zero in the ones place?

Student: Yes.

Teacher: Why do you think this is true? Why is 18 tens 180?

Student: Well, when you multiply 18 by 10 it's like getting 18 ten-dollar bills. Ten of those make $100 and you have $80 more.

Teacher: Do you think this pattern will always be true? Will we always get an answer with a zero in the ones place when we multiply a number by 10?

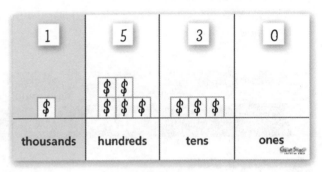

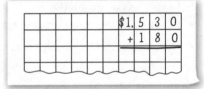

For the End of the Month

Before school closes for break in November, have students predict how much money should be added while school is closed, and update the total when you return.

These questions can be used to encourage an understanding of the patterns that have been part of the Daily Depositor since the beginning of the year.

- How much money did we deposit during November? ($4,650)

- How much did we deposit in September? ($465)

- How can we describe how these two numbers relate to each other? (Some possible responses might include that they use the same digits

© Great Source. Copying is prohibited.

except that the November total has a zero at the end, or that the larger number is 10 times the smaller one, or that you can get the larger number by multiplying the smaller number by 10. Help students see that these two numbers show the result of multiplying a number by 10: a zero in the ones place.)

Place value and number sense:

- How many thousands did we deposit this month? (4) How many hundreds? (6) How many tens? (5) How many ones? (0)

- How can we write the total in expanded notation? (4,000 + 600 + 50 + 0, or 4 thousands + 6 hundreds + 5 tens + 0 ones)

- If we represented 4,650 only with hundreds, how many would we have? (46)

- Is 4,650 closer to 4,000 or 5,000? (5,000)

Prediction and estimation:

- How much money have we deposited since the beginning of the school year? ($6,107)

- Do you think we will have one million dollars by the end of December?

Daily Depositor				
Month	Days in the Month	Total for the Month	Cumulative Total	Daily Deposit Amount
September	30	$465		$1 times date
October	31	$992	$1,457	$2 times date
November	30	$4,650	$6,107	$10 times date
December	31			
January	31			
February	28 or 29			
March	31			
April	30			
May	31			

Number & Operations   Algebra   Geometry   **Measurement**   Data & Probability
Problem Solving   Reasoning   Communication   Connections   Representation

MEASUREMENT

Concepts & Skills

- Convert cups to quarts
- Examine mixed numbers and fractional parts
- Develop referents for cups and quarts

Materials for November

An 8-ounce cup or jar; a 16-ounce container or pint jar; eight 32-ounce containers or quart jars; Measurement Record cardstock or a copy of TR10 in a large clear pocket; watercolor marker; colored water; 8 copies of the Quart/Liter Drawings (TR16)

Setup

- Label the 8-ounce jar *1 cup*. Label the 16-ounce jar *1 pint*. Label each 32-ounce jar *1 quart*. Display all 3 jars where they easily can be seen.
- Display 1 Quart Drawing and the Measurement Record on the board.

Daily Routine

- Pour 1 cup of colored water into one of the quart jars each day.
- Color 1 cup on the Quart Drawing for each cup that is added to the quart containers.
- Whenever a quart container is filled, begin filling the next one and post a new Quart Drawing on the board.
- Every 4 days, write *1 quart* above the Quart Drawing and on the quart jar.

Ongoing Assessment

1. How many cups are in 1 pint? How many pints are in 1 quart? How many cups are in 1 quart?
2. What fraction of a quart is 1 cup?
3. What is another name for 18 cups?

© Great Source. Copying is prohibited.

DISCUSSION

For the Beginning of the Month

Show students the quart jar, the cup container, and the Quart Drawing. Explain that 1 cup (8 oz) of colored water will be added to a quart jar daily. Ask if students know how many cups are in a quart. Demonstrate by actually filling the cup container twice to fill the pint and filling the pint container twice to fill the quart. Ask students to tell where cups, pints, and quarts are used in daily life.

Sample Dialogue

Teacher: If we add 1 cup to the quart jar each day, how many days until we fill it?

Student: I think there are 4 cups in a quart, so it will take 4 days.

Teacher: That is correct. So when we pour 1 cup into the quart, what fraction of the quart are we filling?

Student: We're filling $\frac{1}{4}$ of the quart.

Teacher: If we add 1 cup each day, how many quarts will we fill by the end of the month?

Student: About 4 quarts.

Student: I think we will have about 10 quarts.

Teacher: What's your reasoning?

For the Middle of the Month

On November 19, there will be 19 cups, or $4\frac{3}{4}$ quarts. This is a good time to ask some questions about mixed numbers and fractions.

- How many cups do we have today? (19)
- How many whole quarts do we have today? (4) How many cups are left over? (3)
- How can we write the leftover amount as a fraction? ($\frac{3}{4}$, because 3 out of the 4 cups needed to make another quart are left over.)
- Let's count the fourths and see how many we have. ($\frac{19}{4}$)
- Do you see $4\frac{3}{4}$ cups when you look up here? (yes)

Record this on the Measurement Record.

Measurement Record
Today we added ____1 cup____ to our _____jars_____.
Now we have ___19 cups or___ ___$4\frac{3}{4}$ quarts.___

For the End of the Month

Summarize all the facts that have been observed.

- Review how many cups equal 1 quart.
- Review 1 cup as $\frac{1}{4}$ of a quart.
- Examine how many cups have been added and ask how many quarts in all.
- Compare the estimates of the amount to be measured with the actual amount in the jars after 30 days.

HELPFUL HINTS

- Have students bring empty plastic quart jars from home. Use them as containers for collecting the colored water. Be sure to have a lid for each container because evaporation affects the outcome.

© Great Source. Copying is prohibited.

- Have students cut out the Quart Drawings so they are ready to use when you need them. Also, since updating daily involves adding a cup of water, assign students this task. Then you will lead discussion on those days.

Number & Operations	Algebra	Geometry	Measurement	Data & Probability
Problem Solving	Reasoning	Communication	Connections	Representation

A FRACTION A DAY

Concepts & Skills
- Visualize fractions
- Understand numerator and denominator
- Write improper fractions as mixed numbers
- Find a fraction of a set
- Compute with fractions
- See fractional equivalencies

Materials for November
8 copies of the Giant Inch from TR11, 8 circles from TR11, Fraction Record (TR13), markers or crayons in 2 bright colors, black crayon or marker

Author Notes
A Fraction A Day continues to use different models to help students develop flexibility in comparing and computing with fractions. This month, A Fraction A Day adds one fourth each day using a line model represented by a Giant "Inch" as well as the area model represented by a pizza (or circle).

Setup
- Cut out 8 circles from TR11. Post one, leaving room for more.
- Cut out 8 copies of the Inch. Post one, leaving room for the other 7 Inches to be connected to form a line with no gaps.

Daily Routine
- **The first day,** tell the class that you will draw 4 equal parts of a pizza (or circle). Use the black marker to draw a line from the 3 o'clock position to 9 o'clock and from the 12 to the 6.
- Shade in or outline one fourth of the circle each day, including weekends and holidays. **Use alternating colors to keep the fourths distinct.**
- When a circle is filled, post a new one next to it, and continue to shade one fourth each day.
- Also shade one fourth of the Giant Inch each day. Again use alternating colors to keep the fourths distinct.
- Each day record the total amount displayed as both a fraction and (after day 4) as a mixed number.

Ongoing Assessment
1. If Runner A runs $1\frac{3}{4}$ miles and Runner B runs $1\frac{1}{2}$ miles, who runs farther?
2. Explain how you would change a fraction greater than 1 into a mixed number.
3. What is $\frac{1}{4}$ of a dozen? What does the denominator tell us?

Draw fourths with lines from 3 o'clock to 9 and from 12 to 6.

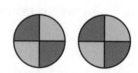

Today we have _____ $\frac{7}{4}$
or 1 whole and $\frac{3}{4}$
or $1\frac{3}{4}$ circles.

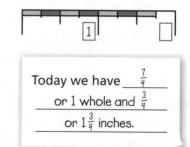

Today we have _____ $\frac{7}{4}$
or 1 whole and $\frac{3}{4}$
or $1\frac{3}{4}$ inches.

© Great Source. Copying is prohibited.

DISCUSSION

For the Beginning of the Month
Sample Dialogue

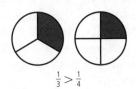

$$\frac{1}{3} > \frac{1}{4}$$

Teacher: This month, we are cutting the pizza into 4 equal parts Are these fourths bigger or smaller than last month's thirds?

Student: Smaller.

Teacher: Then can we say that $\frac{1}{3}$ from last month is more than $\frac{1}{4}$?

Student: Yes.

Teacher: How can we write that sentence with numbers and signs?

Student: $\frac{1}{3} > \frac{1}{4}$ and $\frac{1}{4} < \frac{1}{3}$

Teacher: We also have a giant Inch divided into four equal sections. I'll shade the first part. What is 1 out of 4 equal parts?

Class: One fourth.

Teacher: When we have shaded in 3 of the fourths, what is that?

Student: Three fourths.

Student: That's like 3 fourths of an inch when you're measuring.

Teacher: Very good. How do we write three fourths?

Student: Three over 4. Like this: $\frac{3}{4}$.

For Throughout the Month

The following sample questions can be used on the 18th or adapted for other days. Students will see more patterns and relationships the more often questions like these are posed.

Today we have $\frac{18}{4}$

or 4 wholes and $\frac{2}{4}$

or $4\frac{2}{4}$ or $4\frac{1}{2}$ inches.

"18 fourths is 4 wholes and 2 extra fourths."

Mixed numbers

- How many whole inches are covered by 18 fourth-inches? (4 wholes and 2 extra fourths)
- How many extra fourth-inches beyond 4 whole inches are there? (2)
- How do we write $\frac{18}{4}$ as a mixed number? ($4\frac{2}{4}$, or $4\frac{1}{2}$)

Fraction sense

- How long until we have $5\frac{1}{4}$ inches? (3 days)
- How do you know? (We need 2 more fourths to finish another whole. then we'll have 5 whole, and one more makes $5\frac{1}{4}$.)
- How many people could be served a fourth of a pizza today? (18)
- How do you know? (We have 18 fourths, or, each pizza serves 4 and we have 4 pizzas plus 2 more fourths.)

Equivalent fractions:

- How many one-fourths of a pizza makes a half pizza? (2)
- How do you know? (If you put 2 fourths together and another 2 fourths together that's two equal parts of a whole.)
- How many one-fourths of a pizza make $1\frac{1}{2}$ pizzas? (6)
- How do you know? (Four fourths makes a whole, and two more fourths makes a half.)

"Two fourths are the same as one half."

© Great Source. Copying is prohibited.

HELPFUL HINTS

- *Real-World Fractions* Ask students to brainstorm examples of fourths in the real world. For example, a quarter is a fourth of a dollar, a fourth of an hour is a quarter (so 15 minutes is $\frac{1}{4}$ of 60), one season is a fourth of the year, a football game has 4 quarters, and sandwiches are often cut into fourths by cutting halves in half. After brainstorming your own class list, you might draw from those examples to write or even have the students write related word problems.

"Four quarters make a dollar. A quarter is $\frac{1}{4}$ of a dollar."

- To provide more practice with fourths, consider this activity. Whenever the date is a multiple of 4, have that number of students divide themselves onto 4 equal teams. So on the 16th, students see that $\frac{1}{4}$ of the group of 16 is 4 students, $\frac{2}{4}$ is 8 students, and so on.

- *Fraction Kits* Let students mark, label, and cut their own sets of fourths using copies of TR11 to add to the Fraction Kits they made last month. Use the pieces to act out story problems.

Number & Operations	Algebra	Geometry	Measurement	Data & Probability
Problem Solving	Reasoning	Communication	Connections	Representation

COUNTING TAPE

Concepts & Skills

- Explore multiples and factors
- Count by fours
- Know multiplication facts for 4
- See the relationship between multiples of 2 and 4
- Investigate multiplication and division with remainders
- Write algebraic expressions for multiples of 4

Materials for November

Square Multiple Markers cardstock, copies of Circular Array Paper (TR7), Hundred Chart (TR4), and Equation Chart (TR5)

Daily Routine

- Continue to have students identify and mark multiples of 2 and 3 with Multiple Markers. Begin marking multiples of 4 with purple Square Multiple Markers.

Ongoing Assessment

1. Count by fours from 4 to 40.
2. On what number will we hang our 7th square? Our 9th?
3. What is 6×4? What is 7×4? What is 8×4? What strategy did you use to answer the questions?

DISCUSSION

For the Beginning of the Month

"48 is a multiple of 2, 3, and 4."

Explain that this month, the class will continue marking multiples of 2 and 3 and begin marking multiples of 4. Beginning at 4, ask students to count by fours while you mark the multiples of 4 with the purple squares. It is important that students see the markers placed on the Tape to grasp the evolving pattern.

- What pattern do you see when you look at the numbers in the ones place for the multiples of 4? (4, 8, 2, 6, 0; they're all even numbers.)

© Great Source. Copying is prohibited.

- What other patterns do you see? (Multiples of 4 are every other multiple of 2.)

For the Middle of the Month

The following questions can be used to revisit the concept of common multiples and introduce the term least common multiple.

- What numbers have both heart and square markers and are common multiples of 2 and 4? (4, 8, 12, and so on)
- Look at the Counting Tape. What is the least common multiple of 2 and 4? (4)
- Do numbers that break up evenly into 4s always break up into 2s? Why? (Yes, because there are 2 groups of 2 in each group of 4.)
- What numbers on the Tape have three markers: heart, square, and triangle? (12, 24, 36, and so on)
- What do the markers tell us about these numbers? (They all break up into groups of 2, 3, and 4 with no leftovers.)
- What is the least number of cans of soup that can be packaged by 2s, 3s, and 4s with no leftovers? (12 cans) So what is the least common multiple of 2, 3 and 4? (12)

For the End of the Month

- As at the end of September and October, distribute copies of the Hundred Chart (TR4) and the Equation Chart (TR5). Students should complete these as they have in months past and add them to their Multiplication Books. Multiplication facts for 4, as they are learned and recalled easily, can be shaded on the cover of the books.
- As in previous months, use Circular Array Paper to make Array Flash Cards for facts 4×4 to 10×4. This can help students practice these facts. These models also illustrate the commutative property and help students see that factors of numbers represent the number of equal groups and the number within each group. Finally, they show that if a number is a multiple of 4, it has 4 as a factor and can be broken up into 4 equal groups, with each group being one fourth.

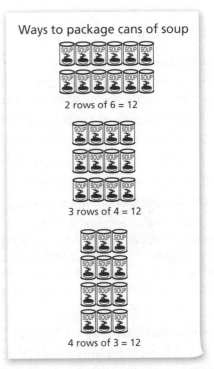

Ways to package cans of soup

2 rows of 6 = 12

3 rows of 4 = 12

4 rows of 3 = 12

12 is the least common multiple of 2, 3, and 4.

Number & Operations	Algebra	Geometry	Measurement	Data & Probability
Problem Solving	Reasoning	Communication	Connections	Representation

COIN COUNTER

Concepts & Skills

- Count mixed coins
- Determine the fewest coins for a given amount
- Solve word problems using mental addition and subtraction
- See pennies and dimes as hundredths and tenths of a dollar
- Use decimal notation for tenths and hundredths

Materials for the Rest of the Year

Shopper Cards cardstock or TR17, Shopping Record cardstock or TR18 in a large clear pocket

Ongoing Assessment

1. If you use 2 quarters to buy a can of juice for 35¢, how much change will you get?
2. How many tenths of a dollar are in today's amount?
3. If you have today's amount and buy an eraser for 37¢, how much money will you have left?

© Great Source. Copying is prohibited.

Setup

- Cut up the Shopper Cards and store them in an envelope near the board.

Daily Routine

- Continue to display the combination with the fewest possible coins in the top pocket.
- Continue to use the 100 Penny Grid (TR9) to see and talk about the day's amount as tenths and hundredths of a dollar.
- Occasionally, have students select a Shopper Card and make a pretend purchase using the day's amount.

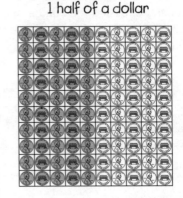

DISCUSSION

Throughout the Month

Show students the Shopper Cards. Ask a volunteer to choose one card. The following questions can be adapted for any day this month.

- What is the price of the Shopper Card item?
- Do we have enough money to pay for it?
- If yes, how much money would we have left?
- If no, how much more money do we need to be able to pay for it?
- Can anyone share how you got your answer using mental math?

It is important to encourage students to share their mental math strategies for subtraction. Most students will share a variety of counting up strategies. Some will use rounding to make the problem simpler and then adjust to get an exact answer. It won't be long before students who lack confidence begin trying strategies learned from others.

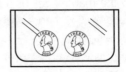
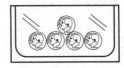
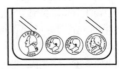

Today we have

$ _0_ . _5_ _0_

5 dimes = 5 tenths or
1 half of a dollar

The Coin Counter on day 50

For the Fiftieth Day of School

On Day 50, show students a real half dollar or a copy of one from Play Money: Coins (TR8). While it is important that students be able to recognize these coins, explain that they are very rarely used. For this reason, we suggest keeping the quarter as the coin of greatest value in the Coin Counter.

Sample Dialogue

Teacher: Let's look at the half dollar with President Kennedy on the "heads" side and an eagle on the "tails" side. How much is half a dollar?

Student: Fifty cents.

Teacher: Yes. We can see that half of our 100 Penny Grid is colored in. What else do you notice?

Student: 50¢ is 5 columns. That's five tenths.

Student: That's the same as 5 dimes.

Teacher: So, when we write $0.50 it can mean 5 dimes or 5 tenths of a dollar and zero extra pennies. What is another way we can read this decimal?

Student: Fifty hundredths.

© Great Source. Copying is prohibited.

Teacher: That's another way to say one half. If someone said they paid 50% of the price of a $20-dollar basketball, how much did they pay?

Student: Half the price, or $10.

Teacher: Yes, 50 percent means 50 out of 100, or one half.

HELPFUL HINT

- To increase the challenge you may want to have students select 2 Shopper Cards for the pretend purchase. Let students share any mental addition strategies they use to determine if they can make the complete purchase.

Number & Operations   Algebra   Geometry   **Measurement**   Data & Probability
Problem Solving   **Reasoning**   **Communication**   **Connections**   **Representation**

CLOCK

Concepts & Skills

- Read and set the minute and hour hands
- Understand passage of time up to an hour

Daily Routine

- Keep the hour hand at 9 again this month.
- Use the number of the day in school to set the minute hand.

DISCUSSION

During the Month

On the 48th day of school, cover the Clock on the board with a piece of paper. Ask what the Clock will look like if the time is 9:48. This will help students to visualize the Clock and to verbalize what they see. Some responses might include:

- The hour hand is close to the 10.
- It looks like it is almost 10:00.
- The minute hand is close to the 10.
- The minute hand is a little past quarter to ten.

HELPFUL HINT

- If your days in school reach 60 before the end of November, refer to December's discussion for activities dealing with more than 60 minutes on the Clock.

Ongoing Assessment

1. Draw what the Clock looks like at 9:42.
2. What is another name for 9:34?
3. What time will it be 5 minutes after 9:38?

The Clock says 9:48, or 12 minutes before 10.

© Great Source. Copying is prohibited.

Every Day Calendar

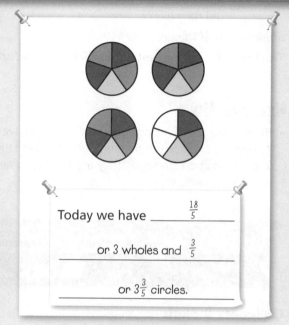

Today we have _____ $\frac{18}{5}$

or 3 wholes and $\frac{3}{5}$ _____

or $3\frac{3}{5}$ circles. _____

A Fraction A Day

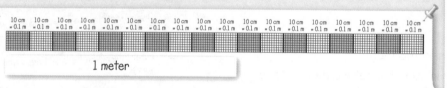

| 10 cm = 0.1 m | 10 cm = 0.1 m | 10 cm = 0.1 m | 10 cm = 0.1 m | 10 cm = 0.1 m | 10 cm = 0.1 m | 10 cm = 0.1 m | 10 cm = 0.1 m | 10 cm = 0.1 m | 10 cm = 0.1 m | 10 cm = 0.1 m | 10 cm = 0.1 m | 10 cm = 0.1 m | 10 cm = 0.1 m | 10 cm = 0.1 m | 10 cm = 0.1 m | 10 cm = 0.1 m | 10 cm = 0.1 m |

1 meter

Measurement

Measurement Record
Today we added 10 cm, or 1 dm
to our _____ length _____ .
Now we have _____ 180 cm, or

18 dm, or $1\frac{8}{10}$ m, or 1.8 m.

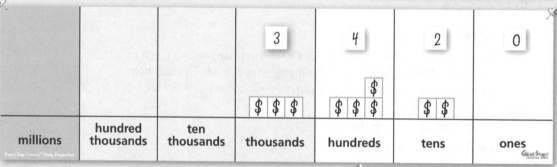

millions	hundred thousands	ten thousands	thousands	hundreds	tens	ones
			3	4	2	0

Every Day Counts® Daily Depositor

Daily Depositor

					$3,	0	6	0
				+		3	6	0
				$3,	4	2	0

53 54 55 56 57 58 59 60 61 62 63 64 65 66 67 68 69 70 71

Counting Tape

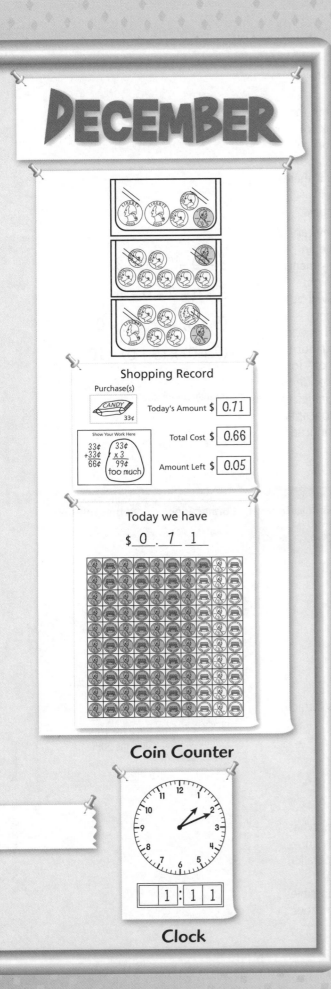

DECEMBER

Shopping Record

Purchase(s)

CANDY 33¢

Today's Amount $ 0.71

Show Your Work Here

33¢	33¢
+33¢	x 3
66¢	99¢
	too much

Total Cost $ 0.66

Amount Left $ 0.05

Today we have

$ 0 . 7 1

Coin Counter

Clock

1 : 1 1

DECEMBER ELEMENTS

CALENDAR **62**

recognize patterns in multiples of 5; compare and analyze attributes of lines and line segments

DAILY DEPOSITOR **63**

multiply by 20; use mental math; perform multi-digit addition; estimate and predict

MEASUREMENT **66**

write centimeters as decimeters and meters; express measurement using fractions and decimals

A FRACTION A DAY **68**

visualize fractions; find a fraction of a set; see equivalence between fifths, tenths, and parts of a dollar

COUNTING TAPE **70**

see relationship between multiples of 5 and 10; investigate multiplication and division with remainders

COIN COUNTER **72**

use estimation and mental math; count mixed coins; use decimal notation for tenths and hundredths

CLOCK **72**

differentiate between A.M. and P.M.; determine minutes greater than an hour

In December, there are fewer school days than in other months, and it is often a hectic month because of the approaching holidays. To minimize preparation time, there are no new elements introduced this month. Emphasis is placed on continuing those elements used previously in the year.

The December chapter begins with a few suggestions for activities related to the end of the calendar year. These are intended to provide some enrichment and excitement for students as they connect the end of the calendar year to mathematics.

ENDING THE YEAR

Suggestions for activities to highlight the end of the calendar year are listed below.

- At the beginning of December, count the number of days left in the calendar year. Have students make a paper chain with one link for each day left until December 31. You can assign different colors to the even and odd numbers. Each day tear off one of the links and record the number of links remaining as a fraction of 365. So if there are 23 links on the chain, there is $\frac{23}{365}$ of a year left. This allows students to see that fractions occur with large and small numbers.

- Challenge students to write as many number sentences as they can, using all four of the numbers in the calendar year. For example, in 2005 they must use 2, 0, 0, and 5. The object is to produce as many different answers as possible. Before beginning the list, you might ask the students to predict how many different answers they will be able to find. Allow students to use all four operations (addition, subtraction, multiplication, and division). Look for the smallest possible number and the largest possible number. This investigation may give you an opportunity to introduce the term "quantity of" for numbers and operations within parentheses, when students decide to use more than one operation. The zeros will give you opportunities to review the identity properties of zero, as well as place value concepts. If the year is 2005, some number sentences that might be produced are shown at the right.

$$5 - 0 - 2 - 0 = 3$$
$$5 + 0 + 2 + 0 = 7$$
$$(5 \times 0) + (2 \times 0) = 0$$
$$(2 + 0) \times (5 + 0) = 10$$

Number sentences for 2005

Number & Operations	Algebra	Geometry	Measurement	Data & Probability
Problem Solving	Reasoning	Communication	Connections	Representation

CALENDAR

Concepts & Skills

- Analyze and predict patterns
- Recognize patterns in multiples of 5
- Compare and analyze attributes of lines and line segments

Daily Routine

- Each day, attach the Calendar Piece for that day. On Mondays, attach pieces for the weekend days.

DISCUSSION

For the Beginning of the Month

Ask students what they remember about lines and line segments. What are some of the words used to describe them? Write these words on the board and ask for definitions. Encourage students to model parallel, intersecting, and perpendicular lines with their arms. Point out that there are many words used in geometry to explain as clearly as possible exactly what we are talking about. Illustrate the notation used to show the difference between a line and a line segment. Continue to encourage students to discover patterns as the month continues.

Ongoing Assessment

1. Draw two perpendicular lines.
2. Which number doesn't belong in this pattern? 2, 4, 5, 6, 8, 10, 12
3. 5, 10, 15, 20, 25, 30 are the first 6 numbers in a pattern. If this pattern continued, what would the 20th number be?

© Great Source. Copying is prohibited.

For the Middle of the Month

Since this is a shorter month in school, you will probably discuss the Calendar only four or five times. Alternate between questions about lines and number patterns. Some possible questions might include:

- How often do the parallel lines appear? (on multiples of 5)
- How many parallel lines will appear in the month? (6)
- What kind of lines will be on today's piece? How do you know?
- What kind of lines will appear one week from today? How do you know? (Students may count out the pattern, but encourage them to find a strategy that uses the fact that the pattern repeats every 5 days and a week is 7 days.)
- What is the number pattern for the perpendicular lines? (4, 9, 14, 19, 24, and so on)
- What other patterns do you notice on the Calendar?
- Describe the difference between intersecting lines and parallel lines. (Intersecting means the lines cross. Parallel lines never meet or cross.)
- Are perpendicular lines intersecting? Why or why not? (Yes, because they cross.)
- How do we mark a line segment to show it is not a line? (We put points at both ends.)
- Describe the angles created when two lines are perpendicular. (They are all 90° or right angles.)
- Do you notice anything special about the angles when two lines intersect? (Students may suggest that opposite angles look equal or congruent. If not, return to this idea later when measuring angles.)

The December Calendar Pieces create an ABCDE pattern using lines and line segments.

HELPFUL HINT

- Use lengths of string or yarn to act out intersecting, perpendicular, and parallel lines.

Number & Operations	Algebra	Geometry	Measurement	Data & Probability
Problem Solving	Reasoning	Communication	Connections	Representation

DAILY DEPOSITOR

Concepts & Skills

- Multiply by 20
- Use mental math
- Perform multi-digit addition
- Understand place value
- Estimate and predict

Author Notes

"This month, one goal for the Depositor activity is to help students see that they can multiply multi-digit numbers mentally. Various strategies should be shared to achieve this result for students. For example, to calculate $20 times 17, demonstrate multiplying 17 times $10 ($170) and doubling that amount to get $340. Also demonstrate doubling 17 first (34) and then multiplying by $10. As students become better

Ongoing Assessment

1. What is the greatest odd number you can make using the digits 4, 5, 6, and 7?
2. What is 1×23? 2×23? 10×23? 20×23? Explain your mental math strategy.
3. What is 6,399 rounded to the nearest thousand?

© Great Source. Copying is prohibited.

mental mathematicians, their calculations with paper and pencil will reflect more reasonableness and accuracy.

Before school closes for winter break, it will be necessary to take time to complete the Depositor transactions through the end of the month. This can be used as an intensive problem-solving activity for the students."

Setup

- Be sure the totals for the 3 preceding months ($465, $992, and $4,650) as well as the cumulative total ($6,107) are in plain view. Empty the Depositor and start fresh on the first of December.

Daily Routine

- Each day in December, add a dollar amount equal to 20 times the date.
- Record the addition and the total every day.

DISCUSSION

For the Beginning of the Month

On December 1st, explain the rule that will be used to determine the daily amount to be added to the Depositor. Here are sample questions for the beginning of the month.

- How much money will we deposit on December 1st? ($20) How much on the 2nd? ($40) How much will we add on December 9th? ($180)
- How much money do you predict we will collect this month?
- How much money do you predict we will have in the Depositor at the end of December? Explain how you got your answer.

Continue to have students use subtraction to solve problems by posing a pretend expenditure once a week. After discussion, return the bills to the Depositor.

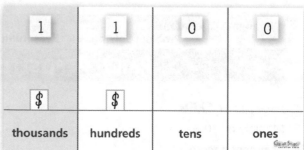

For the Tenth Day of the Month
Sample Dialogue

Teacher: Today is the 10th of December. How much money have we deposited so far this month?

Student: We add $200 to the $900 we had yesterday, so we have $1,100.

Teacher: That's right. I'm going to write the date and that amount on the board. (writes *First ten days of December—$1,100* on the board) Who remembers the rule we used last month to figure out how much we should deposit each day?

Student: We added $10 times the date in November.

Teacher: Yes. Now take a few minutes to figure out how much money we deposited during the first 10 days of November. You can use paper and pencil. Write down how much we added on each of the first 10 days, and then add those amounts together to find out how much we had deposited by November 10th. (pause) What answer did you get?

Student: We had $550 on the 10th of November.

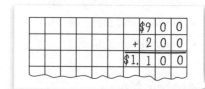

© Great Source. Copying is prohibited.

Teacher:	Good. I'm going to write that on the board. (writes *First ten days of November—$550* on the board) In October, we deposited a daily amount that was $2 times the date. Figure out how much money we had in the Depositor on October 10th. You can do it the same way. (pause) How much did we have? Why don't you come and write it on the board?	
Student:	(writes *First ten days of October—$110* on the board)	
Teacher:	That's correct. Now let's figure out how much we had after the first 10 days in September. Remember that we added $1 times the date in September. (pause) Come and write the amount on the board.	
Student:	(writes *First ten days of September—$55* on the board)	
Teacher:	Right. Looking at the chart we've made on the board, do you see a pattern to the numbers? If you do, try to describe the pattern you see.	
Student:	We had half as much money on November 10th as we do on December 10th.	
Student:	We have 10 times more money today than we had on October 10th.	
Student:	Yes, and on November 10th we had 10 times the amount we had on September 10th.	
Student:	We have 20 times more money today than we had on the 10th of September.	
Teacher:	Those are all good observations. Why do you think there is a pattern?	

Allow students to talk about the pattern and encourage them to express their thinking. Direct student attention to the relationship among the rules for each month.

Can you see a pattern?

On September 10th	–	$55
On October 10th	–	$110
On November 10th	–	$550
On December 10th	–	$1,100

For the Middle of the Month

Many schools close for winter vacation around the 18th of December. This provides an opportunity for a valuable problem-solving activity regarding how to update the amount added to the Depositor over a long period of time. For example, the Depositor will hold $3,420 on the 18th of December. The question to ask students is:

- How much money will be collected in the Depositor from December 19th to December 31st if we continue to add $20 times the date?

Students might work in groups to reach a solution to this problem. Here is one possible solution offered by one group of students.

- We noticed that if you add the first day, 19, to the last day, 31, or if you add the second day, 20, to the second-last day, 30, you get 50 each time. So we began to pair up all the days that are left in the month and got this:

    19 + 31 = 50
    20 + 30 = 50
    21 + 29 = 50
    22 + 28 = 50
    23 + 27 = 50
    24 + 26 = 50

That left 25 without a partner. We knew we had to multiply by $20 because that is the rule for the month. So we multiplied each 50 we had by 10 and then doubled that to get $1,000 for each sum of 50.

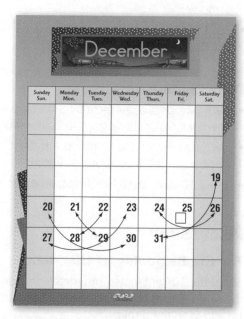

© Great Source. Copying is prohibited.

There are six 50s, so that is $6,000. Then we took the 25th day and multiplied it times $20, which is $500. $6,000 plus $500 is $6,500, so that is how much money will be deposited between now and the end of December.

Point out to the students that this is a difficult way to add large numbers in sequence, but that it works well for smaller numbers. Demonstrate this by showing that 1 + 2 + 3 + 4 = 10, and that 1 + 4 and 2 + 3 make two sums of 5, or 10. Also, 1 + 2 + 3 + 4 + 5 + 6 + 7 + 8 = 36, and that 1 + 8, 2 + 7, 3 + 6, and 4 + 5 make four sums of 9, or 36. Students enjoy practicing this procedure, and it may help them to compute the amount in the Depositor over long periods of time.

	Daily Depositor			
Month	Days in the Month	Total for the Month	Cumulative Total	Daily Deposit Amount
September	30	$465		$1 times date
October	31	$992	$1,457	$2 times date
November	30	$4,650	$6,107	$10 times date
December	31	$9,920	$16,027	$20 times date
January	31			
February	28 or 29			
March	31			
April	30			
May	31			

Number & Operations   Algebra   Geometry   **Measurement**   Data & Probability
Problem Solving   Reasoning   Communication   Connections   Representation

MEASUREMENT

Concepts & Skills
- Write centimeters as decimeters and meters
- Develop referents for centimeters, decimeters, and meters
- Express measurement in fractions and decimals

Materials for December
Thirty-one 10-cm by 8-cm strips of Centimeter Squared Paper (TR15); 3 meter-long strips of adding machine tape; meterstick; scissors; tape; 2 different-colored markers or crayons; Measurement Record (TR10)

Setup
- Cut copies of Centimeter Squared Paper (TR15) into 10-cm by 8-cm strips. Five of these can be made from each copy if the last one is taped together.
- Label each strip *10 cm, $\frac{1}{10}$ m, 0.1 m, 1 dm*.
- Cut 3 meter-long strips of adding machine tape. Label each one *1 meter*.
- Put the Measurement Record in a large clear pocket and post it on the board.

Daily Routine
- Each day, post one 10-cm by 8-cm strip in a line on the wall or on the floor. Color these strips in 2 alternating colors.
- Each day, record the length as a fraction or mixed number and as a decimal on the Measurement Record.
- Every 10 days, post 1 meter strip next to the centimeter strips.

DISCUSSION

For the Beginning of the Month
Show the 10-centimeter and meter-long strips of paper that have been displayed. Explain that each day of the month a 10-centimeter strip will be added to the display.

Ongoing Assessment
1. How many decimeters are in 120 centimeters?
2. If we have 120 centimeters, how can we write that as meters?
3. How many different ways can you express 150 centimeters?

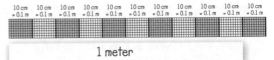

1 meter

Measurement Record

Today we added ___10 cm or 1 dm___
to our _____length_____.
Now we have ___110 cm, or___
___11 dm, or 1.1 m.___

© Great Source. Copying is prohibited.

Sample Dialogue

Teacher: Who knows how many centimeters are in a meter?

Student: There are 100.

Teacher: Yes. We will use these 10-centimeter strips to measure length this month. How many of these strips will equal a meter?

Student: 10.

Teacher: So what part of a meter is a 10-centimeter strip?

Student: It is $\frac{1}{10}$ of a meter.

Teacher: Another name for $\frac{1}{10}$ of a meter is a decimeter. So 1 decimeter is equal to 10 centimeters. There are 10 decimeters in one meter. Can we estimate where the strips will reach in the classroom by the end of the month?

Students give their estimates. Some teachers have students place small pieces of masking tape with their names to mark the estimates.

For the Fifteenth Day of the Month

The following questions are for December 15th. By changing the numbers, you can use these questions any day of the month.

- Look at the display and tell me how many centimeters we have. (150) How many decimeters are there? (15) How many meters are there? (1) How many extra centimeters? (50)

- How can we write the extra amount as a fraction? ($\frac{50}{100}$)

- How can we write the extra amount as a decimal? (0.50)

- How many 10-centimeter strips do we have today? (15) How many meters is that? (1) How many tenth strips are left over? (5)

- How can we write these leftover tenth strips as a fraction? ($\frac{5}{10}$) As a decimal? (0.5)

Record this on the Measurement Record.

For the End of the Month

To review, ask students to:

- Tell how many centimeters equal a meter.
- List objects in the room that are about 10 cm long.
- List things that are about 1 meter and about 1.5 meters long.
- Compare the estimates of where the tape would reach after 31 days to its actual length.

HELPFUL HINTS

- Have students prepare and mount the strips throughout the month.
- On Mondays, show the addition of decimal tenths adding 3 days worth of tenths. For example, if Monday is the 11th day of the month, write *0.8 m + 0.3 m = 1.1 m*. Record the problem vertically as well, as shown at the right.

Measurement Record

Today we added 10 cm or 1 dm to our _____ length _____.

Now we have 150 cm, or 15 dm, or $1\frac{1}{2}$ m, or 1.5 m.

$$\begin{array}{r} 0.8\text{ m} \\ +\ 0.3\text{ m} \\ \hline 1.1\text{ m} \end{array}$$

© Great Source. Copying is prohibited.

A Fraction A Day

Concepts & Skills

- Visualize fractions
- Understand numerator and denominator
- Write improper fractions as mixed numbers
- Find a fraction of a set
- Compute with fractions
- See fractional equivalencies

Ongoing Assessment

1. How many fifths are in $2\frac{3}{5}$?
2. Which is more, $\frac{4}{5}$ or $\frac{4}{4}$? How do you know?
3. How could you find $\frac{1}{5}$ of a dollar?

Materials for December

- 6 circles from TR11, Fraction Record (TR13), markers or crayons in 3 or more bright colors, black crayon or marker

Author Notes

A Fraction A Day continues in December with just the circle model. As students develop confidence with the concept of five equal parts they might be then asked extend their understanding to consider fifths of a nickel, dime, dollar, or fifths of an hour (You might want to avoid discussing fifths of a quarter since the word quarter already implies a fraction, which could lead to confusion.)

Setup

- Display only one circle but leave room for 5 more.
- Post the Fraction Record.

Daily Routine:

- **The first day,** mark fifths of a circle by drawing a line from the 0 minute point to the center, and from 12, 24, 36, 48, and 60 minute points to the center.
- Each day, including weekends and holidays, color in one fifth of a circle. **Use alternating colors to keep the fifths distinct.**
- Each day record the total amount displayed as both a fraction and (after day 5) as a mixed number.

Draw fifths with lines from the 12, 24, 36, 48, and 60 minute points to the center.

DISCUSSION

For the Beginning of the Month

Comparing fractions Begin with the circle model divided into fifths. Ask questions such as:

- This month, into how many equal parts has the circle been cut? (5)
- Is $\frac{1}{5}$ of a circle bigger or smaller than $\frac{1}{4}$ of the circle? (Smaller)
- How can we write a sentence with numbers and signs that compares $\frac{1}{4}$ and $\frac{1}{5}$? ($\frac{1}{4} > \frac{1}{5}$ or $\frac{1}{5} < \frac{1}{4}$)
- Can you put in order from least to greatest $\frac{1}{4}$, $\frac{1}{5}$, and $\frac{1}{3}$? ($\frac{1}{5}$, $\frac{1}{4}$, $\frac{1}{3}$)

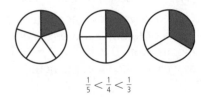

$\frac{1}{5} < \frac{1}{4} < \frac{1}{3}$

© Great Source. Copying is prohibited.

- What do you notice about the size of the fractional pieces and the number in the denominators? (The fractional pieces get smaller when the denominator gets bigger.)
- Can you explain why the number in the denominator gets larger while the fractional pieces get smaller?

For Throughout the Month

Fraction sense Lead the class to find fifths of a dime with a discussion similar to the following. On other days you might explore fifths of a dollar, fifths of an hour, or perhaps fifths of the class itself.

Sample Dialogue

Teacher: What else do you know that comes in five equal parts, or fifths?

Student: There's 5 fingers on a hand but those aren't all the same size.

Student: How about 5 school days in a week?

Student: After 1 day, 1 fifth of the school week is done, and after 2 days, 2 fifths of the school week is done. Five fifths is a whole.

Student: I have another good one. There's 5 pennies in a nickel, so 1 penny is one fifth of a nickel.

Teacher: Those are all good ideas. How do you think we could find one fifth of a dime?

Student: If you think about 10 pennies you could do it.

Teacher: I'll draw 10 pennies on the board. Now what?

Student: Make them into 5 equal groups of 2.

Teacher: So one fifth of a dime is how much?

Student: Two cents.

Teacher: We have 4 fifths of our circle filled. What's 4 fifths of a dime?

Student: Every fifth is 2 cents, so 4 fifths has to be 8 cents.

Teacher: Tomorrow we'll have 5 fifths. What is 5 fifths of a dime?

Student: That's just a whole dime, so 10 cents!

By the 14th students should be able to consider questions such as:

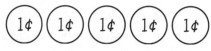

"There are 5 pennies in a nickel, so 1 penny is $\frac{1}{5}$ of a nickel."

Mixed numbers:

- Can you write 14 fifths as a fraction? ($\frac{14}{5}$) as a mixed number? ($2\frac{4}{5}$)
- How does $2\frac{4}{5}$ describe the shaded circles? (There are 2 full circles and $\frac{4}{5}$ of another.)
- If we shade $\frac{2}{5}$ more how much will be shaded? ($\frac{16}{5}$ or $3\frac{1}{5}$)

Fractions of a set:

- How can we find $2\frac{4}{5}$ of a dime? (That would be 2 dimes and 4 groups of 2 cents, or 28 cents.)
- How can we find $2\frac{4}{5}$ of a dollar? (That would be 2 whole dollars and 4 twenties, or $2.80 cents.)

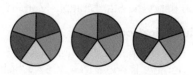

Today we have $\frac{14}{5}$
or 2 wholes and $\frac{4}{5}$
or $2\frac{4}{5}$ circles.

© Great Source. Copying is prohibited.

HELPFUL HINTS

- To provide more practice with fifths, use the same activity presented in November (see p. 56) whenever the date is a multiple of 5.

Number & Operations   Algebra   Geometry   Measurement   Data & Probability
Problem Solving   Reasoning   Communication   Connections   Representation

COUNTING TAPE

Concepts & Skills

- Explore multiples and factors
- Know multiplication facts for 5
- See the relationship between multiples of 5 and 10
- Investigate multiplication and division with remainders
- Write algebraic expressions for multiples of 5

Materials for December

Star Multiple Markers cardstock, copies of Circular Array Paper (TR7), Hundred Chart (TR4), and Equation Chart (TR5)

Daily Routine

- Continue to have students identify and mark multiples of 2, 3, and 4 with Multiple Markers. Begin marking multiples of 5 with yellow Star Multiple Markers.

Ongoing Assessment

1. Count by fives from 5 to 50.
2. On what number will we hang our 7th star? Our 9th star?
3. 6×5 is the same as 3×10. How can we use this idea to find 12×5?

DISCUSSION

51 52 53 54 55 56 57 58 59 60 61 62

"60 is a multiple of 2, 3, 4, and 5."

For the Beginning of the Month

At this point in the year, many multiples of 5 have already been written on the Tape. It is important to identify each one and discuss the pattern of these multiples. Count by fives from the beginning of the Tape up to the present and state the number of groups of 5 and any remainder. As you hang the Star Multiple Markers on the Tape, ask questions such as:

Multiplication:

- Can you name the multiples of 5 that appear on the Tape? Which number is equal to 4×5? Which one is equal to 5×5?
- Which number represents the points on 3 stars? The sides on 4 pentagons? The number of pennies in 2 nickels?
- How can we tell which multiple is 6×5? (Count the multiples of 5; the 6th one shows the product of 6×5.)
- What are the next 4 multiples of 5 after day 50? (55, 60, 65, 70)
- How can we get the answer for 13×5 without counting up by fives? (10 groups of 5 is 50; 3 more 5s is 15. That's $50 + 15 = 65$.)

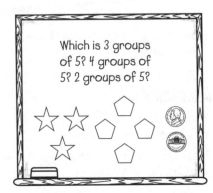

Which is 3 groups of 5? 4 groups of 5? 2 groups of 5?

3 stars have 15 points. 4 pentagons have 20 sides. 2 nickels = 10¢.

© Great Source. Copying is prohibited.

Division:

- How many fives are in 15? In 25? In 30? In 60?
- Which numbers on the Tape have 5 as a factor?
- How many five-dollar bills can you get for $45?
- How many fives are in 33? (6R3) In 42? (8R2) When dividing by 5, how do you know if there will be a remainder? (If the number ends in 5 or 0, there will not be a remainder.)

Remember to use days beyond 50 to practice combining 10 groups of 5 to get 50, and adding groups of 5 to get to larger numbers.

tens	ones
0	0
0	5
1	0
1	5
2	0
2	5
3	0
3	5
4	0
4	5
5	0
5	5
6	0

For the Middle of the Month

Ask students to study the pattern of the multiples of 5. It might be helpful to first make a vertical list on the board, such as the one shown. Ask students to tell any patterns they see. Responses might include:

- They all end in 5 or 0.
- There is a pattern in the ones place: 0, 5, 0, 5, 0, 5, and so on.
- All the multiples of 5 that end in 0 are also multiples of 2. They are common multiples of 2 and 5.
- There is a pattern in the tens place 0, 0, 1, 1, 2, 2, 3, 3, 4, 4, 5, 5, and so on.
- Every two fives make another 10.

In this way, students are beginning to identify how to know if any number is a multiple of 5. Ask students which of the following numbers are multiples of 5: 350, 785, 9,001, 9,005, 10,990, 999,995? By practicing with greater numbers, divisibility rules are revealed.

1 group of 5 = 1 x 5 = 5	6 groups of 5 = 6 x 5 = 30
2 groups of 5 = 2 x 5 = 10	7 groups of 5 = 7 x 5 = 35
3 groups of 5 = 3 x 5 = 15	8 groups of 5 = 8 x 5 = 40
4 groups of 5 = 4 x 5 = 20	9 groups of 5 = 9 x 5 = 45
5 groups of 5 = 5 x 5 = 25	10 groups of 5 = 10 x 5 = 50

1	2	3	4	5	6	7	8	9	10
11	12	13	14	15	16	17	18	19	20
21	22	23	24	25	26	27	28	29	30
31	32	33	34	35	36	37	38	39	40
41	42	43	44	45	46	47	48	49	50
51	52	53	54	55	56	57	58	59	60
61	62	63	64	65	66	67	68	69	70
71	72	73	74	75	76	77	78	79	80
81	82	83	84	85	86	87	88	89	90
91	92	93	94	95	96	97	98	99	100

For the End of the Month

- At the end of the month, pass out copies of the Hundred Chart and the Equation Chart so students can update their Multiplication Books to include the facts for 5. Have students update their books by continuing the patterns for twos, threes, and fours up to the present day of school. Finally, on the Multiplication Facts Progress Record (the cover of their Multiplication Books), have them color yellow the facts for 5 that they can recall easily.
- Using Circular Array Paper (TR7) to create Array Flash Cards for facts 5 × 5 to 10 × 5 can help students practice these facts. These models show that if a number is a multiple of 5, it has 5 as a factor and can be broken up either into groups of 5 or into 5 groups, each worth a fifth of the total.

HELPFUL HINT

- New patterns will emerge this month on the Equation Chart, recording how each day's number can be divided into groups of 5. This month you might use division equations to show that multiples of 5 are divisible by 5 and have 5 as a factor. When students staple their Equation Chart inside their Multiplication Book opposite the new Hundred Chart, they can look for connections between the two.

Day	Groups	Remainder	Equation
1	0	1	1 ÷ 5 = 0R1
2	0	2	2 ÷ 5 = 0R2
3	0	3	3 ÷ 5 = 0R3
4	0	4	4 ÷ 5 = 0R4
5	1	0	5 ÷ 5 = 1
6	1	1	6 ÷ 5 = 1R1
7	1	2	7 ÷ 5 = 1R2
8	1	3	8 ÷ 5 = 1R3
9	1	4	9 ÷ 5 = 1R4
10	2	0	10 ÷ 5 = 2
11	2	1	11 ÷ 5 = 2R1

What patterns do you see?

© Great Source. Copying is prohibited.

COIN COUNTER

Concepts & Skills

- Estimate and use mental math
- See pennies and dimes as hundredths and tenths of a dollar
- Multiply 1-digit by 2-digit numbers

Daily Routine

- Continue to display the coin combination with the fewest possible coins in the top pocket.
- Continue to use the 100 Penny Grid (TR9) to see and talk about the day's amount as tenths and hundredths of a dollar.
- The Shopping problem this month is to have students select a Shopper Card and estimate how many of the item can be purchased with the day's amount.

DISCUSSION

For the Beginning of the Month

Have a volunteer draw 1 Shopper Card and show it to the class. Give students time to estimate how many of the item they can buy using the day's amount in the Coin Counter. For example, if it's day 67 with 67¢ available, and the gum Shopper Card is drawn, the question would be, "How many packs of gum at 16¢ each can we buy for 67¢?" Have 2 or 3 students explain how they estimated the answer. Then let students choose mental math, paper and pencil, or calculators to find the total cost of the gum and the amount that would be left after the purchase. See if their different methods produce the same answers.

During the Month

The following questions focusing on the coin combinations may encourage communication and problem solving.

- How could you explain your way of determining the fewest coins for today's amount?
- How do you know if you will need pennies?
- Can we make today's amount with 5 coins? 6 coins? 7 coins?
- Which numbers on the Counting Tape can be made with 1 coin? Which can be made with 2 coins? With 3 coins? With 4 coins?

Ongoing Assessment

1. How many dimes are in 6 tenths of a dollar?

2. How many cents are in 6 tenths of a dollar?

3. If a pack of gum costs 16¢ and you have today's amount, how many packs can you buy?

Today we have

$ 0 . 6 0

Sixty cents equals 6 dimes or 6 tenths of a dollar.

Shopping Record

Purchase(s)

GUM
16¢

Today's Amount $ 0.67

Total Cost $ 0.64

Amount Left $ 0.03

"We can buy 4 packs of gum with 67¢."

CLOCK

Concepts & Skills

- Differentiate between A.M. and P.M.
- Determine minutes greater than an hour

© Great Source. Copying is prohibited.

Daily Routine

- Set the hour hand at 12 this month.
- Use the number of the day in school to set the minute hand.

Ongoing Assessment

1. If you are eating breakfast, is it most likely A.M. or P.M.?
2. How many hours and minutes is 63 minutes?
3. How many minutes are in 1 hour and 7 minutes?

DISCUSSION

Throughout the Month

Tell students that the hour will be set to 12 this month. Explain that after 12:00, the time changes from A.M. to P.M. or the reverse. Explain that while digital clocks are made to change from A.M. to P.M. at exactly 12:00, it is always better to refer to that time as noon, and to 12:00 at night as midnight. Use the following questions to guide the discussion.

- What do A.M. and P.M. mean?
- What are some things you do in the A.M.? What are some things you do in the P.M.?
- Do you know what 12:00 at lunchtime is called? (12 noon) Are times just before noon A.M. or P.M.? What about times just after noon?
- Do you know what 12:00 at night is called? (12 midnight) Are times just before midnight A.M. or P.M.? What about times just after midnight?
- How can we remember if the time is A.M. or P.M.? (Some teachers like to help students by saying A.M. stands for *after midnight* and P.M. stands for *past morning*.)

Questions to connect measurement of time to fractions:

- How many equal minutes is an hour divided into? (60)
- If we are going to cook something in the microwave for 7 minutes, what fraction of an hour is that?
- If I drive for 30 minutes, what fraction of an hour is that?
- If you have a 20-minute ride on the bus to come to school, what fraction of an hour is that?
- How many 20-minute segments are there in an hour? (3)

12:59 A.M. is the same as one minute before 1 o'clock in the morning.

After the Sixtieth Day of School

As the number of days in school passes 60, the time will be written differently. For example, if the number of days in school is 67, then the time would be 12:67, or 1:07.

Here are some questions to help students understand this concept.

- How many minutes are in an hour? (60)
- Is 62 minutes more or less than an hour? (more)
- How much more? (2 minutes)
- How many hours and minutes is 70 minutes? (1 hour, 10 minutes)
- If it is 12 noon and we must catch a train in 70 minutes, what time will it be when the train arrives? (1:10 P.M.)
- Does anyone have a way to figure out these problems very quickly? (One suggestion might be to subtract 60 minutes from the number of minutes more than 1 hour. Then the amount left over shows the minutes in addition to the hour.)

© Great Source. Copying is prohibited.

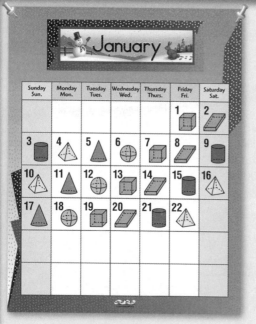

Every Day Calendar

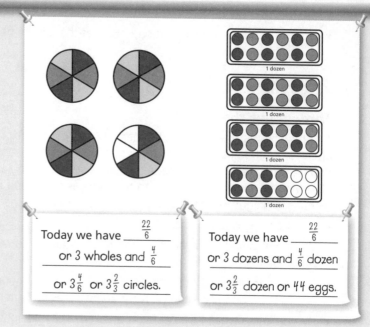

Today we have ___$\frac{22}{6}$___

or 3 wholes and $\frac{4}{6}$

or $3\frac{4}{6}$ or $3\frac{2}{3}$ circles.

Today we have ___$\frac{22}{6}$___

or 3 dozens and $\frac{4}{6}$ dozen

or $3\frac{2}{3}$ dozen or 44 eggs.

A Fraction A Day

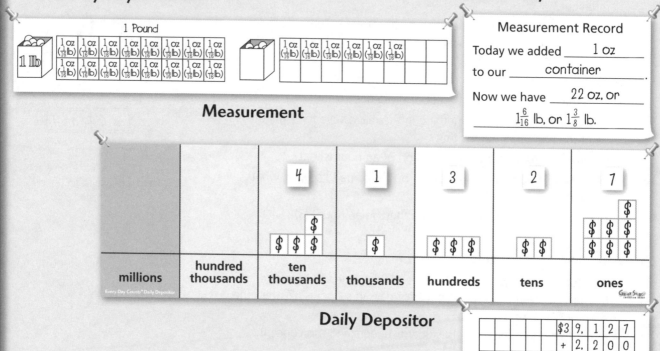

Measurement

Measurement Record

Today we added ___1 oz___

to our ___container___.

Now we have ___22 oz, or___

___$1\frac{6}{16}$ lb, or $1\frac{3}{8}$ lb.___

millions	hundred thousands	ten thousands	thousands	hundreds	tens	ones
		4	1	3	2	7

Daily Depositor

```
   $3 9, 1 2 7
 +    2, 2 0 0
   $4 1, 3 2 7
```

73 74 75 76 77 78 79 80 81 82 83 84 85 86 87 88 89 90 91

Counting Tape

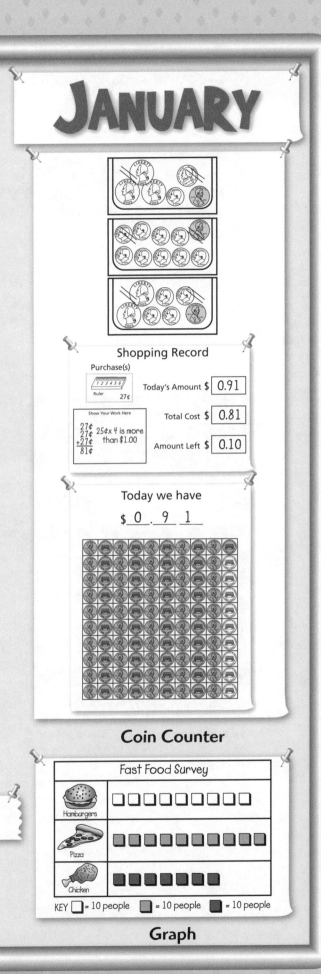

Coin Counter

Shopping Record

Purchase(s)

Ruler 27¢

Today's Amount $ 0.91

Total Cost $ 0.81

Amount Left $ 0.10

Show Your Work Here

27¢
27¢ 25¢ x 4 is more
+27¢ than $1.00
81¢

Today we have

$ 0 . 9 1

Graph

Fast Food Survey

Hamburgers

Pizza

Chicken

KEY ☐ = 10 people ▨ = 10 people ■ = 10 people

JANUARY

JANUARY ELEMENTS

CALENDAR **76**
use tables to represent patterns; compare and analyze attributes of solids; recognize terms used to describe solids

DAILY DEPOSITOR **79**
multiply numbers by 100; perform multi-digit addition; estimate and predict

MEASUREMENT **81**
write ounces as pounds; develop a referent for a pound; think about mixed numbers and fractional parts

A FRACTION A DAY **82**
write improper fractions as mixed numbers; find a fraction of a set; see relationships among sixths, thirds, and halves

COUNTING TAPE **84**
explore multiples and factors; see the relationship between multiples of 6 and 3; investigate multiplication and division with remainders

COIN COUNTER **87**
look for patterns in coins used for the same amount; count mixed coins

GRAPH **88**
collect and organize data; analyze data and interpret results; make predictions

Calendar Math activities in January will present new challenges for students. The Multiple Markers on the Counting Tape will highlight multiples of 6, and the Daily Depositor will be used to examine new ways to add large numbers quickly. The Coin Counter will feature a new problem-solving approach to coin collection. The Measurement element will be used to study ounces and pounds. Using the Every Day Calendar, students will analyze and compare three-dimensional shapes.

CALENDAR

Concepts & Skills

- Use tables to represent patterns
- Recognize patterns in multiples of 6
- Compare and analyze attributes of solids
- Recognize terms used to describe solids

Materials for January

A large piece of paper to make a solids poster

Author Notes

"This month students examine solids. In addition to seeing these shapes displayed on the Calendar, students are encouraged to look for them in their environment. The emphasis throughout the month is modeling and using descriptive geometric language. Terms like *faces* and *edges* are introduced to describe the solids."

Daily Routine

- Each day, attach the Calendar Piece for that day. On Mondays, attach pieces for the weekend days.

DISCUSSION

For the Beginning of the Month

Attach a sample of each of the 6 shapes appearing on the Calendar Pieces to a large piece of paper to make a solids poster. Label each solid. Invite students to search for examples of these three-dimensional shapes in their environment.

To explore the cube:

- Who has found an example of this shape to share with the class?
- What shape do you recognize on this solid? (square)
- Are all of the faces squares? (Yes. While the picture may not make it possible for students to see, be sure they know that 6 congruent square faces is a defining attribute of a cube.)
- How many square faces does the cube have? (6)
- When 2 square faces meet, it is called an edge. How many edges meet at a corner of a cube? (3) How many corners does a cube have? (8)

Record these attributes on the cube poster.

To explore the rectangular prism:

- This shape is called a rectangular prism. What shapes do you recognize on this solid? (rectangles)
- How many faces does a rectangular solid have? (6) How many corners? (8)

Ongoing Assessment

1. Describe the number of faces and the shapes on a square pyramid.
2. What is the least number that is a multiple of both 5 and 6?
3. Which is the shape of a rectangular prism, an orange or a cereal box?

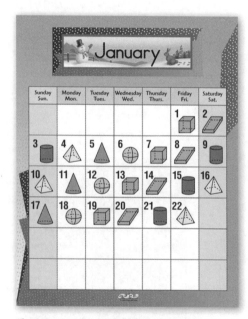

The January Calendar Pieces create an AABCDE color pattern and an overlapping ABCDEF pattern of shapes in the order blue cube, blue rectangular prism, red cylinder, yellow pyramid, green cone, and orange sphere.

© Great Source. Copying is prohibited.

- On this rectangular solid, are all the faces the same size and shape? (no)

- How is the prism the same as the cube? How is it different? (Both have 6 faces, 8 corners, 12 edges, and rectangular faces. A cube has 6 square faces.)

- Why do you suppose the cube and the rectangular prism are the same color on our Calendar Pieces? (Because they are both box shapes with 6 faces. Cubes are special rectangular solids.)

Record these attributes on the rectangular prism poster.

To explore the cylinder:

- How many faces does a cylinder have? (2) What shapes do you see on the ends of the cylinder? (2 circles)

- What are some examples of cylinders? (frozen orange juice cans, soda cans, and so on)

- To make a cylinder out of pieces of paper, what shapes would you need to cut? (A rectangle and two circles. If students do not recognize the rectangle as the outside, cut a paper towel roll along its length to reveal that it is a rectangle.)

Record these attributes on the cylinder poster.

To explore the square pyramid:

- How many faces does this pyramid have? (5)

- What shapes do you recognize on this pyramid? (The bottom may be a square. There are triangles, too.)

- Yes, the bottom of this pyramid is a square. How many triangles and squares do you see? (1 square, 4 triangles)

- How is the pyramid like the rectangular prism and how is it different? (Both have a base and faces, but the prism has two bases and the pyramid only one. The edges meet in a point on the pyramid but not in a prism.)

Record these attributes on the pyramid poster. If available, show some pyramids that have bases that are not squares.

To explore the cone:

- What shape do you recognize on this solid? (circle) How many circles do you see? (1)

- Do all cones have a circular base? (yes)

- What do you think a cone would look like if we cut it the way we cut the cylinder? (a triangular shape with a curved edge)

- What is the same about a pyramid and a cone? (They both have a point at one end and a base on the other.)

Record these attributes on the cone poster.

To explore the sphere:

- Do spheres have any flat surfaces? (no)

- How would you describe a sphere? (round, circular, a ball, one continuous curved surface)

- How is a sphere different from the other shapes? (There are no flat surfaces.)

- What are some examples of spheres? (oranges, globes, balls, and so on)

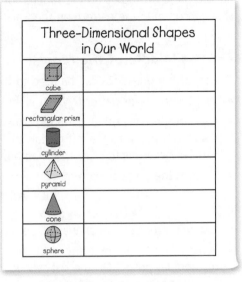

Three-Dimensional Shapes in Our World	
cube	
rectangular prism	
cylinder	
pyramid	
cone	
sphere	

Encourage students to find examples of these shapes in the world around them.

© Great Source. Copying is prohibited.

Record these attributes on the sphere poster. After introducing the shapes, continue the pattern on the Calendar.

For the Middle of the Month

The following questions can be used to foster thinking about patterns.

- What is the color pattern? What is the shape pattern?
- Can you find any other patterns? (Answers may include that moving diagonally down to the left reveals the same shape and that the vertical pattern is the same as the horizontal pattern.)
- What is the number pattern for the blue shapes? (1, 2, 7, 8, 13, 14, and so on) What is the difference between the numbers? (+1, +5, +1, +5, and so on)
- Can you predict what shape will be on day 13? Day 24? Day 29?
- What will the date be on the last cube this month? On the last rectangular prism? On the last cylinder? On the last pyramid? On the last cone? On the last sphere?
- What is the number pattern for the spheres? (6, 12, 18, and so on)
- What will the date be on the 3rd sphere? (18) On the 4th sphere? (24) On the 5th sphere? (30) How do you know? (They appear on multiples of 6.) Let's make a table to show how the spheres appear on the Calendar.
- If this pattern continued beyond the end of the month, what would be the number on the 10th sphere? Why? (60, because 10 × 6 = 60.)

To Sum Up

Ask students to tell what they have noticed about the Calendar. Make a list of the patterns and any observations about the solids.

Algebraic Relationships To continue to support students in developing an understanding of algebraic thinking, use the following questions:

- How can you predict when the cubes appear? (They always appear after the spheres, or 1 more than a multiple of 6.)
- What is the difference between the dates of the cubes? (Beginning on 1, they increase by 6.)
- How can you tell whether a cube will appear on the 25th without looking at the Calendar? (25 is 1 more than a multiple of 6, so there will be a cube that day.)

Draw the table shown at the right on the board. Ask students to complete the table without looking at the Calendar. Tell them that they will extend the pattern beyond the 31 days in January. When they have finished, they can check their work by looking at the Calendar. The cubes appear on 1, 7, 13, 19, 25, 31, 37, and 43.

HELPFUL HINT

- Students enjoy problem solving in the game *Who Am I?* Ask everyone to look at the solids poster. Give them clues to help them identify one of the solids. For example, "I have all flat surfaces. I have 6 of them. All my faces are not the same. Who am I?"

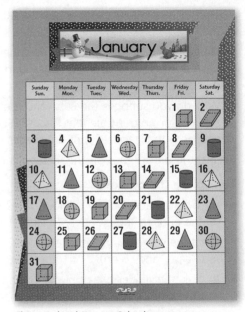

The completed January Calendar

Number of Sphere	Date
1	6
2	12
3	18
4	
5	

Number of Cube	Date
1	1
2	7
3	
4	
5	
6	
7	
8	

Representing patterns in tables

© Great Source. Copying is prohibited.

DAILY DEPOSITOR

Concepts & Skills

- Multiply numbers by 100
- Use mental math
- Perform multi-digit addition
- Estimate and predict

Materials for January

Blocks or cubes

Setup

- Put the entire $16,027 collected during the first 4 months of the school year back into the Depositor, displaying the total.

Daily Routine

- During January and February the amount added to the Depositor each day will be $100 times the day's date and the total will be cumulative.
- After returning from winter break, update the Depositor to the current day.

Ongoing Assessment

1. What is 13 + 14 + 15? Explain your mental math strategy.
2. What is six thousand more than 42,650?
3. How would you write 3,705 in expanded notation?

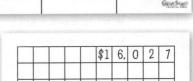

DISCUSSION

For the Beginning of the Month

Explain the rule that will be used to determine the daily amount to be added to the Depositor. Here are some sample questions to help bring the Depositor up to date after the vacation.

- If we add $100 times the date each day, how much money would we have added to the Depositor on January 1st? ($100) How much on the 2nd? ($200) On the 4th? ($400)
- How much would we have added up to today's date?
- If we add $100 times the date between now and May 31st, do you think our total will reach one million dollars? How about $500,000? How about $100,000?

Continue to have students use subtraction to solve problems by posing a pretend expenditure once a week. After discussion, return the bills to the Depositor.

For the Middle of the Month

At the end of the Depositor activity in December, students used the pairing method for adding numbers in sequence. Remind students that updating the Depositor amount after a weekend involves adding 3 consecutive numbers. Ask them if they can describe a quick way to figure out the sum of 3 consecutive numbers each Monday when they

© Great Source. Copying is prohibited.

update the Depositor after the weekend. Offer the following method for adding an odd number of consecutive numbers.

- How much is 1 + 2 + 3? (6) How much is 2 + 3 + 4? (9) How much is 4 + 5 + 6? (15)

- What do you notice about those problems? (They all add 3 consecutive numbers and the sums are multiples of 3.)

Using cubes or blocks, make 3 piles: one with 1 block, another with 2 blocks, and a third with 3 blocks. Ask students to make the stacks the same by moving 1 block. Explain that this is like adding 3 consecutive numbers: 1 + 2 + 3. If you take 1 block off the third stack and put it on the first stack, it will have 2 blocks, as will the second and third stacks. Now all the stacks are the same as the middle number.

After applying this strategy to a few other sums of 3 numbers in sequence, ask students to compose a theory about adding 3 consecutive numbers. Something like this might be the outcome: *The sum of 3 consecutive numbers is equal to 3 times the middle number.*

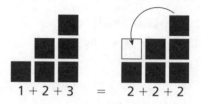

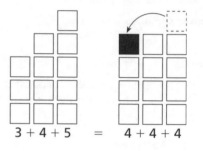

Sample Dialogue

Teacher: Today is Monday, January 18th. Let's use our new method of adding 3 consecutive numbers to update the Depositor after the weekend. The dates are the 16th, 17th, and 18th. How much will we add for these 3 days?

Student: 16 + 17 + 18 equals 51.

Student: 17 × 3 equals 51. So we can use this method every Monday.

Teacher: Yes. If the sum of the 3 numbers is 51, how much do we need to deposit today?

Student: $5,100.

Teacher: What will our total be as of today?

Student: We'll have $33,127.

HELPFUL HINTS

- To strengthen students' mental math skills, use this method every Monday to update the Depositor.

-  This method of adding numbers is a great way to demonstrate the value of mental math. Play the game *Beat the Calculator*. Call out any 3 consecutive numbers. One group of students enters the numbers in the calculator while the other group does the calculation in their heads. Keep score of which group has the solution first. If students can multiply in their heads quickly, they usually beat the calculator, making a strong point for mental math skills.

- This method of adding 3 consecutive numbers applies to calculating the sum of any odd-numbered group of consecutive numbers. Therefore, in the series of 7 numbers, 1 + 2 + 3 + 4 + 5 + 6 + 7, 4 is the middle number and you multiply it by the total number in the series (7) to get the answer, or 7 × 4 = 28.

Daily Depositor				
Month	Days in the Month	Total for the Month	Cumulative Total	Daily Deposit Amount
September	30	$465		$1 times date
October	31	$992	$1,457	$2 times date
November	30	$4,650	$6,107	$10 times date
December	31	$9,920	$16,027	$20 times date
January	31	$49,600	$65,627	$100 times date
February	28 or 29			
March	31			
April	30			
May	31			

© Great Source. Copying is prohibited.

MEASUREMENT

Concepts & Skills

- Write ounces as pounds
- Develop a referent for one pound
- Understand mixed numbers and fractional parts

Materials for January

One pound of clay; bottom half of a plastic milk container; 1 pan balance and ounce weights; Measurement Record (TR10); copy of Inch Squared Paper (TR3); plastic knife

Setup

- Cut the Inch Squared Paper to make two 2" × 8" grids. Label each square *1 oz ($\frac{1}{16}$ lb)* in both grids.
- Post the grids and the Measurement Record on the board.

Daily Routine

- Each day put 1 ounce of clay in the plastic milk container.
- Color a square on the 2" × 8" grid for each ounce added to the container. After 16 days, label the colored grid *1 pound* and begin coloring the second grid on the 17th.
- Record the total on the Measurement Record as a fraction and a mixed number.

© Great Source. Copying is prohibited.

DISCUSSION

For the First Day

Show students the clay and tell them that it weighs 1 pound. Ask them how they think it can be divided evenly. Some students may suggest that you make it into a round ball and cut it approximately in half. Do that and continue questioning and cutting pieces in half until you have 16 approximately equal pieces.

Sample Dialogue

Teacher: This is 1 pound. How many pieces have we cut it into?

Student: 16.

Teacher: We call each section 1 ounce. We will add 1 ounce to this plastic container every day. That will be $\frac{1}{16}$ of a pound. How many days do you think it will take to accumulate a pound?

Student: 16.

Teacher: That's right. How many ounces do you think will accumulate in a month?

Allow students to make their estimates, which will be kept until the end of the month.

Ongoing Assessment

1. How many ounces are in 1 pound?
2. What fractional part of 1 pound is 1 ounce?
3. What is another way to express 25 ounces?

For the Twenty-fifth Day of the Month

The following questions are for January 25th. Use them all month by changing the numbers to match what your classroom total is on any day this month.

- How many ounces do we have today? (25) How many pounds is that? (1) How many extra ounces? (9)
- How can we write the leftover amount as a fraction? ($\frac{9}{16}$, because 9 out of the 16 ounces needed to make another pound are left over.)
- Let's count the sixteenths of pounds and see how many sixteenths we have. ($\frac{25}{16}$)
- Do you see $1\frac{9}{16}$ pounds when you look up here? (yes)

Record this on the Measurement Record.

For the End of the Month

Summarize all the facts that have been observed.

- Review how many ounces equal 1 pound.
- Review an ounce as $\frac{1}{16}$ of a pound.
- Examine how many ounces have been collected and ask how many pounds in all.
- Compare the estimates of the total to be accumulated with the actual amount.

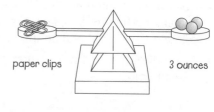

Measurement Record

Today we added _____ 1 oz _____

to our _____ container _____.

Now we have _____ 25oz, or $1\frac{9}{16}$ lb.

_____

The 25th Day

HELPFUL HINTS

- It is important to give students the opportunity to hold items weighing 1 to 16 ounces and compare them to something. Therefore, if you have a pan balance in your school, allow students to find things in the room that weigh the same as the amount accumulated. For management purposes, you might assign each student a day during the month when he or she can explore weight.

- A good activity is to ask students to bring in a 1-pound can of food every day during the month. Each day put one can in a box displayed in the room for this purpose. Allow students to lift the box with 1 pound, 2 pounds, 3 pounds, and so on, until it is too heavy for one student to lift easily. Then ask two students and if necessary, three. This gives students a reference for understanding weight. At the end of the month, donate all the cans to a worthy cause.

paper clips   3 ounces

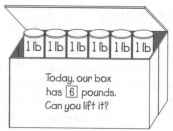

Today, our box has [6] pounds. Can you lift it?

Number & Operations	Algebra	Geometry	Measurement	Data & Probability
Problem Solving	Reasoning	Communication	Connections	Representation

A FRACTION A DAY

Concepts & Skills

- Visualize fractions
- Understand numerator and denominator
- Write improper fractions as mixed numbers
- Find a fraction of a set
- Compute with fractions
- See fractional equivalencies

© Great Source. Copying is prohibited.

Materials for January

6 circles from TR11, two copies of egg carton Dozens (TRxx), Fraction Record (TR13), markers or crayons in 2 bright colors and black

Author Notes

A Fraction A Day explores sixths in January. Circles are used again to provide continuity and dozens are again used as the second model because they nicely show equivalent fractions for thirds and sixths.

Setup

- Cut 6 circles from TR 11 and post one, leaving room for the other 5.
- Cut 6 Dozens from TR12. Post one, leaving room for 5 more.
- Post the Fraction Record.

Daily Routine

- **The first day,** tell the class that you will draw 6 equal parts of a pizza (or circle). Use the black marker to draw sixths on one circle. (Draw a line from the 12 o'clock position through the center to 6 o'clock, from 2 to 8, and from 4 to 10.
- Shade in one sixth of the circle each day, including weekends and holidays. **Use alternating colors to keep the sixths distinct.**
- When a circle is filled, post a new one next to it, and continue to shade one fourth each day.
- Each day also shade in one sixth of the egg carton Dozen. Use alternating colors and dotted lines to keep the sixths distinct.
- Each day record the total on the Fraction Record both as a fraction and (after day 6) as a mixed number.

Discussion

For the Beginning of the Month

Begin with the familiar circle model, divided into sixths. Ask:

- This month, how many equal parts has the circle been cut into? (6)
- Are this month's sixths bigger or smaller than last month's fifths? (smaller) How do you know?
- Looking at this circle divided into sixths, how do you think you could draw twelfths? (Cut every sixth into 2 pieces.)
- Why will that give us twelfths? (because there would be 12 pieces)
- So one half of one sixth is how much? (one twelfth)
- Would you rather have $\frac{1}{3}$, $\frac{1}{4}$, $\frac{1}{5}$, or $\frac{1}{6}$ of a million dollars? Why?

Another day, work with students to complete a table like the one shown on the next page to understand fractions of a dozen.

Sample Dialogue

Teacher: This month we are looking at sixths. Who can remind us, what does one sixth mean?

Student: One out of 6 equal parts.

© Great Source. Copying is prohibited.

Ongoing Assessment
1. How many sixths are in $2\frac{5}{6}$?
2. How can you write $\frac{23}{6}$ as a mixed number?
3. How many eggs are in $\frac{5}{6}$ of a dozen?

Draw sixths with lines from 12 o'clock to 6, from 2 to 8, and from 4 to 10.

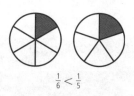

$\frac{1}{6} < \frac{1}{5}$

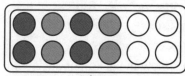

1 dozen

Today we have $\frac{4}{6}$ or $\frac{2}{3}$ dozen or 8 eggs.

Teacher:	When you look at the dozen can you see six equal groups?
Student:	That's pretty easy. There are six pairs of eggs.
Teacher:	If we shade $\frac{1}{6}$ of a dozen each day how many eggs is that?
Student:	Two.
Teacher:	So $\frac{1}{6}$ of 12 is 2. And since we've been coloring sixths for 4 days now, how many eggs should we have shaded?
Student:	Eight.
Teacher:	And so we can say that 4 sixths of 12 is how much?
Student:	Eight.
Teacher:	How much would $\frac{5}{6}$ be?
Student:	Ten.
Teacher:	And on January 12th, when we've shaded $\frac{12}{6}$, what will the egg cartons look like?

Fraction of 12	How Many
$\frac{1}{6}$ of 12	2
$\frac{2}{6}$ of 12	4
$\frac{3}{6}$ of 12	6
$\frac{4}{6}$ of 12	
$\frac{5}{6}$ of 12	
$\frac{6}{6}$ of 12	

"How much is $\frac{4}{6}$ of 12?"

Throughout the Month

By the 14th day there are 14 sixths colored on both models. The following sample questions can be adapted for use on any date.

Mixed numbers:

- Today is the 14th so we have 14 sixths shaded. How many whole circles is that? (2)
- How many extra sixths are there? (2)
- How can we write $\frac{14}{6}$ as a mixed number? ($2\frac{2}{6}$)
- What other fraction is $\frac{2}{6}$ equal to? ($\frac{1}{3}$)
- What will the date be when we have 4 whole circles? (January 24)

Today we have $\frac{14}{6}$
or 2 wholes and $\frac{2}{6}$
or $2\frac{2}{6}$ or $2\frac{1}{3}$ circles.

HELPFUL HINTS

- *Real-World Fractions* Ask students to brainstorm examples of sixths in the real world. Examples might include 1 box of juice from a 6-pack of juice boxes, one player on a volleyball team, one side of a hexagon.

Number & Operations   Algebra   Geometry   Measurement   Data & Probability
   Problem Solving   Reasoning   Communication   Connections   Representation

COUNTING TAPE

Concepts & Skills

- Explore multiples and factors
- Count by sixes
- Know multiplication facts for 6
- See the relationship between multiples of 6 and 3
- Investigate multiplication and division with remainders

Materials for January

Hexagon Multiple Markers cardstock, copies of Circular Array Paper (TR7), Hundred Chart (TR4), and Equation Chart (TR5)

Ongoing Assessment

1. Count by sixes from 6 to 60.
2. On what number will we hang our 6th hexagon? Our 9th hexagon?
3. 7 groups of 3 is 21. How can we use this idea to find 7×6?

© Great Source. Copying is prohibited.

Daily Routine

- Continue to have students identify and mark multiples of 2, 3, 4, and 5 with Multiple Markers. Begin marking multiples of 6 with green Hexagon Multiple Markers.

DISCUSSION

59 60 61 62 63 64 65 66 67 68 69 70 71 72 73

For the Beginning of the Month

In January many multiples of 6 have already been written on the Counting Tape. It is important to have students identify each one and look for patterns as they hang the hexagons on the Tape. As each multiple of 6 is called out, write the multiplication equations on the board.

Ask questions similar to the following to help students see patterns and correlations between the Counting Tape and the equations:

- How do we know by looking at the Counting Tape that 4×6 is 24? (24 is the fourth multiple of 6 on the Tape.)
- What is an easy way to figure out the product of 9×4? (It is 36, one 4 less than $10 \times 4 = 40$.)
- Can we write a multiplication word problem to go with the equation 5×6? (I bought 5 six-packs of soda. How many cans in all?)
- Can we write a division word problem using 30 and groups of 6? (We are having a party for 30 people. How many six-packs of soda do we need if we want 1 can for each person?)

For the Middle of the Month

Here are some sample questions to encourage use of the distributive property. In this example, that property is used to break multiplication facts for 6 into facts for 3 to make them easier to solve and remember.

- What patterns do you see with the triangles and hexagons on the Tape? (All hexagons have triangles and hearts, since 6 is a common multiple of 2 and 3. There are 2 groups of 3 in every group of 6.)
- Can we use that fact to help us figure out 7×6? ($7 \times 6 = 7$ groups of 3 twice, or $21 + 21 = 42$)
- How can we use the times 3 facts we know to help us learn the times 6 facts?

Practice this strategy with students by asking them to supply the answer for multiplication facts for 3 and doubling the product to get answers for facts for 6. Use Circular Array Paper, Centimeter Squared Paper, or any other visual aid that will help students see this connection.

Division and 6 as a factor:

- How many sixes are in 30? In 36? In 42? (continue through 60)
- Which numbers on the Tape have 6 as a factor?
- How many groups of 6 can we make with 30 students? With 38 students? With 45 students? With 48 students?

© Great Source. Copying is prohibited.

- How many sixes are in 33? (5R3) In 43? (7R1)
- Is there a pattern in the digits of the multiples of 6 that can help us know which numbers will have remainders and which will not? (If the number is even and the digits add up to a multiple of 3, the number has 6 as a factor and will not have a remainder.)

Ten groups of 6 and more:

Days after 60 provide opportunities to look for strategies to identify multiples of 6 greater than 60.

- What are the next 5 multiples of 6 after 60? (66, 72, 78, 84, 90)
- How can we get the answer for 13×6 without counting up by sixes? (10 groups of 6 = 60, and 3 more sixes is 18. 60 + 18 = 78.)
- How can we figure out how many sixes are in 85 without counting by sixes? (85 is 10 groups of 6 to 60. That leaves 25. There are enough for 4 more groups of 6 in 25. That leaves 1. So, $85 \div 6 = 14R1$.)

For the End of the Month

Here are some questions about multiples of 6 and common multiples.

- What can you tell us about all the multiples of 6? (Each is a common multiple of 2 and 3.)
- What numbers can you find that can be divided by 2, 4, and 6? (12, 24, 36, 48, 60) What can you say about these numbers? (They are common multiples of 2, 4, and 6; they are all multiples of 12.)
- Look at 60 on the Counting Tape. Why is 60 special? (It has markers for every multiple we have used so far: 2, 3, 4, 5, and 6. It has all those numbers for factors.)

At the end of the month, pass out copies of the Hundred Chart and the Equation Chart so students can update their Multiplication Books to include the facts for 6. Have students update their books by continuing the patterns for twos, threes, fours, and fives up to the present day of school. Finally, on the Multiplication Facts Progress Record (the cover of their Multiplication Books), have them color green the facts for 6 that they can recall easily.

Use Circular Array Paper (TR7) to create Array Flash Cards for facts 6×6 to 10×6 to help students practice these facts. These models show that if a number is a multiple of 6, it has 6 as a factor and can be broken up either into groups of 6 or into 6 groups. They can also be broken into groups of 3 and doubled for easier mental computation.

HELPFUL HINT

- Once students have mastered multiplication facts through 5, the facts from 6×6 to 9×6 provide opportunities to use known facts to learn harder facts. As students break these facts apart into smaller groupings, and then recombine them to find the products, they are making use of the distributive property of multiplication.

1 group of 6 = 1 x 6 = 6	6 groups of 6 = 6 x 6 = 36
2 groups of 6 = 2 x 6 = 12	7 groups of 6 = 7 x 6 = 42
3 groups of 6 = 3 x 6 = 18	8 groups of 6 = 8 x 6 = 48
4 groups of 6 = 4 x 6 = 24	9 groups of 6 = 9 x 6 = 54
5 groups of 6 = 5 x 6 = 30	10 groups of 6 = 10 x 6 = 60

1	2	3	4	5	6	7	8	9	10
11	12	13	14	15	16	17	18	19	20
21	22	23	24	25	26	27	28	29	30
31	32	33	34	35	36	37	38	39	40
41	42	43	44	45	46	47	48	49	50
51	52	53	54	55	56	57	58	59	60
61	62	63	64	65	66	67	68	69	70
71	72	73	74	75	76	77	78	79	80
81	82	83	84	85	86	87	88	89	90
91	92	93	94	95	96	97	98	99	100

Multiplication Facts for 6

© Great Source. Copying is prohibited.

COIN COUNTER

Concepts & Skills

- Determine coin combinations for given amounts
- Look for patterns
- Count mixed coins
- See pennies and dimes as hundredths and tenths of a dollar

Daily Routine

- Continue to display the coin combination with the fewest coins in the top pocket.
- Continue to use the 100 Penny Grid to talk about the day's amount as tenths and hundredths of a dollar.
- Once or twice a week, select a Shopper Card and have students estimate and then calculate how many of the item can be purchased with the day's amount. Conclude by deciding how much money would be left.

Ongoing Assessment

1. How can we show 75 hundredths of a dollar using dimes and pennies?
2. How much money do we need to add to today's amount to reach 1 dollar?
3. If a ruler costs $0.27, and you have today's amount, how many rulers can you buy? How much money will be left?

DISCUSSION

For the Seventy-fifth Day of School

Have students look at the 75¢ on the 100 Penny Grid to see that if the cents are grouped into groups of 25, they are equal to $\frac{3}{4}$ of a dollar. Ask, "How can this help explain why 75 hundredths or 75% of a whole is the same as $\frac{3}{4}$?" See what connections students are able to make between frequently used decimals, fractions, and percents.

Use the Coin Counter to search for all the coin combinations for 75¢. Use an organized list to verify that all the possibilities have been found. To limit the number of possibilities, you might require that all combinations include 1 half dollar. The complete table is provided at the right.

After students have completed the organized list, ask some of the following questions:

- What patterns do you see on the chart?
- What pattern do you see in the pennies column? Can someone explain it?
- Why does the number of coins differ by four when exchanging a nickel for pennies? (Because you trade 1 nickel for 5 pennies.)

Throughout the Month

On days when coin combinations are not the focus, continue to involve the class in shopping problems. Focus on students sharing their mental math strategies for deciding how many of the item shown on the Shopper Card can be purchased with the day's amount and how much money will be left.

Coin Chart for 75¢					
					COINS
1	1	0	0	0	2
1	0	2	1	0	4
1	0	2	0	5	8
1	0	1	3	0	5
1	0	1	2	5	9
1	0	1	1	10	13
1	0	1	0	15	17
1	0	0	5	0	6
1	0	0	4	5	10
1	0	0	3	10	14
1	0	0	2	15	18
1	0	0	1	20	22
1	0	0	0	25	26

Ways to make 75¢

© Great Source. Copying is prohibited.

HELPFUL HINTS

- Generating coin combinations can be time consuming. When planning for these days, focus only on the Coin Counter. Some teachers pose the problem as an evening's homework assignment and use class time to organize solutions into one list.

- You may want to assign a project to explore coin combinations for $1 in preparation for the 100th day of school next month.

Number & Operations	Algebra	Geometry	Measurement	Data & Probability
Problem Solving	Reasoning	Communication	Connections	Representation

GRAPH

Concepts & Skills

- Collect and organize data
- Analyze data and interpret results
- Make predictions

Materials for January

Three sentence strips, 3 envelopes, Inch Squared Paper (TR3), crayons

Setup

- Make a copy of Inch Squared Paper for each student.
- Make a set of 3 different-colored crayons for each student.
- Label the 3 envelopes *hamburgers*, *pizza*, and *chicken*. You can include a colored square for each choice once the class has decided what colors to use. Attach the envelopes to the board to collect data as students bring in their results.
- Use the sentence strips, labeled with the choices for the opinion poll, to display the results.

Daily Routine

- Assign each student a due date for their data to be turned in.

DISCUSSION

For the Beginning of the Month

Begin by explaining that students will be conducting a survey of people's preferences given 3 choices of food: chicken, hamburgers, or pizza. Other foods can be used, but limit the number of choices to 3. Poll the class. Ask if there is enough data to decide what kind of food a restaurant in the neighborhood should serve. Would the results be the same if we polled people in the neighborhood? How can we get a larger sample?

Ongoing Assessment

1. Look at the Graph. How many people chose pizzas as their favorite food?

2. Did more people choose pizza or hamburgers?

3. What food did people choose most often? What food was chosen least often?

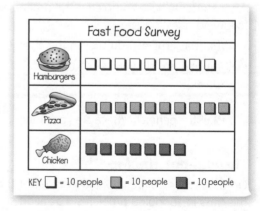

Fast Food Survey

© Great Source. Copying is prohibited.

Sample Dialogue

Teacher: I am going to assign each of you a date this month when you will bring in the opinions of 10 people about their favorite food of 3 given choices. You may count yourself as one of the 10.

Student: Should we bring in 10 pieces of paper?

Teacher: Good question. I am going to give you this Inch Squared Paper. For each person you interview, color in 1 square for his or her choice of chicken, hamburgers, or pizza. What color shall we make each food?

Student: Let's make chicken yellow, hamburgers brown, and pizza red.

Teacher: Great. Now, Lucia, you bring in your results in 2 days. Jeremy, your results are due in 3 days.

For the Second Week in January

As students bring their results to the classroom, they will cut apart their squares and put them in the correct envelopes on the board. After about a week has passed, call attention to the accumulated responses. Explain that the 3 sentence strips on the board will help organize the results into a graph. As 10 of any one color accumulate, they will be stacked on top of each other and attached to the Graph next to the proper category.

- How many red squares do we have in the envelope today?
- Count them. If there are 10 or more, take 10, stack them in a pile, and pin them to the Graph next to the word *pizza*.

Repeat this process for all 3 foods about 4 times during the month.

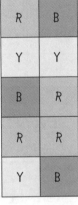

Possible survey results for one student

For the End of the Month

These questions can help make good use of the collected data.

- How many people chose pizza? Hamburgers? Chicken?
- How many more people chose _____ than _____?
- What fraction of the whole group chose pizza? Hamburgers? Chicken?
- If you were a restaurant owner, what kind of food would you choose to serve to this group of people?
- If we asked people in a different community, would the results be the same?

HELPFUL HINTS

- Continue adding more data than just the 10 people polled by each student. Discuss what happens to the results of the graph as the sample size grows.
- Using a food poll is just a suggestion. You can use any question of interest to you and your students. The most important thing is to have your students conduct a survey throughout the month and report their findings back to the class.
- Some students may want to continue making graphs and conducting interviews. Encourage them!

© Great Source. Copying is prohibited.

Every Day Calendar

FEBRUARY

Area 23

P = 48

Measurement

11:02 plus 23 minutes =

| 1 | 1 | : | 2 | 5 |

Clock

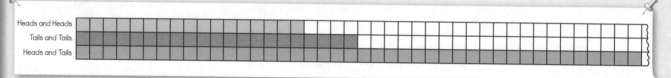

Heads and Heads
Tails and Tails
Heads and Tails

Graph

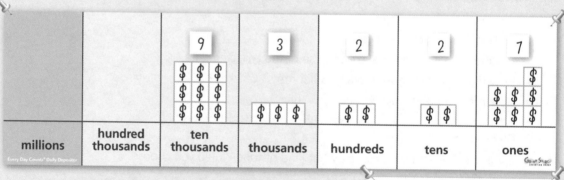

		9	3	2	2	7
millions	hundred thousands	ten thousands	thousands	hundreds	tens	ones

Daily Depositor

				$9	0,	9	2	7
			+		2,	3	0	0
				$9	3,	2	2	7

89 90 91 92 93 94 95 96 97 98 99 (100) 101 102 103 104 105 106 107

Counting Tape

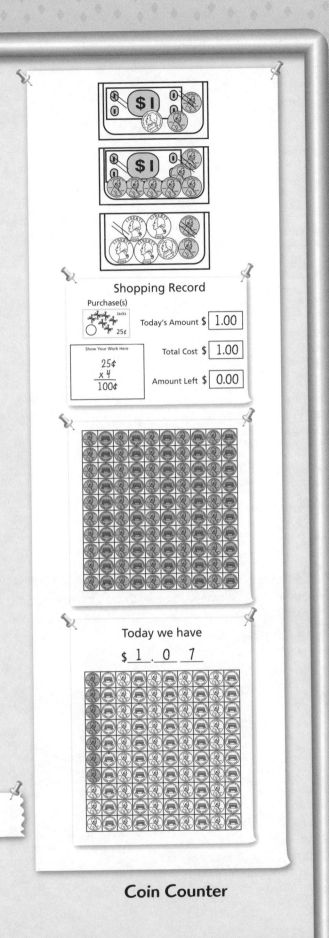

Coin Counter

FEBRUARY ELEMENTS

ONE HUNDREDTH DAY CELEBRATION . . 92
find two addends for 100; write number sentences

CALENDAR 92
recognize patterns in multiples of 6; compare and classify angles

DAILY DEPOSITOR 94
multiply numbers by 100; round to the thousands place; perform multi-digit addition

MEASUREMENT 95
develop an understanding of area and perimeter; discover if figures with the same area have the same perimeter

COUNTING TAPE 97
find multiples of 7; know multiplication facts for 7; look at factors of 100

COIN COUNTER 99
count mixed coins; see pennies as hundredths and dimes as tenths of a dollar; use mental math to compute change

CLOCK 100
add on time in increments up to 30 minutes; understand elapsed time

GRAPH 101
compare experimental probability to theoretical probability; analyze the results of tossing 2 quarters a total of 100 times

During February, the One Hundredth Day of school occurs. February is also special because it is shorter, but sometimes gets an added day. Activities related to the One Hundredth Day of school and leap year follow. The Calendar features a discussion of angles and their names. The Daily Depositor focuses on rounding to the nearest thousand. Multiple Markers indicate multiples of 7 on the Counting Tape. The Clock focuses on adding time in random amounts. The Measurement element examines the relationship between area and perimeter.

LEAP YEAR EXPLANATION

Leap year happens every 4 years because each calendar year is actually 365 days and about 6 hours. When 4 years have passed, these 6 hours add up to 24 hours, thereby creating an extra day. You can illustrate this by folding a circle into fourths and writing 6 hours on each fourth. When demonstrating, color in one fourth for each year. This way students can see that after 4 years, the entire circle is colored and there is one more whole. This is the day added to the calendar in February every fourth year. Leap year occurs every year that is divisible by 4 except centenary years not exactly divisible by 400.

ONE HUNDREDTH DAY CELEBRATION

Here are some activities for the One Hundredth Day of school.

- *Can You Make 100?* The purpose of this game is to identify two numbers that add up to 100. Each team makes a list of numbers less than 100 and has a captain standing by the Counting Tape. Team A's captain points to a number on the Tape, and a member of Team B must tell what number can be added to make a sum of 100. For example, if Team A points to 35, then a member of Team B must quickly respond "65." Then Team B's captain points to a number and a member of Team A must tell the missing addend to make 100. For every correct answer, the team scores 1 point. The game ends when a team scores 10 points.

- *Number Sentences for 100.* As in December, this can be a great way to practice writing number sentences with 100 as the answer. For example, $25 \times 4 = 100$ or $400 \div 4 = 100$. Make a big chart and allow students to display their solutions as they discover them. See if the class can generate 100 number sentences for the 100th day.

Number & Operations	Algebra	Geometry	Measurement	Data & Probability
Problem Solving	Reasoning	Communication	Connections	Representation

CALENDAR

Concepts & Skills

- Analyze and predict patterns
- Recognize patterns in multiples of 6
- Compare and classify angles

Author Notes

"Angles are difficult for many students. Often, students confuse measuring angles with measuring distance, asking, "Which number do I read on the protractor?" Angles are measures of turn. Ask students to explain what a *360* means in basketball. Encourage students to stand and turn 90, 180, and 360 degrees. Students will probably not all turn in the same direction. Explain that degrees tell how far to turn, not in what direction. Demonstrate angles with a door in your classroom, changing the number of degrees as you open and close the door. As you begin the Calendar this month, be sure to refer back to these known benchmarks in explaining acute and obtuse angles. Always emphasize that angles are turns measured in degrees."

Ongoing Assessment

1. In your own words, define an obtuse angle.

2. Draw a right angle. Then draw what that angle would look like if you rotated it 90° in a clockwise direction.

3. In the number pattern 4, 8, 12, 16, 20, 24, and so on, what will the 10th number be?

© Great Source. Copying is prohibited.

Discussion

For the Beginning of the Month
Sample Dialogue

Teacher: There are different-sized angles on the Calendar. Who can describe them?

Student: The 1st one is the smallest and the 3rd one is the biggest. I don't think the 4th one is an angle.

Teacher: What is an angle ?

Student: (holds both arms at an angle) They look like this.

Student: They are where 2 lines meet.

Teacher: You are both right in a way, but let's explore a bit. When Michael Jordan spun around and "did a 360," what did that mean? What did he do?

Student: He turned around completely.

Teacher: Exactly. He turned 360°, or 1 complete circle. There are 360° in a circle. What actually happens when a skateboarder "does a 180"?

Student: That means turning half way around, like turning in the other direction.

Teacher: Yes. Angles measure how far you turn. When we measure angles between two rays like these (pointing to the Calendar), we are measuring how far one ray has turned from the other ray. Let me show you with a door. If the door makes a right angle like this, how many degrees is that?

Student: 90°, like in a square.

Teacher: An angle greater than 0° and less than 90° is called an acute angle . Are any of these angles acute?

Student: The first one.

Teacher: An angle greater than 90° but less than 180° is called an obtuse angle . An angle of exactly 180° looks like a straight line. Do you see any of those?

Student: The 3rd angle is obtuse.

Student: And the 4th one is 180°.

The February Calendar Pieces create an ABCD pattern defined by the kinds of angles. The pattern is acute, right, obtuse, straight (180°) angle. The sizes of the acute and obtuse angles change so students see a variety. The angles are rotated 90° clockwise so students can recognize the angles no matter what the orientation.

To Sum Up

Some questions to support students' understanding of angles and patterns might include the following.

- What patterns do you notice on the Calendar?
- What kind of angle will appear today? How do you know?
- What kind of angle will appear one week from today?
- How many 180° angles will appear this month? How do you know?
- What is the number pattern for right angles? (2, 6, 10, and so on)
- Explain why all the angles on the 2nd, 6th, 10th, and so on, are called right angles even though some of them may turn to the left? (A right angle has nothing to do with direction but simply means it is the measure of a 90° turn.)
- Do you think the angle on the 25th is greater than or less than 45°? (less than) About how many degrees is that angle? How do you

© Great Source. Copying is prohibited.

know? (For example: It looks about the same as the distance between 6 and 7 on a clock. It may be about 30°.)

- These acute angles increase by 10° each time. Do you think the obtuse angles do the same? (yes)
- If you put 2 right angles together, what size angle do you get? (180°)

HELPFUL HINT

- Continue to ask students to create angles with their arms and with the door. Have them say the name of the angle they form: acute, right, obtuse, straight (180°) angle.

Number & Operations	Algebra	Geometry	Measurement	Data & Probability
Problem Solving	Reasoning	Communication	Connections	Representation

DAILY DEPOSITOR

Concepts & Skills

- Multiply numbers by 100
- Perform multi-digit addition
- Estimate and predict
- Round to the thousands place

Daily Routine

- During February, the amount added to the Depositor each day will be $100 times the date. At the end of January there was $65,627 in the Depositor.

Ongoing Assessment

1. What is the value of the 6 in 26,310?
2. Start with 16,200 and count up by hundreds to 17,000.
3. Is the sum of 1,500 + 2,250 + 3,010 closer to 6,000 or 7,000?

DISCUSSION

Throughout the Month

Ask students what number is halfway between 0 and 1,000. (500) Review the definition of rounding. (A rounded number tells about how many. To round to the nearest hundred, round up if the digit with the next smallest place value is halfway or more to the next hundred. Otherwise round down.)

1	0	6	2	2	7
hundred thousands	ten thousands	thousands	hundreds	tens	ones

Some questions for discussion might include the following:

- If you were rounding 28 to the nearest ten, what would you do? (Since I am rounding to the tens place, I would look at the number in the ones place and think that 8 is close to the next 10, so I will round up to 30. The 8 helps me make up my mind.)
- If you were rounding 141 to the nearest 10, what would the answer be? (The 1 helps me remember to round down to 140.)
- Suppose you are rounding 800 to the nearest thousand. Would it round to 0 or 1,000? (800 is closer to 1,000, so I would round up.)

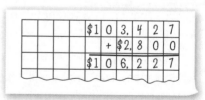

The Depositor on February 28th

© Great Source. Copying is prohibited.

- Our Depositor contains $65,627 through the end of January. Before we add any more money, let's try to round that number to the nearest thousand. (It rounds up to $66,000 because 600 is closer to 1,000 than to 0.)
- After we deposit our money on February 3rd, there is a total of $66,227 in the Depositor. How can we round that number to the nearest thousand? (It also rounds to $66,000. The 200 helps me remember to round down because it is less than halfway.)
- How can 2 numbers that are $600 apart round to the same number? (Because you round one number up and one number down, and both end up in the same place.)

While the discussion continues during the month, it is important to record the rounding that you are doing. Write the number being rounded and indicate with an arrow the column to which you are rounding. Circle the part of the number that determines the direction of the rounding.

To promote subtraction practice, remember to pose an expenditure problem once a week using the amount in the Daily Depositor.

			Daily Depositor		
Month	Days in the Month	Total for the Month	Cumulative Total	Daily Deposit Amount
September	30	$465		$1 times date
October	31	$992	$1,457	$2 times date
November	30	$4,650	$6,107	$10 times date
December	31	$9,920	$16,027	$20 times date
January	31	$49,600	$65,627	$100 times date
February	28 or 29	$40,600 or $43,500 in leap year	$106,227 or $109,127 in leap year	$100 times date
March	31			
April	30			
May	31			

Daily Depositor totals through the end of February

We are rounding this number
$65,627

Does this number round up or down?

Number & Operations   Algebra   Geometry   Measurement   Data & Probability
Problem Solving   Reasoning   Communication   Connections   Representation

MEASUREMENT

Concepts & Skills
- Develop an understanding of area and perimeter and the ability to distinguish between the two
- Discover if figures with the same area have the same perimeter

Materials for February
Several copies of Inch Squared Paper (TR3); about 20 pieces of construction paper

Author Notes
"The purpose of this element is to provide an opportunity for students to explore the relationship between area and perimeter. By constructing figures with an area equal to the day's date, students have the opportunity to investigate whether these figures have the same perimeter. For example, on February 6, students use 6 paper inch squares to make designs with an area of 6 square inches. Each design must have tiles with full sides touching."

Setup
- Cut copies of Inch Squared Paper into individual one-inch squares. Store these in an envelope so students can use them.

Daily Routine
- About 20 times during the month, have students investigate the area and perimeter of figures constructed with the number of paper inch squares equal to the day's date.

Ongoing Assessment
1. How would you describe what the word *area* means?
2. How would you describe what the word *perimeter* means?
3. What happens to the relationship between area and perimeter as the shape of a figure becomes closer to a square?

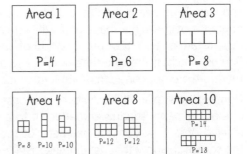

What is the relationship between area and perimeter?

© Great Source. Copying is prohibited.

- As students find figures, have them attach them to the construction paper at the front of the room, labeling the area and the perimeter for each figure. No two figures can be congruent.
- Discuss the relationship between the area and perimeter of each figure revealed through students' explorations. Look to see if any patterns are emerging.

DISCUSSION

For the First Day
Sample Dialogue

Teacher: This month we will be making figures using these paper inch squares. We will use the day's date to determine how many squares to use. Then we will try to find the perimeter of each figure we make. On some days we will try to make more than one figure to see if the perimeter is always the same when the area is the same. What does area mean?

Student: The amount of space covered by something.

Student: The top of my desk.

Teacher: Those are good answers. *Area* is the measure of how much surface is covered by a figure. So each day the number of squares we use to construct our figures will be the area of that figure. When we find the area, we always measure in square units. Why do you think we use square units?

Student: Well, when you measure a line, you can only go in one direction. If you use square units you can fill in the space something takes up in two directions.

Teacher: That's right. Since the squares we are using are an inch long on each side, we call one of them a square inch. So if we use 5 of them to make a shape, its area is 5 square inches. Does anyone know what perimeter means?

Student: Perimeter is the outside of a circle.

Student: It's the distance around the outside of a figure.

Teacher: Yes. We will measure the perimeter of the figures we construct. Do we need to use square units?

Student: No, because we're only trying to measure in one direction.

Teacher: We want to find out if 2 or more figures that have the same area also have the same perimeter.

Explain that each figure the students make has to be a different shape and size. That means the figures cannot be congruent. To make sure a figure is not the same shape and size—or congruent—you can flip it over, rotate or turn it, or put it on top of another figure to see if the figures match. If they are the same, the two figures are congruent, and therefore are not considered different shapes.

Continue to explain the activity by demonstrating with 1 square. Take one of the paper squares and attach it to a piece of construction paper labeled *Area 1*. Ask for the perimeter of the figure. Write $P = 4$ beneath the square to show that its perimeter is 4 inches. Take 2 squares and arrange them next to each other horizontally. Take 2 more squares and arrange them next to each other vertically. Rotate one rectangle and lay it on top of the other to show that they are in fact the same size and shape, or congruent.

© Great Source. Copying is prohibited.

Throughout the Month

Here are some questions to help students decide whether two figures can have the same area and different perimeters.

- What is today's date? How many squares did you use?
- What is the area of your figure? Remember to use square inches.
- What is the perimeter of your figure?
- Do all the figures constructed today have the same area? Do all the figures constructed today have the same perimeter?
- Which figures have the longest perimeters? The shortest perimeters?

For the End of the Month

These questions can be used to provide a good summation.

- Do figures with the same area always have the same perimeter? (no) How do you know? (We made figures with the same area and different perimeters.)
- Was there a day this month when you could not find figures with the same area and different perimeters? (the 1st, 2nd, and 3rd days)
- Were there any 2 days where the area was different and the perimeter was the same? (The response will depend on the number of shapes constructed each day in your classroom, but the answer should be yes. On days 3 and 4, you can make figures with different areas and the same perimeters. The same is true many other days, depending on what figures your class constructs.)
- What have we noticed during the month about the shapes that have the longest perimeter? (They seem to be very long in one direction and narrow in the other direction.)
- What about the shapes that have the shortest perimeter? (They are squares or more like squares than the others.)

Number & Operations	Algebra	Geometry	Measurement	Data & Probability
Problem Solving	Reasoning	Communication	Connections	Representation

COUNTING TAPE

Concepts & Skills

- Explore multiples and factors
- Know multiplication facts for 7
- Look at the factors of 100

Materials for February

Days-of-the-Week Multiple Markers cardstock, copies of Circular Array Paper (TR7), Hundred Chart (TR4), Centimeter Squared Paper (TR15), and Equation Chart (TR5)

Daily Routine

- Continue to have students identify and mark multiples of 2, 3, 4, 5, and 6 with Multiple Markers. Begin marking multiples of 7 with Days-of-the-Week Multiple Markers.

Ongoing Assessment

1. Count by sevens from 7 to 70.
2. What is the 9th multiple of 7? Can you use 10×7 to find it quickly?
3. 5 groups of 7 is 35. How can we use this fact to find 7×7?

© Great Source. Copying is prohibited.

93 94 95 96 97 98 99 (100) 101 102 103 104 105 106 107

For the Beginning of the Month

Many multiples of 7 have already been written on the Counting Tape by the time February begins. Hang the Days-of-the-Week Multiple Markers as students tell you the numbers. Ask questions like these:

- Are there any numbers like 7 that have only one Multiple Marker hanging from them? (2, 3, 5, and 7) You can introduce the term prime number for these numbers and for all numbers with no markers so far that have only 2 factors, 1 and the number itself.

- What numbers are multiples of 7 but have just 2 Multiple Markers? (14, 21, 35) Why can we refer to each of those numbers as a least common multiple?

- What multiples of 7 have more than 2 Multiple Markers? (28, 42, 56, 63, 70, 84, and 98.) What do the markers tell us about these numbers?

Invite students to share how they can combine groups of 7 to find products greater than 70. Using days in a week is one way to help students think about groups of 7. This can lead to students discovering ways to solve some of the more difficult facts easily.

For the One Hundredth Day of School

Focus attention on the Counting Tape to review the concept of factors. You may want to have counters available so students can prove their answers to the following questions:

- What Multiple Markers will we hang from 100? (2, 4, and 5)

- How many twos are in 100? (50) Then 2 and 50 are both factors of 100. Let's make a list of the factors of 100.

- How many fours are in 100? (25) Then 4 and 25 are factors of 100. Let's add them to the list.

- How many fives are in 100? (20) Then 5 and 20 are factors of 100.

- What other numbers divide 100 into equal groups? (10, 1, and 100) Let's add them to the list.

For the End of the Month

Distribute all the materials (Hundred Chart and Equation Chart) students will need to update their Multiplication Books to include facts and remainder equations for 7. They should also color the facts for 7 they can recall easily on their Multiplication Facts Progress Records and update multiple patterns for 2, 3, 4, 5, and 6 from previous months.

HELPFUL HINT

- Students can create Array Flash Cards for facts 7×7 to 7×10 using Centimeter Squared Paper (TR15). These arrays can also provide practice with the concept of area.

Factors of 100
100 x 1 and 1 x 100
50 x 2 and 2 x 50
25 x 4 and 4 x 25
20 x 5 and 5 x 20
10 x 10
Factors: 1, 2, 4, 5, 10, 20, 25, 50, 100

Factors are the number of equal groups and the number within each group.

1 group of 7 = 1 x 7 = 7	6 groups of 7 = 6 x 7 = 42
2 groups of 7 = 2 x 7 = 14	7 groups of 7 = 7 x 7 = 49
3 groups of 7 = 3 x 7 = 21	8 groups of 7 = 8 x 7 = 56
4 groups of 7 = 4 x 7 = 28	9 groups of 7 = 9 x 7 = 63
5 groups of 7 = 5 x 7 = 35	10 groups of 7 = 10 x 7 = 70

1	2	3	4	5	6	7	8	9	10
11	12	13	14	15	16	17	18	19	20
21	22	23	24	25	26	27	28	29	30
31	32	33	34	35	36	37	38	39	40
41	42	43	44	45	46	47	48	49	50
51	52	53	54	55	56	57	58	59	60
61	62	63	64	65	66	67	68	69	70
71	72	73	74	75	76	77	78	79	80
81	82	83	84	85	86	87	88	89	90
91	92	93	94	95	96	97	98	99	100

Multiplication Facts for 7

© Great Source. Copying is prohibited.

COIN COUNTER

Concepts & Skills

- Count mixed coins
- See pennies and dimes as hundredths and tenths of a dollar
- Estimate and multiply 1-digit by 2-digit numbers
- Use mental math to figure change

Materials for February

Play Money: Bills (TR2) or a dollar bill from cardstock

Setup

- On day 101, add a second 100 Penny Grid to the board.

Daily Routine

- Continue to display the coin combination with the fewest coins in the top pocket.
- Continue to use the 100 Penny Grid to talk about the day's amount as tenths and hundredths of a dollar.
- From day 101 forward, show the day's amount with one dollar accompanied by the fewest additional coins in the top pocket, one dollar, dimes, and pennies only in the middle pocket; and a combination that uses only coins in the bottom pocket.
- About twice a week, continue to use a Shopper Card and the Shopping Record to make multiple purchases and determine how much would be left.

DISCUSSION

For the One Hundredth Day

Have students look at the 100 Penny Grid to see that the whole grid has been colored. You might ask, "How can we use the 100 Penny Grid to help explain why 100%, 100 hundredths, and 10 tenths are each the same as 1 whole?" Listen to the variety of explanations. As you write the amount at the top of the grid, explain that a *1* to the left of the decimal point means 1 whole dollar, the *decimal point* divides the quantity so that wholes appear to the left and fractional parts to the right, and that today you have *zero* tenths and *zero* hundredths. Tell students that when reading decimals, the decimal point stands for *and*.

Direct students' attention to the Coin Counter. Have a volunteer exchange the 4 quarters appearing in the top pocket for one play money dollar. Explain that from now on, the top pocket will always have a $1 bill plus the fewest coins to make the day's amount. The second pocket will show the day's amount with a dollar, dimes, and pennies to show tenths and hundredths of the next dollar. The bottom pocket will show coins only. Invite suggestions of coin combinations for one dollar that use 10 or fewer coins excluding half dollars. Some students may

© Great Source. Copying is prohibited.

Ongoing Assessment

1. How can we show 93 hundredths of a dollar using dimes and pennies?

2. How many hundredths are in a dollar? How many tenths?

3. Pens cost 39¢ and you have $1. How many pens can you buy? What will be your change?

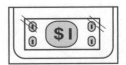

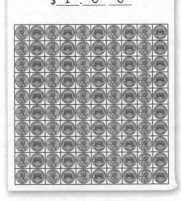

"We have 100¢, or 100 hundredths, and that's a whole dollar."

want to find all possible coin combinations for one dollar that use 10 coins or less.

For Throughout the Month

After Day 100, on shopping problem days, limit the amount available for making the day's total purchase to $1. Focus students on sharing their mental math strategies for deciding how many of an item can be purchased and determining the change due. If some students need more practice with this, ask, "How much change will we get back from a dollar if we buy only 1 of the item? What if we buy 2?"

"I multiplied 4 x 23¢. Four 20s = 80 and four 3s = 12. That's 92¢. There's not enough left for another ball."

© Great Source. Copying is prohibited.

Number & Operations	Algebra	Geometry	Measurement	Data & Probability
Problem Solving	Reasoning	Communication	Connections	Representation

CLOCK

Concepts & Skills

• Add on time in increments up to 30 minutes
• Understand elapsed time

Daily Routine

• Each day, set the Clock to the actual time on the classroom clock.
• Add the number of minutes equal to the date to the time on the Clock.

DISCUSSION

For the Beginning of the Month

Explain to students the procedure that will be used to set the Clock in February. Here are some questions to provide discussion:

• What is the time on the classroom clock right now? (8:26)

• What is the date today? (the 4th) Can you add 4 minutes to the time? (It would be 8:30.) Tell me how to place the hands on the Clock to show 8:30.

If you do Calendar Math at the same time every day, you may want to generate some different starting times by asking different questions like, "What time do we eat lunch? Go to gym class? Go home?"

For the End of the Month
Sample Dialogue

Teacher: Today is February 24th. What is the time?

Student: 8:46.

Teacher: We need to add 24 minutes to the present time. Can anyone tell me what time it will be 24 minutes from now?

Student: It will be past 9:00, I think.

Teacher: Why do you say that?

Student: Because if the time is 8:46, then there are only 14 minutes until 9:00, and you asked us to add on 24 minutes. I guess it will be 9:10.

Ongoing Assessment

1. If it is 11:14, what time will it be 7 minutes from now?

2. If it is 11:25 now, what time was it 23 minutes ago?

3. Draw a picture of what the clock looks like at 11:40.

Advance 24 minutes to:

Teacher: Excellent explanation. Did anyone else figure this out another way?

Student: Well, I knew that 24 minutes was almost one-half hour, so I added on half an hour and took off a few minutes. I got an approximate time of 9:13.

Teacher: That was a great response. I am glad you did it differently.

These conversations help to indicate if students have an understanding for telling time and looking ahead in time.

HELPFUL HINTS

- If you are drawing the time on the Clock, use a black watercolor marker for the present time and a different-colored marker to shade in the time ahead.

- Practice adding on time regularly in the classroom. Ask students what time it will be 17 minutes from now, 26 minutes from now, 7 minutes from now. The more students experience these questions, the more they will begin to develop understanding.

| Number & Operations | Algebra | Geometry | Measurement | Data & Probability |
| Problem Solving | Reasoning | Communication | Connections | Representation |

GRAPH

Concepts & Skills
- Collect and record data
- Compare experimental probability to theoretical probability
- Analyze the results of a coin toss experiment

Materials for February
Two quarters, several 3" × 10" strips of Inch Squared Paper (T3), marker

Setup
- Cut copies of Inch Squared Paper into 3" × 10" strips.
- To make the Graph, post several of the strips next to each other horizontally on the board. Label the 3 rows *Heads and Heads*, *Tails and Tails*, and *Heads and Tails*.

Daily Routine
- Toss 2 quarters 5 times a day, or 25 times a week, for 4 weeks, for a total of 100 tosses.
- Record the result of each toss on the grid strips.

DISCUSSION

For the First Day of the Month
Explain that students will be doing an experiment this month. They will toss 2 quarters together a total of 100 times and record the result of

Ongoing Assessment

1. If you tossed Heads and Heads 23 times out of 100, what fraction would show that result?

2. If you tossed Tails and Tails 27 times out of 100, what decimal would show that result?

3. If you tossed Heads and Tails 53 times out of 100, what percent would show that result?

© Great Source. Copying is prohibited.

each toss. Draw the table shown at the right on the board before
discussing possible outcomes.

	Heads	Tails
Heads	Heads and Heads	Heads and Tails
Tails	Tails and Heads	Tails and Tails

"Heads and Tails or Tails and Heads
has a 2 out of 4 chance of occurring."

Sample Dialogue

Teacher: When you toss 2 quarters, what are the possible outcomes? Look at this table to help answer that question.

Student: You could get heads on both, or you could get tails on both.

Student: You could get heads on 1 coin and tails on the other, or the other way around.

Teacher: It doesn't matter which coin shows heads or tails in that case; the result is that one coin shows heads and the other shows tails. So the possible outcomes of tossing 2 quarters are getting 2 heads, 2 tails, or 1 heads and 1 tails. Looking at the table, is there any combination of Heads and/or Tails that is impossible?

Student: No, you will either get both heads, both tails, or a combination of heads and tails.

Teacher: Is there any toss that is certain to happen every time you toss 2 coins?

Student: No, because the table shows different possibilities.

Teacher: Looking at the table, what are the chances of tossing Heads and Heads?

Student: One out of 4.

Teacher: What are the chances of tossing Tails and Tails?

Student: The same, 1 out of 4.

Teacher: What are the chances of tossing a combination of heads and tails?

Student: Two out of 4.

Teacher: Let's toss 2 quarters 5 times today to see what actually happens. We'll toss the quarters a total of 100 times this month and record the result of each toss on this grid paper.

Throughout the Month
Sample Dialogue

Teacher: What fraction of 100 tosses do you think will be Heads and Heads?

Student: About 25 out of 100 times.

Teacher: How do you know that?

Student: The table we made shows that Heads and Heads should happen 1 out of every 4 times. One fourth of 100 is 25.

Teacher: (writing $\frac{25}{100}$) Then you think that 25 out of 100 tosses will be Heads and Heads. We can also write that two other ways. We can write *0.25*, which is the decimal name for 25 out of 100. Think about how we write 25 cents out of a dollar as $0.25. We can also write *25%* because that is what percent means. Percent means how many out of 100. If 25 out of 100 tosses are Heads and Heads, it is 25%.

Student: $\frac{25}{100}$ can also be written as $\frac{1}{4}$.

Teacher: Yes. What fraction of 100 tosses then do you think will be Tails and Tails?

Heads and Heads

Tails and Tails

Heads and Tails

© Great Source. Copying is prohibited.

Student: That should also happen 25 out of 100 times, or $\frac{1}{4}$.

Teacher: What fraction of 100 tosses do you think will be a combination of Heads and Tails?

Student: That should happen 50 out of 100 times, because $25 + 25 = 50$.

Teacher: How would we write that as a fraction, a decimal, and a percent?

Student: $\frac{50}{100}$, or $\frac{1}{2}$, or 0.50 or 50%.

Teacher: That's great!

For the End of the Month

After 100 tosses, have students write the results in fraction, decimal, and percent forms. Compare the experimental results with the theoretical or expected results.

Sample Dialogue

Teacher: What does our graph show after 100 tosses of 2 quarters?

Student: We tossed Heads and Heads 24 times.

Student: We tossed Tails and Tails 27 times.

Student: So we tossed a combination of Heads and Tails 49 times.

Teacher: Is that close to what you expected?

Student: Yes, we thought about half of the tosses would be a combination.

Teacher: Yes, the chances of getting a combination of Heads and Tails is half of the time. As we did the experiment, it was not always half of the total tosses, but our results came out closer and closer to half of the total tosses the more we tossed the coins. So what fraction of the tosses were Heads and Heads?

Student: $\frac{24}{100}$.

Teacher: And what decimal and percent is that?

Student: 0.24 or 24%.

Teacher: Is this close to what we expected?

Student: Yes, we predicted $\frac{25}{100}$ or $\frac{1}{4}$.

Teacher: And what about Tails and Tails?

Student: $\frac{27}{100}$, which is about what we thought was likely to happen.

HELPFUL HINT

- Coin toss experiments provide fun family math. You might ask that students work at home to tally the results of 20 more tosses of any 2 coins. The student's tallies can then be combined in class to create a very large sample. Students can begin to see that the larger the sample, the more likely the actual results will reflect the theoretical probability.

© Great Source. Copying is prohibited.

MARCH

Every Day Calendar

Sunday Sun.	Monday Mon.	Tuesday Tues.	Wednesday Wed.	Thursday Thurs.	Friday Fri.	Saturday Sat.
	1	2	3	4	5	6
7	8	9	10	11	12	13
14	15	16	17	18	19	20
21	22	23	24	25		

Clock

8 : 5 0

Graph

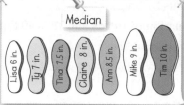

Median

Lisa 6 in. | Ty 7 in. | Tina 7.5 in. | Claire 8 in. | Ann 8.5 in. | Mike 9 in. | Tim 10 in.

Measurement

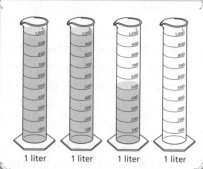

1 liter | 1 liter | 1 liter | 1 liter

Measurement Record

Today we added ___100 mL___

to our ___container___.

Now we have ___2.5 L___, or

$2\frac{1}{2}$ L, or 2,500 mL.

Daily Depositor

millions	hundred thousands	ten thousands	thousands	hundreds	tens	ones
	1	3	8	7	2	7

$$\begin{array}{r} \$136{,}227 \\ +\ 2{,}500 \\ \hline \$138{,}727 \end{array}$$

Counting Tape

112 113 114 115 116 117 118 119 120 121 122 123 124 125 126 127 128 129 130

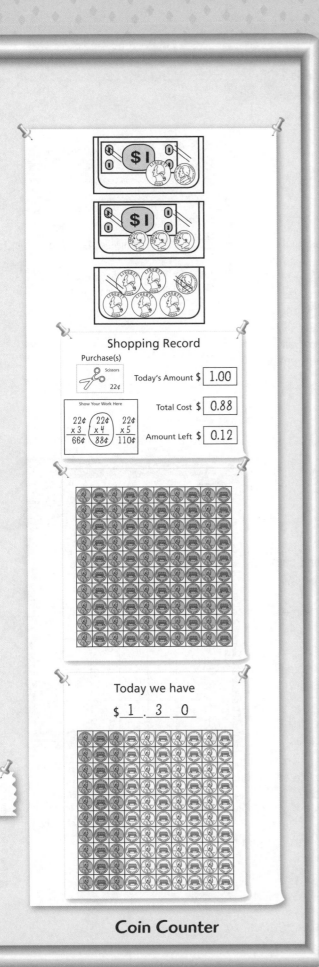

Coin Counter

MARCH ELEMENTS

CALENDAR **106**

analyze and predict patterns; use tables to represent a pattern; compare polygons; develop geometric language

DAILY DEPOSITOR **108**

multiply numbers by 100; perform multi-digit addition; round to the ten thousands place

MEASUREMENT **109**

write milliliters as liters; express measurement using fractions and decimals

COUNTING TAPE **111**

count by eights; know multiplication facts for 8; observe relationships among multiples

COIN COUNTER **113**

see pennies as hundredths and dimes as tenths of a dollar; estimate and multiply 1-digit times 2-digit numbers

CLOCK **113**

subtract time in increments up to 30 minutes

GRAPH **115**

collect and organize data into a bar graph; explore mean, median, mode, and range

March shows steady growth. The Calendar Pieces display different kinds of polygons and the Daily Depositor emphasizes rounding to the nearest ten thousand. The Counting Tape features the multiples of 8 and the relationship between 8 and 4. Purchasing quantities of the same item is the topic for the Coin Counter, while the Clock features counting backward in time. The class is involved in a group project in the Graph activity. The Measurement element focuses on liters and milliliters.

CALENDAR

Concepts & Skills

- Analyze and predict patterns
- Recognize patterns of multiples of 2, 4, and 6
- Use a table to represent a pattern
- Compare and analyze attributes of polygons
- Develop geometric language

Author Notes

"The March Calendar provides the opportunity for students to analyze a variety of irregular polygons to develop the understanding that it is the number of sides that distinguish one kind of polygon from another. Students often see only regular hexagons and don't realize that not all hexagons are regular. This month's Calendar activity allows enough time for all students to identify a polygon by the number of its sides."

Daily Routine

- Each day, attach the Calendar Piece for that day. On Mondays, attach pieces for the weekend days.

DISCUSSION

For the Beginning of the Month

Post Calendar Pieces from the beginning of March, but wait several days before asking students to describe patterns they see. At first they may be confused, because each figure is different from the prior one. Suggest that this month's pattern uses different kinds of shapes. Some questions to stimulate discussion might include the following:

- How are these figures alike? (They are all closed. They all have straight sides.)

- What single name includes all the shapes we see on the Calendar? (polygon)

- What is different about the first 2 shapes and the next 2? (The first 2 have 3 sides and are triangles. The next 2 are four-sided and called quadrilaterals.)

- Describe the triangles on the 1st and 2nd. (The first one looks like an equilateral triangle. All the sides look congruent. The second one looks like an isosceles triangle. Two sides look congruent.)

- Do those triangles have any lines of symmetry? (An equilateral triangle has 3; an isosceles triangle has 1.)

- Does anyone remember the name of the shape on the 5th? (pentagon)

- What do we call the shape on the 6th? (hexagon)

- Both *pent* and *hex* come from the Greek, and mean five and six, respectively. What do you think *quad* means? (four)

Ongoing Assessment

1. Describe a quadrilateral in the most precise terms possible.

2. Name two common multiples of 4 and 6 that are greater than 12.

3. If a shape has 5 sides that are not all equal, is it still called a pentagon?

The pattern this month is a sequence of polygons: triangle, triangle, quadrilateral, quadrilateral, pentagon, hexagon, or an AABBCD pattern. Students are presented with a variety of figures so they identify the number of sides as the critical attribute for distinguishing them.

© Great Source. Copying is prohibited.

- What do you notice about the figures on days 1, 2, 7, and 8? (All of them are purple triangles.)
- What is the same about the triangles on the 7th and 8th? (They both have right angles.)
- Do those triangles have lines of symmetry? (Only the one on the 8th; it's an isosceles right triangle.)

For the Middle of the Month
Sample Dialogue

Teacher: What kind of polygon do we expect to post today? How do you know?

Student: A triangle, because the pattern is triangle, triangle, quadrilateral, quadrilateral, pentagon, hexagon.

Student: A triangle always comes after a hexagon.

Student: The hexagons show up on the multiples of 6, and then there are 2 triangles. Thirteen is one more than 12.

Teacher: (adding the Calendar Piece for the 13th) Describe the triangle.

Student: All 3 sides are different lengths, so it's a scalene triangle.

Teacher: Does this triangle have a line of symmetry?

Student: No.

Teacher: Are any of the angles greater than 90°?

Student: No.

Teacher: So how can we describe this triangle in terms of its angles?

Student: It's acute, like me!

Teacher: Do you see an obtuse triangle anywhere on the Calendar?

Student: On the 14th.

Teacher: Yes. As the pattern unfolds this month, see if you can find something the same and something different about each pair of triangles and each pair of quadrilaterals. Which shapes have at least one line of symmetry? Do any shapes have more than one line of symmetry?

The completed March Calendar

To Sum Up

At the end of the month, review what has been presented about attributes that determine the names of polygons. To encourage observations you might ask:

- What are some of the differences between the quadrilaterals? (Students should use terms such as congruent sides, lines of symmetry, and size of angles.)
- What are some of the differences between the hexagons? (Some have at least 1 line of symmetry and some don't.)
- What is the same about all the pentagons? (They all have 5 sides. They are all pink.)
- On which dates do the hexagons appear? (6, 12, 18, 24, and 30)
- What kinds of numbers are these? (multiples of 6)
- If this pattern continued, what are the next 3 numbers that would have hexagons? (36, 42, 48)

© Great Source. Copying is prohibited.

- What is the number pattern for the quadrilaterals? (3, 4, 9, 10, 15, 16, and so on)

- Describe this pattern in words. (Beginning with 3, you add 1, then 5, then 1, then 5, and so on.)

Draw the table shown at the right on the board. Ask questions like those that follow to help students see how patterns can be recorded in tables. Also, students can begin to see how to write algebraic expressions to make predictions about future appearances of particular Calendar shapes.

Number of Pentagon	Date or Number
1	5
2	11
3	
4	
5	
6	
7	

- This table shows the number pattern of the pentagons. What are the missing dates or numbers? (17, 23, 29, 35, 41) How can you describe this pattern? (The pentagons occur on dates 1 less than a multiple of 6.)

- If the pattern continued what number would be on the 10th pentagon? Is there a rule you can use to figure it out? (59, because the pentagon appears on a number that is 1 less than the 10th multiple of 6. So $(10 \times 6) - 1 = 59$.)

- Can anyone find another pattern on the Calendar? Can you describe the pattern in words? Can you describe it with a rule?

Number & Operations	Algebra	Geometry	Measurement	Data & Probability
Problem Solving	Reasoning	Communication	Connections	Representation

DAILY DEPOSITOR

Concepts & Skills
- Multiply numbers by 100
- Use mental math
- Perform multi-digit addition
- Estimate and predict
- Round to the ten thousands place

Daily Routine
- During March, the amount added to the Depositor each day will be $100 times the date.

- At the end of February, there was $106,227 ($109,127 in leap year) in the Depositor.

- To promote subtraction practice, pose an expenditure problem once a week using the amount in the Daily Depositor. Remember to reinstate the money after the discussion.

DISCUSSION

Throughout the Month

Students should be asked frequently to round the amount to the nearest ten thousand. Ask students what number is halfway between 0 and 10,000. Remind them of the practice they have had rounding numbers to the nearest thousand. To round a number to the nearest 10,000, check the digit in the thousands place. If it is 5,000 or greater, round up. If it is less than 5,000, round down.

Ongoing Assessment

1. How is fifty-two thousand, three hundred sixty-three written in standard notation?

2. Round 52,675 to the nearest ten thousand.

3. Write 125,840 in expanded notation.

© Great Source. Copying is prohibited.

- If you are rounding $8,000 to the nearest ten thousand, would you round it to 0 or to $10,000? (8,000 is closer to 10,000 than to 0, so I would round up.)

- At the end of February, we had $106,227 in the Depositor. Round that number to the nearest ten thousand. (It rounds to $110,000 because 6,227 is closer to 10,000 than 0, so I round up. The 6,000 helps me remember to round up because it is more than halfway between 0 and 10,000.)

- On March 2nd, we had $106,527 in the Depositor. How would we round that number to the nearest ten thousand? (It also rounds to $110,000.)

- On March 9th, the Depositor holds $110,727. Will that round to $110,000 or $120,000? (It will round to $110,000 because 727 is less than halfway between 0 and 10,000.)

- On the 17th, we have $121,527 in the Depositor. Will that round to $120,000 or $130,000? (It will round to $120,000 because 1,527 is closer to 0 than 10,000, so we round down.)

Write the numbers to be rounded on the board. Indicate with an arrow or a box the number in the column to which you are rounding and circle the part of the number that determines the direction of the rounding. Remember to ask students if they think there will be one million dollars in the Depositor by the end of the school year. There will be $155,827 by the end of March, or $158,727 if it is a leap year. With 2 or 3 months left in the school year, ask for predictions now that the end of the year is closer.

Rounding to the ten thousands place

Number & Operations	Algebra	Geometry	Measurement	Data & Probability
Problem Solving	Reasoning	Communication	Connections	Representation

MEASUREMENT

Concepts & Skills
- Write milliliters as liters
- Develop referents for milliliters and liters
- Express measurement using fractions and decimals

Materials for March

Two copies of Quart/Liter Drawings (TR16); 100 mL measure or tablespoon and teaspoon measures; 3 empty 2-liter bottles; Measurement Record (TR10); marker; masking tape; colored water

Setup
- Display the 2-liter bottles where students can easily see them. Remove labels so water level can be indicated.
- Post 4 Liter Drawings from TR16 on the board. Post the Measurement Record nearby.

Ongoing Assessment
1. How many milliliters equal one liter?
2. What are two other ways to write 100 mL?
3. How many liters is 1,200 mL?

© Great Source. Copying is prohibited.

Daily Routine

- Add 100 ml of colored water to a 2-liter bottle each day. Include weekend days and any other days students are not in school. **TIP:** A good approximation for 100 mL is 6 tablespoons plus 2 teaspoons. Since a teaspoon is very close to 5 mL, and there are 3 teaspoons in a tablespoon, you'll be close to 100 mL if you add this amount.

- Mark each 100 mL addition with masking tape to show the new amount. When the container is filled to 1 liter, write *1 liter* on the top piece of masking tape. Begin filling the next container the next day.

- Color 100 mL on the Liter Drawings each day. Update the Measurement Record daily.

1 liter

Discussion

For the Beginning of the Month

Show students the 2-liter container, the Liter Drawings, and your tablespoon/teaspoon measures. Explain that the capacity of containers to hold liquid will be measured this month, using the metric system. Demonstrate adding 100 mL on the first day. Be sure to explain that a liter is equal to 1,000 milliliters. Ask students to give examples of how milliliters and liters are used in daily life. Following this introduction, this conversation might take place.

Measurement Record

Today we added ___100 mL___

to our _____container_____.

Now we have ___0.9 L or___

___900 mL.___

Sample Dialogue

Teacher: If we add 100 milliliters each day, how many days will it be until we have 1 liter? How many milliliters will that be?

Student: 10 days or 1,000 milliliters.

Teacher: That's correct. When we pour 100 milliliters into the liter, what fraction of the liter are we filling?

Student: One tenth of a liter.

Teacher: How many liters do you think we will have at the end of the month?

Student: I think we will have about 3 liters.

Student: I think we will have about 5 liters.

Continue collecting estimates for the outcome at the end of the month. If time permits, ask how students made their estimates. Record their estimates so that they can be compared to the actual amount accumulated by the end of the month.

For the Twenty-third Day of the Month

Adapt these questions as needed by changing the numbers. On April 23, there will be 2,300 mL or 2.3 L.

- How many milliliters do we have today? (2,300)

- How many whole liters is that? (2)

- How many extra milliliters? (300)

- How can we write the leftover amount as a fraction? ($\frac{300}{1,000}$, or $\frac{3}{10}$, or 0.3, because we have filled three tenths of the next liter.)

Record this on the Measurement Record.

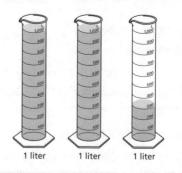

1 liter   1 liter   1 liter

Measurement Record

Today we added ___100 mL___

to our _____container_____.

Now we have ___2.3 L, or___

___$2\frac{3}{10}$ L, or 2,300 mL.___

© Great Source. Copying is prohibited.

For the End of the Month

Summarize all the facts that have been presented:

- Review how many milliliters equal 1 liter.
- Review 100 milliliters as $\frac{1}{10}$ of a liter.
- Examine how many milliliters have been collected and ask how many liters in all.
- Compare the estimates of the amount to be accumulated with the actual amount in the containers.

HELPFUL HINTS

- Have students bring empty 2-liter soda bottles from home. Be sure to have a lid for each container because evaporation affects the outcome.
- Since updating involves pouring water every day, assign students this task. Then you will lead discussion on those days.
- To make colored water, just add drops of food coloring to the water.

Number & Operations	Algebra	Geometry	Measurement	Data & Probability
Problem Solving	Reasoning	Communication	Connections	Representation

COUNTING TAPE

Concepts & Skills

- Explore multiples and factors
- Know multiplication facts for 8
- Observe relationships among multiples

Materials for March

Octagon Multiple Markers cardstock, copies of Circular Array Paper (TR7), Hundred Chart (TR4), Centimeter Squared Paper (TR15), and Equation Chart (TR5)

Daily Routine

- Continue to have students identify and mark multiples of 2, 3, 4, 5, 6, and 7 with Multiple Markers. Begin marking multiples of 8 with Octagon Multiple Markers.

Ongoing Assessment

1. Count by eights from 8 to 80.
2. What is the 9th multiple of 8? Can you use 10×8 to find it quickly?
3. 5 groups of 8 is 40. How can we use this fact to find 7×8?

DISCUSSION

For the Beginning of the Month

Have students call out multiples of 8 beginning at 8 as volunteers attach an octagon marker below each one up to the present day of school.

108 109 110 111 112 113 114 115 116 117 118 119 120 121

"120 has lots of factors."

© Great Source. Copying is prohibited.

Create a list of the multiples of 8 on the board and examine the pattern in the tens column and the ones column. The pattern in the ones place (8, 6, 4, 2, 0) makes sense to many students when they see that going ahead 8 on the Counting Tape is the same as going ahead 10 and back 2.

Since many students find the multiplication facts for 8 difficult, take the time to show them the relationship between 4s and 8s. Have students use Centimeter Squared Paper (TR15) to cut out rectangles, 8 by 8, 9 by 8, and 10 by 8. Fold them in half to change the 8-cm side to a 4-cm side. For example, 8×8 folded in half shows 8 rows of 4 on each half. If a student knows this product is 32, then 8×8 will be twice as much, 64. The doubling can be illustrated by opening the rectangle.

Some questions to ask about the Counting Tape are:

- If you did not know every multiple of 8, how could you find them by looking at the Counting Tape? (Every multiple of 8 has a heart (because they are all multiples of 2), a square (because they are all multiples of 4), and an octagon.

- What other common multiples stand out on the Tape? (Multiples of 6 have both triangles and hexagons. Multiples of 10 have hearts and stars. Multiples of 12 have hearts, triangles, squares, and hexagons.)

- What do we know about numbers with no Multiple Markers? (They are prime numbers, having only 1 and the number itself as factors.)

- How many eights are in 121? ($10 \times 8 = 80$, and 41 more is enough for 5 more eights. That's 15 eights and 1 left over.)

For the End of the Month

Distribute all the materials (Hundred Chart and Equation Chart) students will need to update their Multiplication Books to include facts and remainder equations for 8. They should also color the facts for 8 they can recall easily on their Multiplication Facts Progress Records and update multiple patterns for 2, 3, 4, 5, 6, and 7 from previous months.

HELPFUL HINTS

- You might want to have the class make a list of equations to show how their collection of Array Flash Cards for the harder times 8 facts can be folded in half to show the easier times 4 facts doubled to get the total. Remind students they can read "$\times$" as "groups of."

$8 \times 6 = (4 \times 6) + (4 \times 6) = 24 + 24 = 48$

$8 \times 7 = (4 \times 7) + (4 \times 7) = 28 + 28 = 56$

$8 \times 8 = (4 \times 8) + (4 \times 8) = 32 + 32 = 64$

$8 \times 9 = (4 \times 9) + (4 \times 9) = 36 + 36 = 72$

- Another strategy for remembering 9×8 is to multiply 10×8 and then take 1 group of 8 away. $9 \times 8 = (10 \times 8) - 8 = 80 - 8 = 72$.

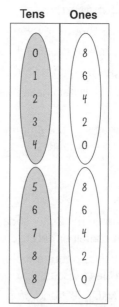

Tens	Ones
0	8
1	6
2	4
3	2
4	0
5	8
6	6
7	4
8	2
8	0

What patterns do you see?

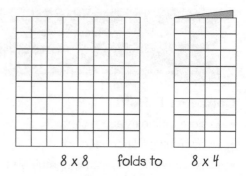

8×8 folds to 8×4

8×8 is 4×8 doubled. $32 + 32 = 64$.

1 group of 8 = 1 x 8 = 8   6 groups of 8 = 6 x 8 = 48
2 groups of 8 = 2 x 8 = 16   7 groups of 8 = 7 x 8 = 56
3 groups of 8 = 3 x 8 = 24   8 groups of 8 = 8 x 8 = 64
4 groups of 8 = 4 x 8 = 32   9 groups of 8 = 9 x 8 = 72
5 groups of 8 = 5 x 8 = 40   10 groups of 8 = 10 x 8 = 80

1	2	3	4	5	6	7	8	9	10
11	12	13	14	15	16	17	18	19	20
21	22	23	24	25	26	27	28	29	30
31	32	33	34	35	36	37	38	39	40
41	42	43	44	45	46	47	48	49	50
51	52	53	54	55	56	57	58	59	60
61	62	63	64	65	66	67	68	69	70
71	72	73	74	75	76	77	78	79	80
81	82	83	84	85	86	87	88	89	90
91	92	93	94	95	96	97	98	99	100

"The pattern really stands out as go ahead 10 and back 2."

© Great Source. Copying is prohibited.

COIN COUNTER

Concepts & Skills

- Count mixed coins
- See pennies and dimes as hundredths and tenths of a dollar
- Estimate and multiply 1-digit times 2-digit numbers
- Use mental math to determine change

Daily Routine

- Continue to display a $1 bill and the fewest coins in the top pocket, a $1 bill and only dimes and pennies in the middle pocket, and a combination that uses only coins in the bottom pocket.

- Continue to use the 100 Penny Grid to talk about the day's amount as tenths and hundredths of a dollar.

- When doing shopping problems once or twice a week, limit the total that can be spent to one dollar.

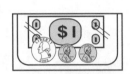
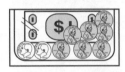

The Coin Counter on day 127

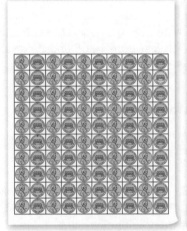

Today we have

$ _1_ . _2_ _7_

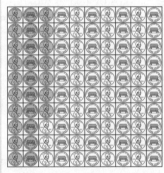

Ongoing Assessment

1. How many dimes would it take to make today's amount?

2. If you used $1 to buy some trail mix that costs 59¢, how much change would you get back?

3. Scissors cost 22¢. How many scissors can you buy with today's amount?

CLOCK

Concepts & Skills

- Subtract time in increments up to 30 minutes

Daily Routine

- In March, set the Clock to the actual time on the classroom clock. Subtract the number of minutes equal to the day's date each day. For example, on March 5 at 1:07, subtract 5 minutes to get 1:02.

Ongoing Assessment

1. If it is 9:23 now, what time was it 8 minutes ago?

2. If it is 9:17 now, what time was it 22 minutes ago?

3. How many minutes are there between 9:15 and 9:32?

© Great Source. Copying is prohibited.

DISCUSSION

For the Beginning of the Month

Explain to students the procedure that will be used for the Clock this month. Here are some questions to provide discussion when getting started.

- What is the time on the classroom clock right now? (1:13)
- What is the date today? (March 3rd)
- What time was it 3 minutes ago? (1:10)
- How do I place the hands on the Clock to show 1:10?

If you use Calendar Math at the same time every day, generate some different starting times by asking questions like the following:

- What time is it when we eat lunch? (12:05)
- What is the date today? (March 9th)
- If we went to lunch 9 minutes earlier today, what time would that be? (11:56)

This is one of the most difficult problems students have with time. It means going backward before the hour. Demonstrate this by moving the hands on the Clock back 4 minutes before the hour. Some students will have to practice this many times to get an understanding. For others, it will be enough to provide the explanation of subtracting 9 minutes by taking 5 minutes off first from 12:05 and then subtracting the remaining 4 minutes from 12:00 or 60.

For the End of the Month
Sample Dialogue

Teacher: Today is March 23rd. What is the time?

Student: 9:17.

Teacher: Let's pretend that 23 minutes before 9:17 the fire alarm rang at our school. What time did the alarm sound? Can anyone tell me what time it was 23 minutes ago?

Student: Well, I know it was after 8:30 because the school bell had already rung.

Teacher: That is helpful information.

Student: If it was 23 minutes ago, it was just before 9:00 because it's 17 minutes after 9:00 now.

Teacher: Well, let's look at the Clock. If we move the minute hand back 17 minutes, it will be 9:00. How many more minutes will we have to move the minute hand back?

Student: 6 more minutes, because 17 + 6 = 23. So the time will be 6 minutes before 9:00.

Teacher: Then what time will it be?

Student: It will be 8:54.

Teacher: A.M. or P.M.?

Student: A.M.

While these conversations do not take much time in the classroom, their influence in developing understanding of time is powerful. While participating in these conversations, you can learn a lot about what students do and do not know about time.

9:17 A.M.
Wall Clock

8:54 A.M.

The actual time is 9:17. 23 minutes ago it was 8:54.

The Clock on March 23rd

© Great Source. Copying is prohibited.

HELPFUL HINTS

- If you are drawing the time on the Clock, use a black marker for the present time and a different-colored marker to shade the minutes subtracted.

- Working backward in a system based on the number 60 is difficult. Be patient and practice this as frequently as you can.

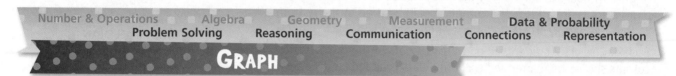

Number & Operations   Algebra   Geometry   Measurement   **Data & Probability**

Problem Solving   **Reasoning**   **Communication**   **Connections**   **Representation**

GRAPH

Concepts & Skills

- Represent data visually
- Predict, collect, and organize data into a bar graph
- Analyze data and interpret graphs
- Explore the definitions of *mean*, *median*, *mode*, and *range*

Materials for March

One light-colored piece of construction paper; 1 piece of construction paper and a crayon for each student; copies of Inch Squared Paper (TR3); copies of the 4 recording sheets shown on page 116; pins or sticky tack; one index card; scissors; glue sticks; calculators

Author Notes

"This activity combines number and measurement with data and statistics in a real-world context. These ideas are presented to students in a meaningful way, not as abstract concepts. It allows students to collect, organize, and analyze data, and make predictions. Interpreting graphs is a useful skill in this information age. In this activity, students create cutouts of their shoes and collect data about the length of their shoes. This gives students the opportunity to explore the meaning of *mean*, *median*, *mode*, and *range* as these terms apply to their collection of shoe-length data."

Setup

- Label the light-colored piece of construction paper *Shoe Length Estimates*.
- Label the index card *Median*.
- Cut a 1" × 10" strip of Inch Squared Paper for each student.
- Ask students to predict how long their shoe is in inches.
- Students record their estimates on the *Shoe Length Estimates* chart.
- Students work in pairs to create shoe cutouts. One student centers one foot on a piece of construction paper. The other student traces around the outside of that student's shoe with a crayon. Students trade places and repeat the process.
- Students cut out the shoe tracings and fold them lengthwise to show the greatest length of the shoe.

Ongoing Assessment

1. What is the median of the data shown? The mean? Is there a mode?

2. What is the range of the data shown on the Graph?

3. Describe how you would find the mean age of the students in your class.

© Great Source. Copying is prohibited.

- Students measure the length of their shoe on the fold by gluing a 1" × 10" strip of Inch Squared Paper along the fold. Students record their name and shoe length to the nearest half-inch on the cutout.

Daily Routine

- Early in the month, choose 3 students to display the shoe cutouts in order from shortest to longest. These should be attached to the wall or bulletin board in such a way that they can be easily rearranged as more cutouts are added. The cutouts should be even at the bottom so that the bar graph created is a scientific bar graph.
- Each day, select 2 students to add their cutouts to the display. The cutouts should be rearranged each time data is added so they are always in order from shortest to longest.
- As new information is added, take time to discuss how it changes the range, median, mode, and mean of the data. Record this information each time you discuss it.

DISCUSSION

For the Beginning of the Month

Explain that students will be measuring their shoe lengths, graphing the information, and making interpretations and predictions with the data. Have students create their shoe cutouts. Begin the month using informal language in your discussion about the data.

Sample Dialogue

Teacher: We have 3 shoe cutouts displayed in order from shortest to longest. Lisa's measures 6 inches, Tina's measures $7\frac{1}{2}$ inches, and Mike's measures 9 inches. What is the difference between the shortest and the longest length?

Student: 3 inches.

Teacher: Whose shoe is in the middle?

Student: Tina's shoe.

Teacher: Do any measurements show up more than once?

Student: No, they are all different lengths.

Teacher: What if we wanted to make these 3 lengths all the same by evening them out so that no one was shorter or longer? What could we do?

Student: We could take some inches away from Mike's cutout and give them to Lisa and Tina.

Teacher: Then everyone's cutout would be $7\frac{1}{2}$ inches long.

For the Middle of the Month

There should be 7 or more shoe cutouts displayed in order from shortest to longest by the middle of the month. Now move the discussion from informal language to formal language by asking the following questions. Record the day's information on the 4 recording sheets pictured above.

Today's RANGE (the difference between the longest and shortest cutouts) is

_____ in.

Today's MEDIAN (middle) length is

_____ in.

Today's MODE (most often appearing length) for our lengths is

_____ in.

Today's MEAN (average) length is

_____ in.

These are important words to know when discussing data.

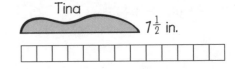

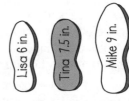

© Great Source. Copying is prohibited.

- What is the difference between the shortest and the longest lengths today? (4 inches) That is called the range of the data.

- Whose cutout is exactly in the middle today? (Claire's) The number in the middle of a set of numbers that are in order from least to greatest is called the median. How can we be sure Claire's cutout is in the middle? (Count in by ones from the right and left ends until you get to the middle. If there are two cutouts in the middle, then the number halfway between them is the middle.)

- Has the median changed every day? Why or why not? (It did not change if the 2 new cutouts were placed on either side of the existing median. It could change if the cutouts were both placed on one side or the other of the existing median.)

- Do any lengths show up more than once? (no) The number that appears most often in a set of data is called the mode. Some data sets, like the one we have today, don't have a mode because no number shows up more often than any other number. As our data changes, we may have a set with a mode during the month.

- What if we evened out all the lengths so they were all the same and no cutout was shorter or longer than any other cutout? When we do that mathematically, we are finding the mean, or average, of the data. About what would that length be? (Have students estimate the mean. Then explain how to find the actual mean by adding the lengths and dividing by the number of lengths. For the data given here, the mean is 8 inches.)

The following questions help students to apply this knowledge in the real world:

- Why is it useful to know the mean or average shoe length, the median shoe length, or the range of shoe lengths for a group of fourth graders? Who might want to know this kind of data? (Answers might include doctors, people who manufacture shoes, people who design skates for them, and so on.)

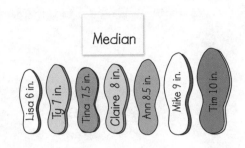

Median

Lisa 6 in. · Ty 7 in. · Tina 7.5 in. · Claire 8 in. · Ann 8.5 in. · Mike 9 in. · Tim 10 in.

HELPFUL HINT

- Use the first day of the month for all students to make their shoe cutouts. Collect the cutouts and post them throughout the month.

© Great Source. Copying is prohibited.

Every Day Calendar

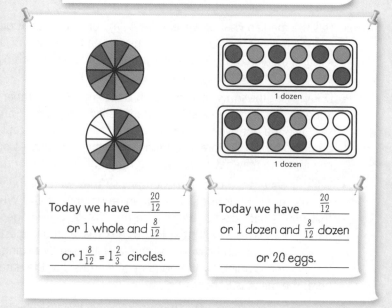

Today we have $\frac{20}{12}$

or 1 whole and $\frac{8}{12}$

or $1\frac{8}{12} = 1\frac{2}{3}$ circles.

Today we have $\frac{20}{12}$

or 1 dozen and $\frac{8}{12}$ dozen

or 20 eggs.

A Fraction A Day

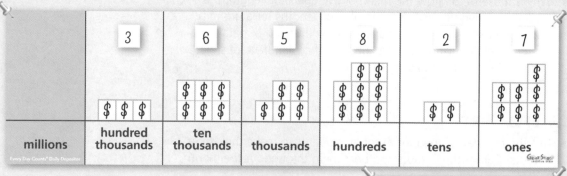

millions	hundred thousands	ten thousands	thousands	hundreds	tens	ones
	3	6	5	8	2	7

Daily Depositor

$$
\begin{array}{r}
\$3\;4\;5,\;8\;2\;7 \\
+\;\;\;\;2\;0,\;0\;0\;0 \\
\hline
\$3\;6\;5,\;8\;2\;7
\end{array}
$$

127 128 129 130 131 132 133 134 135 136 137 138 139 140 141 142 143 144 145

Counting Tape

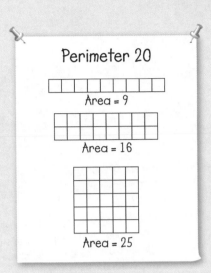

Perimeter 20

Area = 9

Area = 16

Area = 25

Measurement

5 : 0 5 A.M.

It is 9:05 A.M.
on April 20th
right now.
In 20 hours,
it will be 5:05 A.M.
on April 21st.

Clock

APRIL ELEMENTS

CALENDAR **120**

analyze and predict patterns; recognize patterns that grow in a regular way; use logical thinking

DAILY DEPOSITOR **122**

multiply numbers by 1,000; perform multi-digit addition; estimate and predict; write large numbers

MEASUREMENT **124**

understand how to find the perimeter of a rectangle; determine if figures with the same perimeter have the same area

A FRACTION A DAY **126**

associate simplifying with finding equivalent fractions; write improper fractions as mixed numbers; identify equivalent fractions

COUNTING TAPE **128**

explore multiples and factors; know multiplication facts for 9; observe relationships among multiples

CLOCK **130**

add hours in random amounts to the time shown on the clock

In April, the Calendar Pieces highlight a different type of pattern, one that increases in a regular way. The Daily Depositor examines different methods to calculate an end-of-the-year total, and the Clock features adding on hours in random amounts. A Fraction A Day returns and uses twelfths to demonstrate equivalent fractions and simplifying fractions. The Counting Tape highlights the multiples of 9. The Measurement element focuses once again on the relationship between perimeter and area of rectangles.

CALENDAR

Concepts & Skills

- Analyze and predict patterns
- Recognize patterns that increase in a regular way
- Use appropriate notation to represent mathematical reasoning

Daily Routine

- Each day, attach the Calendar Piece for that day. On Mondays, attach pieces for the weekend days.

Discussion

For the Beginning of the Month

Inform students that the pattern this month will be different from others they have seen. After several days, these questions may stimulate discussion about this new type of pattern.

- What shapes do you see this month? (regular pentagons) What colors? (blue and green)
- What does the pattern look like so far this month?
- Can you predict what color pentagon will appear tomorrow? How about the day after tomorrow?
- How is this pattern different from other months? (The pattern does not repeat in a regular way, but rather increases in a regular way.)
- By the 6th, how many green pentagons are on the Calendar? (3)

Encourage students to study the pattern this month and to keep track of the total number of green pentagons. Ask them to carefully keep track of the numbers on the blue pentagons.

For the Fifteenth Day of the Month
Sample Dialogue

Teacher: What is the pattern of the green pentagons?

Student: First there is 1, then 2, then 3, and now 4.

Teacher: Yes, so how many green pentagons are there?

Student: 10.

Teacher: How do you know it is 10?

Student: Well, 1 + 2 is 3, and 3 + 3 is 6, and 4 more is 10.

Teacher: Is there any other way to add those numbers?

Student: Add 1 + 4 and 2 + 3, which are both 5, so that's 10.

Teacher: That is an efficient way to add them. (writing on the board) Let's write this as *(1 + 4) + (2 + 3) = 10*. The parentheses mean "the quantity of." What is the quantity inside each set of parentheses?

Student: Five in each, or 10 altogether.

Ongoing Assessment

1. What are the next 3 numbers in the pattern that begins 1, 3, 6, 10, 15, ___, ___, ___?

2. What are two different ways to quickly add the numbers 1, 2, 3, 4, 5, 6, 7, 8, 9, and 10?

3. On the first day Maria found 1 seashell. On the second day she found 2 seashells. On the third day she found 3 seashells. If this pattern continues, how many seashells will she have after 6 days?

The April Calendar Pieces introduce a pattern that increases in a regular way. Students will see a pattern that increases by 1 each time. One blue pentagon is followed by 1 green pentagon; 2 green pentagons follow the next blue pentagon; the next blue pentagon is followed by 3 green pentagons; and so on.

© Great Source. Copying is prohibited.

Teacher: Yes. How many green pentagons will appear after the next blue one?

Student: 5.

Teacher: And how many will we have altogether then?

Student: 15.

Teacher: What do you notice about the dates for the blue pentagons?

Student: The numbers are 1, 3, 6, 10, 15. They tell you how many green ones there will be until the next blue one. That's really amazing.

To Sum Up

At the end of the month, be sure to review the growing pattern. This is a pattern that students will see many times in their school math careers. The sequence 1, 3, 6, 10, 15, and so on, is the sum of consecutive numbers and is often a sequence that can be used to solve problems. Notice that the blue pentagons contain these numbers, the sum of consecutive numbers. Here are some questions that can be used to deepen this understanding.

- What is the pattern of green pentagons this month? (First 1, then 2, then 3, and so on.)

- Who can tell us the pattern of numbers on the blue pentagons? (1, 3, 6, 10, 15, 21, 28)

- What is the difference between these numbers? (They increase by 1 each time.)

- The numbers 1, 2, 3, 4 are called consecutive numbers. What are the next 4 consecutive numbers? (5, 6, 7, 8)

- What is the sum of the first 5 consecutive numbers? (15)

- What is the sum of the first 7 consecutive numbers? (28) How do you know? (Possible strategies include:
  add (6 + 7) to the sum of the first 5 consecutive numbers;
  add (1 + 7) + (2 + 6) + (3 + 5) + 4 = 28;
  add (1 + 6) + (2 + 5) + (3 + 4) + 7 = 28;
  multiply 7 four times to get 28.)

- What patterns do you see in adding these consecutive numbers? (You can pair them up easily to add them.)

- If the Calendar pattern continued all the way up to 10 consecutive green pentagons, how many pentagons would there be? How do you know? (55. Some students will add to the previous total, while others may pair numbers to make sums of 11 or 10.)

- Look at the blue pentagons. What numbers do you see? (1, 3, 6, 10, 15, 21, 28) What numbers are these? (the sums of consecutive numbers)

Draw arrangements of oranges on the board, as shown at the right. Indicate each grouping as you mention it.

- Oranges are often stacked into these triangle shapes at grocery stores. For instance, one orange looks like this. Three oranges look like this, and 6 oranges look like this. If this pattern continued, how many oranges would be in the next arrangement? (10) What about the arrangement after that? (15) Because these sums of consecutive numbers can be arranged in triangular shapes, they are often called triangular numbers.

The April Calendar shows a growing pattern.

These oranges illustrate the pattern of triangular numbers.

© Great Source. Copying is prohibited.

HELPFUL HINTS

- Students will see this pattern in many contexts. Problems like, "How many games are played by 5 teams if each team plays every other team once?" involve this number pattern, as do many other counting problems.

- A story that may not have happened, but could have happened, involves the 18th century mathematician, Gauss, whose fourth-grade teacher tried to keep him quiet by sending him to the back of the room to add the numbers 1 to 100. Gauss quickly returned with the answer 5,050. He figured out there would be 101 fifty times, because he could pair 1 with 100, 2 with 99, and so on.

- Be sure to spend some time showing students how to write mathematically what they are doing when adding numbers. Writing equations and understanding that the equals sign means both sides are equal quantities is an important algebraic skill for fourth- and fifth-grade students. Write $(1 + 4) + (2 + 3) = 10$, instead of $1 + 4 = 5 + 2 + 3 = 10$.

Number & Operations	Algebra	Geometry	Measurement	Data & Probability
Problem Solving	Reasoning	Communication	Connections	Representation

DAILY DEPOSITOR

Concepts & Skills

- Multiply numbers by 1,000
- Use mental math
- Perform multi-digit addition
- Estimate and predict
- Write large numbers

Daily Routine

- In April, the amount to be added to the Depositor each day will be $1,000 times the day's date.

Ongoing Assessment

1. Start at 145,000 and count up by ten thousands to 205,000.

2. What is the greatest even number you can make with the digits 2, 3, 4, 5, 6, and 7?

3. Using the digits 3, 4, 5, 6, 7, and 8, make two 3-digit numbers whose sum is close to 1,000.

DISCUSSION

Throughout the Month

Point out that the end of the school year is approaching. Ask students to make new estimates of how much money will be in the Depositor by the end of the school year. Spend some time taking estimates. After a sufficient number of students have offered their opinions, suggest a challenge: If you know the monthly rule for how much money will be added to the Depositor from now on, can you figure out how much we will have by May 31st? Tell students they can figure out the amount any way they like, but remind them of the strategies they have studied:

- Using partners to match the first and last numbers in a sequence. (See December, page 65.)

- Using an odd sequence of numbers to find the total. (See January, page 80.)

© Great Source. Copying is prohibited.

millions	hundred thousands	ten thousands	thousands	hundreds	tens	ones
	6	2	0	8	2	7

Remind students that the cumulative total has been recorded each day since January, and that on the last day of March there was $155,827 (or $158,727 if it is a leap year) in the Depositor. We will add $1,000 times the date during the months of April and May. Also, remind students that not all months have the same number of days. After students have had time to work on this problem for a couple of days, ask them what they think the total amount in the Depositor will be by May 31st.

```
   $5 9 0, 8 2 7
 + $3 0, 0 0 0
   $6 2 0, 8 2 7
```

Sample Dialogue

Teacher: How much money will be in the Depositor by May 31st?

Student: I figured $620,827.

Student: I got $1,085,827.

Student: I think it will be $1,116,827.

Teacher: How did you get your answers?

Student: I used the partner method for April because it has 30 days, an even number. I figured out that in a month with 30 days, the Depositor collects $465,000 when $1,000 is added each day. I know that there is 1 more day in May than in April, and since we are adding $1,000 times the date, I knew we would add $31,000 on the last day of May. So in months with 31 days we add $496,000 to the Depositor.

Teacher: Then what did you do?

Student: I added those 2 numbers together to get $961,000 and added that to what we have in the Depositor from March, for a total of $1,116,827 by May 31st.

Teacher: That's very good! Did anyone do this a different way?

Student: I did. I used the total of an odd number of sequential numbers. In a month with 31 days, I found that 16 was the middle number. I multiplied $16,000 times 31 days and got $496,000. I subtracted $31,000 from that to find out how much is collected in a month with 30 days, and I got $465,000.

Teacher: You have done very well in using the strategies we have discussed. Did anyone try something different? **MORE ▶**

© Great Source. Copying is prohibited.

Student: Yes. I added up all the day's dates in a month and multiplied that times $1,000. I got $465,000 for April that way, but I didn't get any further than that.

Teacher: You did great. You can see that there are lots of different ways to solve this problem.

Keep in mind that the main point of this discussion is the sharing of ideas and strategies. Discussions about strategies and approaches to problem solving are ways of communicating our mathematical ideas to each other. It is hoped that this will strengthen students' thinking and their ability to approach large problems.

Number & Operations		Algebra		Geometry		Measurement		Data & Probability
	Problem Solving		Reasoning		Communication		Connections	Representation

MEASUREMENT

Concepts & Skills
- Find the perimeter of rectangles
- Discover if figures with the same perimeter have the same area

Materials for April
Copies of Inch Squared Paper (TR3); 15 pieces of construction paper

Author Notes
"The purpose of this element is to have students continue to explore the relationship between the area and the perimeter of rectangles. In February, students made figures with areas equal to the day's date. In April, they will make figures with perimeters equal to the day's date. Since the figures must be rectangles or squares, this activity is used only on even-numbered days. The question this month is, 'Do rectangles with the same perimeter have the same area?'"

Setup
- Label the pieces of construction paper *Perimeter 2*, *Perimeter 4*, *Perimeter 6*, and so on.
- Make copies of Inch Squared Paper available so students can use them.
- You may want to create groups of students to investigate perimeters on different days.

Daily Routine
- On even-numbered days, have students investigate rectangles with perimeters equal to the day's date. They should begin by drawing the outline of any possible rectangles on a piece of Inch Squared Paper.
- As students find different rectangles, have them attach them to the construction paper at the front of the room, labeling the perimeter and area for each one. No two figures can be congruent.
- Discuss the relationship between the perimeter and area of each rectangle revealed through students' exploration. Look to see if any patterns are emerging.

Ongoing Assessment
1. In your own words, describe the relationship between rectangles and squares.

2. Draw a rectangle with an area of 6 square units. Draw a congruent rectangle that has been rotated 90°.

3. What is the perimeter of a 3 in. × 8 in. rectangle?

© Great Source. Copying is prohibited.

- Discuss on even-numbered days.
- Make sure students understand that a rectangle with a perimeter of 2 inches cannot be made with the Inch Squared Paper, since a rectangle with an area of 1 square inch will have a perimeter of 4 inches.
- Point out that on some even-numbered days, more than one rectangle will be possible. Students should try to find as many of these as possible.

DISCUSSION

For the Beginning of the Month
Sample Dialogue

Teacher: This month volunteers will outline rectangles on Inch Squared Paper. On even-numbered days we will try to make at least 1 rectangle with a perimeter equal to the day's date. Does anyone know what *perimeter* is?

Student: It is the distance around the outside of a figure.

Teacher: That is correct. The perimeter is the distance around the outside of a closed figure. We will measure the distance around the perimeter of the rectangles we construct by counting each exposed side of the one-inch squares used to make the rectangle. We want to find as many different rectangles each day as possible. Rectangles cannot be congruent. What are congruent rectangles?

Student: Congruent means same size and same shape.

Teacher: Yes. Each rectangle has to be a different shape and size. To make sure 2 figures are not congruent, you can flip them over, rotate them, or lay one on top of the other to see if they match. If the 2 figures are congruent, they are considered to be the same shape. After we find a rectangle with a perimeter equal to the day's date, we will find the area of the rectangle. So, how would you define *area*?

Student: The amount of space covered by something.

Teacher: Yes. Area is the measure of how much surface a figure covers. So to find the area of our rectangle, we will count the number of squares used to make the rectangle. What is the area of a rectangle with one of our squares?

Student: One square inch.

Teacher: Yes, and what is the perimeter of that rectangle?

Student: It's 4 inches. So we can't make a rectangle like this that has a perimeter of 2 inches.

Teacher: Right. The first one we can make will be on the 4th.

Student: That rectangle will be a square!

Teacher: Is a square a rectangle?

Student: Yes, a square is a special rectangle with all 4 sides the same length.

Teacher: So for today, we will have to write *Not Possible* on the chart for Perimeter 2.

Can you draw a figure with the same area and perimeter?

© Great Source. Copying is prohibited.

Throughout the Month

Below are some questions to help students decide which date's rectangles can be made and how to determine the perimeter of a rectangle.

- What is today's date?
- Is it possible to make a rectangle?
- On what dates is it not possible to make a rectangle? (on the 2nd; also on all dates that are odd numbers)
- If you know the length and width of a rectangle, how can you find the perimeter? (Add the length of all 4 sides. Students may come up with other ways, such as doubling the length, doubling the width, then adding the two together.)
- On what dates will you make a square rectangle? (4th, 8th, 12th, 16th, 20th, 24th, and 28th)
- Look at the rectangles we have made. Which ones have the greatest area? Which ones have the least area?

For the End of the Month

At the end of the month, ask questions like these to provide a good summation.

- Could you make a rectangle with a perimeter equal to the day's date every day during this month? (no)
- Do rectangles with the same perimeter always have the same area? (no) How do you know? (We made rectangles with the same perimeter, and some of them had different areas.)
- What have you noticed during the month about the shapes that have the greatest area with the day's given perimeter? (Those in the shape of a square have the greatest areas and the shortest perimeters.)
- What about the shapes that have the smallest area with the day's given perimeter? (Rectangles with one row have the smallest areas and the greatest perimeters.)

Number & Operations	Algebra	Geometry	Measurement	Data & Probability
Problem Solving	Reasoning	Communication	Connections	Representation

A FRACTION A DAY

Concepts & Skills

- Visualize fractions
- Understand numerator and denominator
- Write improper fractions as mixed numbers
- Find a fraction of a set
- Compute with fractions
- See fractional equivalencies

Ongoing Assessment

1. How many eggs are in $\frac{1}{2}$ of a dozen? In $\frac{1}{3}$ of a dozen?
2. What is another way to write $\frac{18}{12}$?
3. How many eggs are in $1\frac{3}{4}$ dozen? How do you know?

Materials for April

3 circles from TR11, two copies of egg carton Dozens (TR12), Fraction Record (TR13), markers or crayons in 2 or more bright colors, black crayon or marker

© Great Source. Copying is prohibited.

Author Notes

"In April, A Fraction A Day explores twelfths by using the Dozens model, because that model makes it easy to see equivalent fractions. Each day as another twelfth is colored, students look to see if the twelfths can be arranged into larger equal groups. When this is possible, students simplify the day's fraction."

Setup

- Cut 3 circles from TR11 and post one, leaving room for the other two.
- Cut 3 Dozens from TR12. Post one, leaving room for the other two.

Daily Routine

- **The first day,** tell the class that you will draw 12 equal parts of a pizza (or circle). Use the black marker to draw twelfths on one circle. (Draw a line from the 12 o'clock position through the center to 6 o'clock, from 1 to 7, 2 to 8, 3 to 9, 4 to 10 and 5 to 11.
- Shade in one twelfth of the circle each day, including weekends and holidays. **Alternate colors to keep the twelfths distinct.**
- When a circle is filled, post a new one next to it, and continue to shade one twelfth each day.
- Each day also shade in one twelfth of an egg carton Dozen, posting new ones as needed.
- Each day record the total on the Fraction Record both as a fraction and (after day 12) as a mixed number.

DISCUSSION

For the Beginning of the Month

With the circle divided into twelfths, review fraction vocabulary:

- This month, how many equal parts has the circle been cut into? (12)
- When we write one twelfth as a fraction, which number is the denominator? (12) Which is the numerator? (1)

By now, the dozens model is also familiar. Remind student that they used the dozens model when they were collecting thirds and sixths.

Sample Dialogue

Teacher: Here's the familiar egg carton again. Why do you suppose we're using the egg carton with a dozen eggs to look at twelfths?

Student: Because there are 12 eggs, so each egg is 1 twelfth.

Teacher: Good. But we also used the egg carton when we were collecting thirds. Can someone remind us what 1 third of the dozen looked like?

Student: One third was a group of 4 eggs. Each dozen had 3 thirds.

Teacher: Very good. We just said that 1 egg is the same as 1 twelfth. What can we call 4 eggs?

Student: Four eggs is 4 twelfths of a dozen. So $\frac{4}{12}$ is the same as $\frac{1}{3}$.

Teacher: Can someone show me what $\frac{1}{4}$ of a dozen would look like?

Draw twelfths by connecting the 12 and 6, 1 and 7, 2 and 8, 3 and 9, 4 and 10, and 5 and 11.

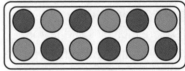

Today we have $\frac{14}{12}$
or 1 whole and $\frac{2}{12}$
or $1\frac{2}{12}$ or $1\frac{1}{6}$ circles.

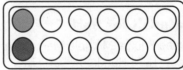

1 dozen

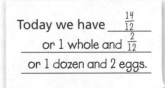

1 dozen

Today we have $\frac{14}{12}$
or 1 whole and $\frac{2}{12}$
or 1 dozen and 2 eggs.

© Great Source. Copying is prohibited.

Student: That's half of a half, so take the first three eggs on the top.

Teacher: What about 1 sixth? What did that look like?

Student: A sixth was a pair of eggs. Two. So, that should be 2 twelfths.

Teacher: Good. This month as we collect twelfths, every time we have a group that can be named by thirds or sixths or even fourths or halves we will use those names too. When we rename a fraction using larger equal groups, there are fewer groups. We call that simplifying a fraction.

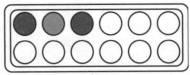

1 dozen

"You can see that $\frac{3}{12}$ equals $\frac{1}{4}$."

For Throughout the Month

It will often be possible to simplify the day's fraction. To provide practice, use questions like those that follow. Use either the circle, the dozen or both to demonstrate equivalencies.

- How can we show $\frac{6}{12}$ as a simpler fraction, or write it with fewer, larger groups? ($\frac{3}{6}$ or $\frac{1}{2}$) How did you figure that out? (If you shade 6 out of 12, then you see another 6 unshaded, showing 2 equal parts, or halves. One half is shaded, so $\frac{6}{12}$ is $\frac{1}{2}$.)

- How can we simplify $\frac{3}{12}$? ($\frac{1}{4}$) How did you figure that out? (Altogether there are 4 groups of 3 in 12, so one group of 3 is $\frac{1}{4}$.)

- How can we simplify $\frac{8}{12}$? ($\frac{4}{6}$ or $\frac{2}{3}$) How did you figure that out? (Look at groups of four. Eight is 2 groups of four, and 12 is 3 groups of four. If you shade 8 out of 12 you shade 2 out of 3 larger groups.)

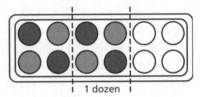

1 dozen

"Each group of four eggs is $\frac{1}{3}$ of a dozen, so 8 eggs is $\frac{2}{3}$ of a dozen."

HELPFUL HINT

- This month on the 12th, invite 12 volunteers to stand and take direction from classmates who will divide them into groups to create equal teams. See how many possibilities can be found.

Number & Operations	Algebra	Geometry	Measurement	Data & Probability
Problem Solving	Reasoning	Communication	Connections	Representation

COUNTING TAPE

Concepts & Skills

- Explore multiples and factors
- Know multiplication facts for 9
- Observe relationships among multiples

Materials for April

Dotted Square Multiple Markers cardstock, copies of Circular Array Paper (TR7), Hundred Chart (TR4), Centimeter Squared Paper (TR15), and Equation Chart (TR5)

Ongoing Assessment

1. Count by nines from 9 to 90.

2. On what number will we hang our 7th dotted square? Our 9th dotted square?

3. How can we use 10 groups of any number to easily find 9 groups of the same number?

© Great Source. Copying is prohibited.

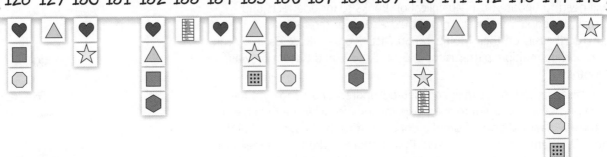

128 129 130 131 132 133 134 135 136 137 138 139 140 141 142 143 144 145

Daily Routine

• Continue to have students identify and mark multiples of 2, 3, 4, 5, 6, 7, and 8 with Multiple Markers. Begin marking multiples of 9 with Dotted Square Multiple Markers.

DISCUSSION

For the Beginning of the Month

In April, discuss the patterns of the multiples of 9. All of the multiples of 9 to 90 will already be on the Counting Tape when April begins. As students call them out and each marker is placed on the Tape, point out that 9 is one less than 10, so the 2nd nine is 2 less than 20, or 18. Becoming familiar with this pattern may make these facts easier for some students.

Write the multiples of 9 on the board vertically, as shown at the right, and examine the pattern in the tens column and in the ones column. These questions will help students examine the pattern of nines.

• What pattern do you see? (As the tens digit increases by 1, the ones digit decreases by 1.)

• Why do you think that is true? (Each time we add 9, we go ahead 10 and take away 1.)

• What do you see in the tens and the ones columns? (The tens go up 0, 1, 2, 3, 4, 5, 6, 7, 8, 9 at the same time the ones go down 9, 8, 7, 6, 5, 4, 3, 2, 1, 0.)

• What do you notice about the digits in these multiples of 9? (The sum of the digits for all these multiples is 9.)

Some questions to ask about the Counting Tape are:

• What markers are attached to every multiple of 9? (triangles and dotted squares) Why? (Each multiple of 9 is also a multiple of 3.)

• Look at every other multiple of 9: 18, 36, 54, 72, 90, and so on. What do they all have in common? (They all are multiples of 2, 3, 6, and 9 and can be divided into groups of 2, 3, 6, and 9 without remainders.)

© Great Source. Copying is prohibited.

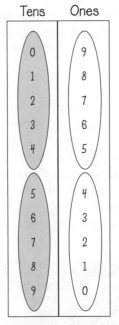

The tens and ones digits in these multiples of 9 add up to 9.

1 group of 9 = 1 x 9 = 9		6 groups of 9 = 6 x 9 = 54		
2 groups of 9 = 2 x 9 = 18		7 groups of 9 = 7 x 9 = 63		
3 groups of 9 = 3 x 9 = 27		8 groups of 9 = 8 x 9 = 72		
4 groups of 9 = 4 x 9 = 36		9 groups of 9 = 9 x 9 = 81		
5 groups of 9 = 5 x 9 = 45		10 groups of 9 = 10 x 9 = 90		

1	2	3	4	5	6	7	8	9	10
11	12	13	14	15	16	17	18	19	20
21	22	23	24	25	26	27	28	29	30
31	32	33	34	35	36	37	38	39	40
41	42	43	44	45	46	47	48	49	50
51	52	53	54	55	56	57	58	59	60
61	62	63	64	65	66	67	68	69	70
71	72	73	74	75	76	77	78	79	80
81	82	83	84	85	86	87	88	89	90
91	92	93	94	95	96	97	98	99	100

Can you explain why the multiples of 9 make this diagonal pattern?

For the End of the Month

Distribute all the materials (Hundred Chart and Equation Chart) students will need to update their Multiplication Books to include facts and remainder equations for 9. They should also color the facts for 9 they can recall easily on their Multiplication Facts Progress Records. They can also update multiple patterns for 2, 3, 4, 5, 6, 7, and 8 from previous months.

Ask students to look at their completed Hundred Chart showing the multiples of 9. Ask them to share explanations for why the multiples of 9 form a diagonal going from the upper right to the lower left. Point out, if students do not mention it, that on the Hundred Chart, each row shows 10 numbers. If you go down one row adding 10 and go back one square taking away 1, it is the same as adding 9. Going down 1 row and back 1 square makes the diagonal.

HELPFUL HINT

- The Hundred Chart and Counting Tape provide different models, helping students to see 2 different ways of thinking about multiplying by 9. Some may find one easier to embrace than the other. The Hundred Chart pattern for nines can help students see adding 9 as adding 10 and taking 1 away each time. On the Counting Tape, locating the 9th of any of the Multiple Markers (heart, star, hexagon, and so on) can be done in an instant when students go to the 10th marker and then find the preceding marker.

Number & Operations	Algebra	Geometry	Measurement	Data & Probability
Problem Solving	Reasoning	Communication	Connections	Representation

CLOCK

Concepts & Skills

- Add hours in random amounts to the time shown on the clock

Daily Routine

- In April, set the Clock to the actual time on the classroom clock. Add the number of hours equal to the day's date each day. For example, if it is 9:35 A.M. on April 6th, add 6 hours to 9:35 A.M. to get 3:35 P.M.

Ongoing Assessment

1. How do you remember the difference between A.M. and P.M.?

2. If it is 9:23 A.M. now, what time will it be 7 hours from now?

3. If you start school at 7:30 A.M. and leave school at 2:45 P.M., how much time have you spent in school?

© Great Source. Copying is prohibited.

DISCUSSION

For the Beginning of the Month

Explain that this month the Clock will be set to the same time as the classroom clock. The students will then add the number of hours equal to the day's date to the time shown on the classroom clock. Here are some questions to stimulate discussion when getting started:

- What is the time on the classroom clock right now? (9:15 A.M.)
- What is the date today? (April 6)
- What time will it be 6 hours from now? (3:15 P.M.)
- Can you tell me how you got the new time?
- Can you tell me how to place the hands on the Clock to show 3:15?

Since you are most likely to use problems that require going from A.M. to P.M., make up some stories going from P.M. to A.M. For example, if it is 8:30 A.M. at school when you are doing Calendar Math, create a story for 8:30 P.M. instead, so that when time is added to 8:30 P.M., it will change to A.M.

A.M.
Time on the wall clock

5:23 A.M.
Time 19 hours later

The Clock on April 19th at 10:23 A.M. Adding 19 hours makes it 5:23 A.M. tomorrow morning.

For the Middle of the Month
Sample Dialogue

Teacher: Today is April 19th. What is the time?

Student: 10:23 A.M.

Teacher: Let's say that 19 hours from now we are all going on a special trip. What time will it be and what will the date be? How did you solve the problem?

Student: First I thought about the problem. Then I added on 12 hours to the time to give me 10:23 P.M. That still left me with 7 hours to add on, so I added 2 hours to make it 12:23 A.M. I knew I had 5 more hours to add on. So, then I got 5:23 A.M.

Student: I added on 24 hours first and then took off 5 hours because 19 is 5 less than 24.

Teacher: Either of these is a fine strategy.

HELPFUL HINT

- Practice as often as you can because the concept of adding on time from A.M. to P.M. is very abstract. Have students share their strategies with the class.

© Great Source. Copying is prohibited.

Every Day Calendar

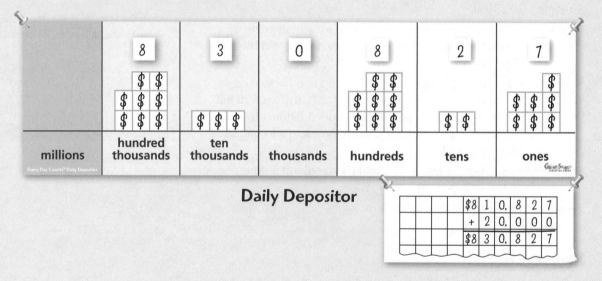

Daily Depositor

		$8	1	0,	8	2	7
		+		2	0,	0	0	0
		$8	3	0,	8	2	7

149 150 151 152 153 154 155 156 157 158 159 160 161 162 163 164 165 166 167

Counting Tape

Calendar Math Favorites

Every Day Calendar	//
Daily Depositor	//// //
Counting Tape	////
Coin Counter	//
Clock	//
Measurement	///

Graph

MAY/JUNE ELEMENTS

CALENDAR **134**
sort shapes by attributes; recognize patterns;
develop logical thinking

DAILY DEPOSITOR **136**
multiply numbers by 1,000; perform
multi-digit addition; write large numbers;
investigate the size of one million

COUNTING TAPE **137**
know multiplication facts through nine;
identify and describe relationships among
multiples; understand math terms:
*prime number, least common multiple,
greatest common factor*

GRAPH **139**
collect and organize data; analyze data and
interpret results; make predictions

If your school year extends into June, continue to
use any of the elements of Calendar Math that
you want. If you need to cut back, you may want
to use only the five elements used at the
beginning of the school year. Select elements that
focus on math topics that students may find
difficult. As the year comes to a close, question
students about what they remember or enjoyed
most in Calendar Math. A fitting end-of-the-year
activity might be to create a graph of the variety of
responses to that question. Although no two
groups are alike, student responses might help you
evaluate your successes and plan for next year.

Number & Operations	Algebra	Geometry	Measurement	Data & Probability
Problem Solving	Reasoning	Communication	Connections	Representation

CALENDAR

Concepts & Skills

- Sort shapes by attributes
- Recognize patterns
- Develop logical thinking

Author Notes

"This month's Calendar activity emphasizes attributes of shapes and is intended to foster logical thinking and problem-solving skills. The Calendar Pieces for May are used to create a different kind of pattern, one in which each piece differs from the one before in just one way. The pattern that will appear on your Calendar will be determined by the piece selected to post on the first day of the month. For example, if that piece is a large red triangle, then the piece for the next day can be a small red triangle because it differs in just one way. The piece on the second day could also be a large yellow triangle or a different large shape of the same color.

To create the pattern, 4 different shapes are used (triangles, circles, squares, and rhombuses) in 2 different sizes. Each of those shapes will appear in one of 4 colors (red, green, blue, and yellow). The focus of the Calendar this month is on classifying and distinguishing by attributes of size, color and shape."

Setup

- Since the pieces added to the Calendar are chosen on a day-to-day basis, they are not numbered. You can write the dates on small self-stick notes and attach them to the posted Calendar Pieces, or you can decide not to number the pieces at all.
- The initial lesson for the May Calendar will take longer than most other Calendar Math lessons.

Daily Routine

- Each day, students will choose one of the Calendar Pieces to post on the Calendar. Each piece that is chosen must differ from the preceding piece in just one way.
- There are 36 Calendar Pieces from which to choose, and it is possible that at the end of the month the pieces left will not fit the attribute required. This may necessitate trying to fit a piece somewhere in the already established pattern and having to move other pieces around to continue the pattern. For this reason, you may not want to number the Calendar Pieces at all.

DISCUSSION

For the Beginning of the Month

Put all the Calendar Pieces on display where students can see them. Ask

Ongoing Assessment

1. Given the pieces used on the May Calendar, which piece could follow a small yellow square if it must change by only one attribute?

2. How is a square both a rectangle and a rhombus?

3. Which two shapes vary by only one attribute, a hexagon and a rhombus, or a rectangle and a square?

The May Calendar Pieces are used to present a logic puzzle in the form of an attribute chain.

© Great Source. Copying is prohibited.

them to describe what they see. Some will say squares, triangles, circles, and rhombuses. Others will say that they see shapes of red, blue, green, and yellow. And still others will say that they see big and small shapes. Put all the pieces in a small box. Pull one out and initiate a discussion to see if students can begin to remember what pieces are left in the box. As students correctly identify the pieces, remove them from the box.

Sample Dialogue

Teacher: I have a large yellow circle. What other pieces are left in the box?

Student: A small green triangle.

Student: A large blue square.

Student: A large green triangle.

Conversation will continue like this for some time. As fewer pieces remain in the box, students will have to think ahead to determine which ones are left.

Explain that this month the Calendar will be used to display a logic puzzle. Questions like these should follow:

- How can we sort these shapes? (by color, shape, and size)
- What colors are there? (red, blue, green, yellow)
- What sizes are there? (big and small)
- What shapes are there? (triangles, circles, squares, rhombuses)
- Let's pick one piece. Can you describe another piece that is different from this one in just one way?
- How is a large green triangle different from a large red triangle? (only in color)
- How is a small red triangle different from a large red triangle? (only in size)
- If we started with a small yellow rhombus, what could be used the next day? (any small yellow shape, or a small rhombus of any color besides yellow, or a large yellow rhombus)

Students are now ready to begin the daily task of filling the Calendar with the Calendar Pieces. Randomly choose one piece with which to start. Ask students to identify another piece that is the same except for one attribute. What are some possibilities?

For the Middle of the Month

This is a good time to review the geometry terms. Some questions that might help students review these terms include:

- What polygons appear in the Calendar pattern this month? (rhombus, square, triangle)
- What do we call a four-sided polygon? (quadrilateral)
- What quadrilaterals appear in the Calendar pattern this month? (rhombus and square)
- Why is a square a rhombus? (It is a parallelogram with all four sides congruent.)
- Are all rhombuses squares? (No, only a rhombus with right angles is a square.)

Pieces that differ from a large yellow rhombus in only one way

 small yellow rhombus

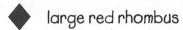 large red rhombus

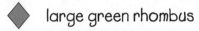 large green rhombus

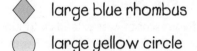 large blue rhombus

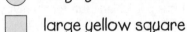 large yellow circle

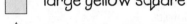 large yellow square

 large yellow triangle

The Calendar Pieces differ in terms of shape, color, and size.

© Great Source. Copying is prohibited.

- What kind of triangle is used in this month's Calendar pattern? (equilateral)
- Why isn't a circle a polygon? (It does not have sides with straight lines.)

Finally, be sure to ask students what other shapes could be used each day.

For the End of the Month

Conclude the month with general observations about the patterns students see on the Calendar. This month, the pieces follow a logical order, differing by only one attribute, but there are still number patterns to study.

HELPFUL HINT

- If your school year extends into June, allow students to create their own pattern using Calendar Pieces they can make or you can supply. This is particularly fun for them if you allow them to do this independently and if you try to predict their pattern as the month unfolds.

Number & Operations   Algebra   Geometry   Measurement   Data & Probability
Problem Solving   Reasoning   Communication   Connections   Representation

DAILY DEPOSITOR

Concepts & Skills

- Multiply numbers by 1,000
- Use mental math
- Perform multi-digit addition
- Write large numbers
- Answer September's dilemma

Daily Routine

- In May, the amount to be added to the Depositor each day will be $1,000 times the day's date.

Ongoing Assessment

1. Start at 979,500 and count up by thousands to 1,000,500.

2. How many thousands are in one million? How many ten thousands?

3. Which is a more reasonable estimate, $1,450 - 695 = 287$, or $23,890 + 16,450 = 40,000$. Explain your thinking.

millions	hundred thousands	ten thousands	thousands	hundreds	tens	ones
1	1	1	6	8	2	7

How does this total match your prediction?

© Great Source. Copying is prohibited.

DISCUSSION

Throughout the Month

To begin final discussions about the Depositor, remind students what the original challenge was:

In September, we wondered if we would collect one million dollars in the Daily Depositor by the end of the school year. We deposited $1 times the date in September, $2 times the date in October, $10 times the date in November, $20 times the date in December, $100 times the date from January through March, and $1,000 times the date since April 1st. Here we are at the end of the school year. Did we collect one million dollars?

By the end of May, there will be $1,116,827 (or $1,119,727 in leap year) in the Depositor.

- What are the totals for each month since January?
- Who can tell me why the totals for every month end in 27?
- How much more do we need to reach $2,000,000?

How much is a million? As an end-of-the-year project, challenge students to explore the quantity of one million. Have students work in groups, and have each group solve one of the following problems. Allow students time to explain their answers to the other groups.

- An elephant eats about 300 pounds of food every day. How long will it take that elephant to eat one million pounds of food?
- How many years would it take for you to live for one million hours?
- How many days would it take your school to sell one million cartons of milk at lunch?
- How many ten-dollar bills would it take to equal $1,000,000?
- The distance from Los Angeles to Atlanta is about 2,000 miles. How many times would you have to make this trip to equal 1,000,000 miles?

	Daily Depositor			
Month	Days in the Month	Total for the Month	Cumulative Total	Daily Deposit Amount
September	30	$465		$1 times date
October	31	$992	$1,457	$2 times date
November	30	$4,650	$6,107	$10 times date
December	31	$9,920	$16,027	$20 times date
January	31	$49,600	$65,627	$100 times date
February	28 or 29	$40,600 or $43,500 in leap year	$106,227 (or $109,127 in leap year)	$100 times date
March	31	$49,600	$155,827 (or $158,727 in leap year)	$100 times date
April	30	$465,000	$620,827 (or $623,727 in leap year)	$1,000 times date
May	31	$496,000	$1,116,827 (or $1,119,727 in leap year)	$1,000 times date

---

Number & Operations	Algebra	Geometry	Measurement	Data & Probability
Problem Solving	Reasoning	Communication	Connections	Representation

COUNTING TAPE

Concepts & Skills

- Continue patterns of multiples
- Know multiplication facts through nine
- Identify and describe relationships among multiples
- Understand terms: *prime number, least common multiple,* and *greatest common factor*

Daily Routine

- Continue to have students identify and mark multiples of 2, 3, 4, 5, 6, 7, 8, and 9 as they have in previous months.
- Since there are no new Multiple Markers to add this month, examine multiples of 10 that have been circled on the Counting Tape since the beginning of the year.

Ongoing Assessment

1. In your own words, describe what makes a number prime.
2. What is the least common multiple of 3 and 4? Of 5 and 3?
3. What is the greatest common factor of 12 and 16? Of 20 and 24? Of 10 and 25?

© Great Source. Copying is prohibited.

DISCUSSION

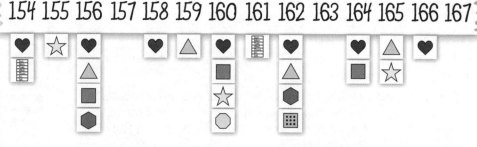

Throughout the Month

In May the focus will be on observations that can be made by looking at the Counting Tape. Focus attention on the first 30 numbers on the Tape and ask questions similar to the following ones:

- Which numbers less than 10 have only one Multiple Marker on them? (2, 3, 5, and 7)

- Which numbers between 10 and 30 have no markers on them? (11, 13, 17, 19, 23, and 29)

- What do these numbers have in common? (The only equal groups that can be made with these numbers are groups of 1 or the number itself. They are prime numbers and have only 2 factors.

Have students make arrangements of counters for these numbers. Challenge them to find more than one way to arrange the counters in equal rows and columns.

What's the next multiple of 7 that will appear on the Counting Tape?

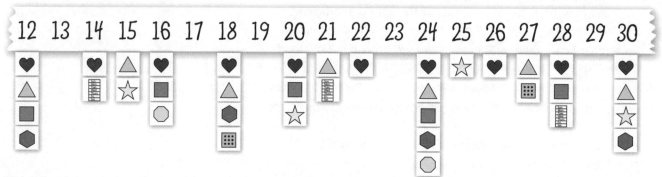

The following questions focus on least common multiples:

- What is the least number on the Tape that can be broken up evenly into twos and threes? (6. Look on the Tape for the place where the Multiple Markers for 2 and 3 appear together for the first time.)

- What is the least common multiple of 2 and 4? (4)

- What is the least common multiple of 2 and 5? (10)

- What is the least common multiple of 2, 3, and 4? (12)

To focus attention on greatest common factors, examine 2 numbers on the Counting Tape, for example, 12 and 18. What Multiple Markers appear on both numbers? (hearts for 2, triangles for 3, hexagons for 6) These are all common factors of 12 and 18. Which of those is the greatest common factor? (6) Look at several pairs of numbers less than 25 and see what Multiple Markers they have in common: 9 and 12 both have triangles and can be broken up into threes. 8 and 12 both have hearts and squares and can be divided into groups of 2 or 4, so 4 is the greatest common factor. 15 and 10 both have stars, so 5 is their greatest common factor.

Here are some questions to help students think about the divisibility of larger numbers.

- What numbers above 100 have stars? (105, 110, 115, 120, and so on) What is their pattern? (They all end in 0 or 5.)

The Multiple Markers are helpful for finding greatest common factors.

© Great Source. Copying is prohibited.

- Look at the number 96. What markers are on it? (2, 3, 4, 6, and 8.)
- Can you tell how many twos are in 96? How many threes? How many fours? How many sixes? How many eights? Can you write a multiplication sentence and a division sentence for each one of these?

HELPFUL HINTS

- Encourage any students who have difficulty with some multiplication facts to use their Array Flash cards to practice.
- Some teachers include students' Multiplication Facts Progress Records in end-of-the-year reports so parents can see how their children are doing. The Records can also provide review and practice during the summer.

Number & Operations		Algebra		Geometry		Measurement		Data & Probability
Problem Solving		Reasoning		Communication		Connections		Representation

GRAPH

Concepts & Skills

- Collect and organize data
- Analyze data and interpret results
- Make predictions

Materials for May

A variety of materials to create graphs, such as different-sized grid paper, plain paper, crayons

Daily Routine

- If you want to make a Graph during the last days of school, it would be fun to poll students about what they enjoyed most in Calendar Math. Or you can poll them about what they plan to do during the summer. Be sure to make a Graph and analyze the data should you decide to add this spark of fun during this last month of school.

HELPFUL HINT

- Students can create their own Graph, polling people on subjects such as favorite food for lunch, favorite recess activity, hours spent watching TV or playing video games, hours of sleep at night, or any other appropriate topic.

  Students should choose the type of graph that will best display their data: a bar graph, a bar graph requiring a key to explain that each unit is equal to something other than 1, a line graph used to show change over time, or a stem-and-leaf plot.

Ongoing Assessment

1. How many students liked the Every Day Calendar best?
2. How many more students liked the Daily Depositor than the Counting Tape?
3. What other ways could the information on the Graph be presented?

Calendar Math Favorites

Every Day Calendar	//
Daily Depositor	##//
Counting Tape	##
Coin Counter	//
Clock	//
Measurement	///

Which was your favorite part of Calendar Math?

© Great Source. Copying is prohibited.

BIBLIOGRAPHY

Baratta-Lorton, Mary. "The Opening," *Math Their Way Newsletter* 1977–78. Saratoga, CA: The Center for Innovation in Education.

Baratta-Lorton, Mary. *Mathematics Their Way*. Dale Seymour Publications, 1995.

Baratta-Lorton, Mary. *Workjobs II*. Pearson Learning, 1987.

Burk, Donna, Allyn Snider, and Paula Symonds. "The Calendar," *Box It or Bag It*. Salem, OR: Math Learning Center, 1988.

Burns, Marilyn and Kathy Richardson. "Making Sense out of Word Problems," *Learning*. January, 1981.

Burns, Marilyn. *The Math Solution*. Sausalito, CA: Marilyn Burns Assoc.

Greenwood, Jay. *Developing Mathematical Thinking*. Portland, OR: Multnomah County Education Service District, 1991.

National Council of Teachers of Mathematics. *Curriculum and Evaluation Standards for School Mathematics*. Reston, VA: The National Council of Teachers of Mathematics, 1989.

Parker, Tom. *In One Day: The Things Americans Do in a Day*. Boston, MA: Houghton Mifflin, 1984.

Richardson, Kathy. *Developing Number Concepts Using Unifix Cubes*. Reading, MA: Addison-Wesley, 1984.

Wirtz, Robert. *Banking on Problem Solving* and *Think, Talk, Connect*. Washington, DC: Curriculum Development Assoc., Inc., 1980.

Wirtz, Robert. *Drill and Practice at a Problem-Solving Level*. Washington, DC: Curriculum Development Assoc., Inc., 1976.

Wirtz, Robert. *Making Friends with Numbers*. Washington, DC: Curriculum Development Assoc., Inc., 1977.

© Great Source. Copying is prohibited.

To the Teacher:

The Assessment component of *Every Day Counts® Calendar Math* includes four tests: Pretest, Winter Test, Spring Test, and Post Test. This arrangement enables you to monitor student progress at significant times during the year. Each test includes an answer key and an accompanying list of tested skills.

The Pretest and Post Test are parallel tests, measuring skills for the whole year. They include questions in various standardized-test formats, including short answer, multiple choice, and in the upper grades, extended response questions.

The Winter and Spring Tests are structured similarly. The Winter Test focuses on skills presented in September, October, and November, and might be given in December or January. The Spring Test covers skills taught in December, January, and February, and might be given in March or April.

Any of these tests will be useful as practice at various times during the year before students take regular standardized tests. They can also be given in shorter form—a page or a few questions at a time.

Following each test is an answer key that includes a list of tested skills, the corresponding test item numbers, and a list of Calendar Math Elements where the skills are presented. This allows you to find places within the program where individual skills can be reinforced in a variety of contexts.

The tests are cumulative in nature, testing skills in ways similar to the way they are taught in Calendar Math, but in slightly different contexts. Students should be able to apply the skills they have learned and experienced in a variety of situations.

© Great Source. Copying is prohibited.

NAME _____

Directions: Write your answer to each question.

1. What are the next three numbers in this pattern?

   4, 8, 12, 16, 20, _____, _____, _____

2. Draw the next two shapes in this pattern.

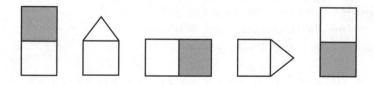

   _____ _____

3. Write the numbers to complete the pattern in this table.

Week	1	2	3	4	5	6	7
Amount	$8	$16	$24	$32			

4. What is the greatest common factor of 8, 32, 40, and 52? _____

5. What is 57×10? _____

6. What is 34×100? _____

7. What is 6,845 rounded to the nearest thousand? _____

8. The Larsons drove 245 miles on Thursday and 196 miles on Friday. How many miles did they drive altogether?

   _____

9. What is the greatest even number you can make with the digits 1, 3, 5, 6?

   _____

© Great Source. Copying is permitted; see page ii.

10. Write $\frac{19}{4}$ as a mixed number. _____

11. Jamal mixed $1\frac{1}{2}$ cups of whole wheat flour with $1\frac{3}{4}$ cups of cake flour. How much flour did he mix in all?

_____

12. Mr. Lambert's new fence is 32 feet long. How many yards is that?

_____

13. Mina is 145 centimeters tall. How many meters is that? _____

14. Tonya's boots weigh 40 ounces. How many pounds is that? _____

15. Garrett started playing the drums at the time shown on the clock. He played for 45 minutes. At what time did he finish?

_____

16. What is the value of these coins? _____

17. Using quarters, dimes, nickels, and pennies, how can you make $0.47 with the fewest possible coins?

_____

18. Kirsten bought a marker for $0.39. She paid for it with 2 quarters. How much change should she get?

_____

© Great Source. Copying is permitted; see page ii.

Directions: Choose the best answer to each question. Mark your answer.

19. Which of these figures is a trapezoid?

 **A** 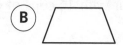 **B**  **C** 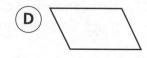 **D**

20. Which lines appear to be parallel?

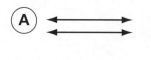 **A** **B** 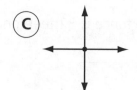 **C** 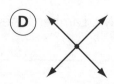 **D**

21. Which figure has exactly 8 edges?

 A 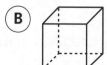 **B** 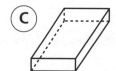 **C** **D**

22. What is the perimeter of this rectangle?

- **A** 16 units
- **B** 26 units
- **C** 32 units
- **D** 60 units

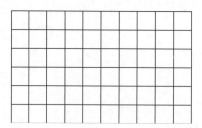

23. What is the value of the **2** in 1**2**,750?

A 2 ones   **B** 2 tens   **C** 2 hundreds   **D** 2 thousands

24. Of the 20 houses on Elm Street, 12 are painted white. What fraction of the houses are painted white?

A $\frac{3}{5}$ **B** $\frac{3}{4}$ **C** $\frac{2}{3}$ **D** $\frac{1}{2}$

25. Raymond bought 7 boxes of pencils. Each box has 6 pencils. Which expression can be used to find how many pencils he bought in all?

A $7 + 6$ **B** 7×7 **C** $7 \div 6$ **D** 7×6

© Great Source. Copying is permitted; see page ii.

26. Which picture shows $\frac{2}{5}$ shaded?

(A) **(B)** **(C)** **(D)**

27. Cam spent 20 minutes eating lunch. He finished at 12:05 P.M. At what time did he start eating lunch?

(A) 11:45 A.M.   **(B)** 11:50 A.M.   **(C)** 11:45 P.M.   **(D)** 12:25 P.M.

28. Which is the best estimate of 19×21?

(A) $200   **(B)** $300   **(C)** $400   **(D)** $500

29. Which is the greatest common factor of 15 and 20?

(A) 10   **(B)** 5   **(C)** 4   **(D)** 3

30. Dennis plans to toss a coin 60 times and record the results. About how many times will he probably get heads?

(A) 20   **(B)** 25   **(C)** 30   **(D)** 60

Use the chart and your graph to answer questions 31 and 32.

31. The chart shows the favorite foods of the students in Ms. Hodgdon's class. Use the grid to make a bar graph of the data. Label each part of your graph.

Favorite Foods

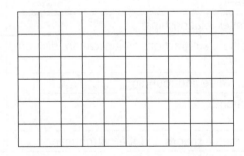

Kind of Food	Number of Students
Chinese	6
Italian	5
Mexican	8
Japanese	2

32. What is the range of the data shown on the graph?

(A) 4   **(B)** 5.5   **(C)** 6   **(D)** 21

© Great Source. Copying is permitted; see page ii.

1. 24, 28, 32

2.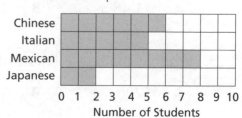

3. $40, $48, $56

4. 4

5. 570

6. 3,400

7. 7,000

8. 441

9. 5,316

10. $4\frac{3}{4}$

11. $3\frac{1}{4}$ cups

12. $10\frac{2}{3}$

13. 1.45

14. $2\frac{1}{2}$

15. 5:25

16. $0.76 or 76¢

17. 1 quarter, 2 dimes, 2 pennies

18. $0.11 or 11¢

19. B

20. A

21. D

22. C

23. D

24. A

25. D

26. B

27. A

28. C

29. B

30. C

31. Example:

Chinese										
Italian										
Mexican										
Japanese										

0 1 2 3 4 5 6 7 8 9 10
Number of Students

32. C

Tested Skills	Item Numbers	Every Day Counts Element(s)
Patterns	1, 2, 3	Calendar, Counting Tape
Number relationships	4, 29	Calendar, Counting Tape
Addition, subtraction, multiplication, division	5, 6, 8, 25, 28	Daily Depositor, Counting Tape, Coin Counter
Place value and rounding	7, 9, 23	Daily Depositor
Fractions	10, 11, 24, 26	Coin Counter, Measurement, A Fraction A Day
Geometric shapes and their attributes	19, 20, 21, 22	Calendar
Analyzing data and making predictions	30, 31, 32	Calendar, Daily Depositor, Graph
Solving problems with time	15, 27	Clock
Solving problems with money	16, 17, 18	Daily Depositor, Coin Counter
Measuring length, weight, and capacity	12, 13, 14	Measurement

© Great Source. Copying is prohibited.

NAME _____

Directions: Write your answer to each question.

1. What are the next three numbers in this pattern?

| 12 | 14 | 16 | 18 | | | |

2. 10, 15, 35, and 100 are all multiples of what number? _____

3. Draw the next two shapes in this pattern.

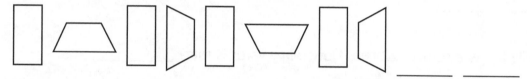 _____ _____

4. On Monday, 382 people visited the aquarium. On Tuesday, 275 people visited the aquarium. How many people visited the aquarium in all?

_____

5. 9,000 + 70 + 3 = _____

6. What is 300 more than 1,750? _____

7. What is 26 × 10? _____

8. Write $\frac{13}{4}$ as a mixed number. _____

9. Alex jogged $3\frac{1}{2}$ miles on Saturday and $2\frac{1}{4}$ miles on Sunday. How far did she jog altogether?

_____

© Great Source. Copying is permitted; see page ii.

10. What is the value of these coins? _____

11. Using the fewest possible coins, which coins would you use to make 48¢?

_____

12. Jamie buys a juice box for 33¢. He pays for it with 2 quarters. How much change should he get?

_____

13. Kelly threw a softball 22 feet. How many yards is that? _____

14. Martin poured 11 cups of lemonade. How many quarts did he pour? _____

15. What time is shown on the clock?

_____

16. Giselle started reading at 7:45. She stopped reading at 8:34. How many minutes did she read?

_____

17. Sam has 2 nickels and 5 dimes. How many tenths of a dollar does he have?

_____

18. Mrs. Neilson bought 9 boxes of granola bars. Each box has 4 bars. Write a number sentence showing how many granola bars she bought in all.

_____

© Great Source. Copying is permitted; see page ii.

NAME _____

Directions: Choose the best answer to each question. Mark your answer.

19. What is the value of the **7** in 4,**7**95?

    A 7 ones   **B** 7 tens   **C** 7 hundreds   **D** 7 thousands

20. Which of these figures is a rhombus?

 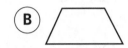  

21. Which figure is an isosceles triangle?

 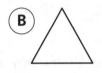 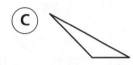

22. Which figure has exactly two lines of symmetry?

   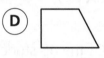

Use the graph to answer questions 23–25.

The graph shows daily average temperatures in Seattle, Washington, in September.

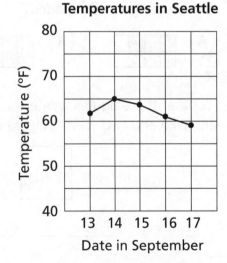

23. What was the average temperature on September 16?

    A 58°   **C** 64°

    B 61°   **D** 67°

24. Which day had the highest temperature?

    A 14th   **C** 16th

    B 15th   **D** 17th

25. Based on the graph, which is the most likely temperature for September 18?

    A 70°   **B** 66°   **C** 62°   **D** 58°

© Great Source. Copying is permitted; see page ii.

26. Which number is a multiple of both 3 and 6?

(A) 27   (B) 32   (C) 39   (D) 42

27. What is the least common multiple of 3, 4, and 6?

(A) 9   (B) 12   (C) 18   (D) 24

28. Ahmed started watching a movie at 4:15. The movie lasted 93 minutes. At what time did the movie end?

(A) 4:48   (B) 5:38   (C) 5:48   (D) 6:08

29. Reno can make a paper airplane in 4 minutes. How many airplanes can he make in 30 minutes?

(A) 7   (B) 8   (C) 9   (D) 10

30. Of the 45 students eating lunch at noon, 30 were girls. What fraction of the students were girls?

(A) $\frac{3}{4}$ (B) $\frac{2}{3}$ (C) $\frac{1}{2}$ (D) $\frac{3}{5}$

31. Which picture has $\frac{3}{4}$ shaded?

(A)   (B)   (C)   (D)

32. Look at these figures. Write the name of each figure. List two ways they are alike and two ways they are different.

_____   _____

_____

_____

_____

© Great Source. Copying is permitted; see page ii.

1. 20, 22, 24

2. 5

3.

4. 657

5. 9,073

6. 2,050

7. 260

8. $3\frac{1}{4}$

9. $5\frac{3}{4}$ miles

10. 61¢ or $0.61

11. 1 quarter, 2 dimes, 3 pennies

12. 17¢

13. $7\frac{1}{3}$

14. $2\frac{3}{4}$

15. 6:22

16. 49

17. 6 tenths, or $0.60

18. $9 \times 4 = 36$

19. C

20. D

21. A

22. C

23. B

24. A

25. D

26. D

27. B

28. C

29. A

30. B

31. A

32. square, rhombus

Similarities: Each figure has four sides; the sides are of equal length; opposite sides are parallel.

Differences: The square has four right angles; the rhombus has none. The square has four lines of symmetry; the rhombus has two.

Tested Skills	Item Numbers	Every Day Counts Element(s)
Patterns	1, 3	Calendar, Counting Tape
Place value	5, 6, 19	Daily Depositor
Number relationships	2, 26, 27	Calendar, Counting Tape
Addition, subtraction, multiplication, division	4, 7, 18, 29	Daily Depositor, Counting Tape, Coin Counter
Fractions	8, 9, 30, 31	Coin Counter, Measurement, A Fraction A Day
Geometric shapes and their attributes	20, 21, 22, 32	Calendar
Analyzing data and making predictions	23, 24, 25	Calendar, Daily Depositor, Graph
Solving problems with time	15, 16, 28	Clock
Solving problems with money	10, 11, 12, 17	Daily Depositor, Coin Counter
Measuring length and capacity	13, 14	Measurement

© Great Source. Copying is prohibited.

NAME _____

Directions: Write your answer to each question.

1. What are the next three numbers in this pattern?

   6, 12, 18, 24, 30, _____, _____, _____

2. Draw the next two figures in this pattern.

               _____ _____

3. 9, 21, 30, and 66 are all multiples of what number? _____

4. Last year the Rosebud Garden Center sold 347 apple trees and 195 plum trees. What was the total number of trees sold?

   _____

5. What is 8,748 rounded to the nearest thousand? _____

6. What is 14 × 20? _____

7. What is 29 × 100? _____

8. Write $\frac{17}{5}$ as a mixed number. _____

9. Emilio mixed $\frac{3}{4}$ cup of vinegar with $1\frac{1}{2}$ cups of oil to make salad dressing. How many cups of salad dressing did he make?

   _____

10. What is the greatest number you can make using the digits 0, 1, 2, and 3?

    _____

© Great Source. Copying is permitted; see page ii.

11. 150 centimeters is the same as _____ decimeters or _____ meters.

12. Meredith took two steps forward. One step measured 0.7 meter and the other measured 0.6 meter. How far did she move forward altogether?

_____

13. Randy bought 8 ounces of pears and 12 ounces of peaches. How many pounds of fruit did he buy in all?

_____

14. What is the value of these coins? _____

15. Using quarters, dimes, nickels, and pennies, how can you make $0.68 with the fewest possible coins?

_____

16. Fernando bought a yo-yo for $0.87. He gave the clerk 4 quarters. How much change should he receive?

_____

17. Jessie's soccer practice started at the time shown on the clock. If practice lasted $1\frac{1}{2}$ hours, at what time did it end?

_____

18. Karen bought 8 packs of hair ties. There were 5 hair ties in each pack. Write a number sentence showing how many hair ties Karen bought.

_____

© Great Source. Copying is permitted; see page ii.

Directions: Choose the best answer to each question. Mark your answer.

19. Which lines appear to be perpendicular?

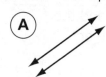 A   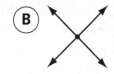 B   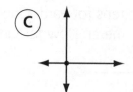 C   D

20. Which of these figures has exactly 5 corners?

 A   B   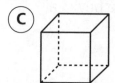 C   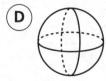 D

21. Which figure has two round faces?

 A   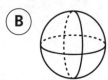 B   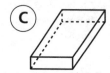 C   D

22. Which figure is an acute angle?

 A   B   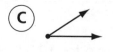 C    D

23. What is the value of the **1** in 7,512?

    (**A**) 1 one   (**B**) 1 ten   (**C**) 1 hundred   (**D**) 1 thousand

24. 9×18 is closest to —

    (**A**) 140   (**B**) 160   (**C**) 180   (**D**) 200

25. Of the 24 players on a baseball team, 18 are right-handed. What fraction of the players are right-handed?

    (**A**) $\frac{3}{4}$ (**B**) $\frac{2}{3}$ (**C**) $\frac{1}{2}$ (**D**) $\frac{1}{4}$

© Great Source. Copying is permitted; see page ii.

26. Which picture shows $\frac{1}{3}$ shaded?

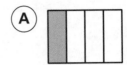

(A) (B) (C) (D)

27. A group of 50 fourth graders are going on a field trip. If one van can take 8 students, how many vans will be needed for the trip?

(A) 6   (B) 7   (C) 8   (D) 9

28. What is the least common multiple of 6 and 9?

(A) 18   (B) 27   (C) 36   (D) 45

29. Jody started cleaning her room at 4:25. She finished at 5:40. How much time did she spend cleaning her room?

(A) 15 min   (B) 55 min   (C) 1 hr 5 min   (D) 1 hour 15 min

Use the graph to answer questions 30 and 31.

The graph shows the results of a survey of students' favorite movies.

30. How many people chose *Ice Age*?

(A) 5   (C) 25

(B) 20   (D) 30

Favorite Movies	
Lord of the Rings	★★★★
Finding Nemo	★★★★★★
Ice Age	★★★★★
Key: ★ = 5 people	

31. How many more people chose *Finding Nemo* than *Lord of the Rings*?

(A) 2   (B) 10   (C) 20   (D) 30

32. Find the perimeter and the area of each figure below. Figure 1 is made of 1-inch squares. Figure 2 is a rectangle.

Figure 1

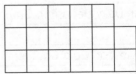

P = _____

A = _____

Figure 2

8 cm

10 cm

P = _____

A = _____

© Great Source. Copying is permitted; see page ii.

1. 36, 42, 48

2.

3. 3

4. 542

5. 9,000

6. 280

7. 2,900

8. $3\frac{2}{5}$

9. $2\frac{1}{4}$

10. 3,210

11. 15 dm, 1.5 m

12. 1.3 m

13. $1\frac{1}{4}$

14. $0.92 or 92¢

15. 2 quarters, 1 dime, 1 nickel, 3 pennies

16. 13¢ or $0.13

17. 4:45

18. $8 \times 5 = 40$

19. C

20. A

21. D

22. C

23. B

24. B

25. A

26. D

27. B

28. A

29. D

30. C

31. B

32. Figure 1:
   $P = 18$ in.; $A = 17$ sq. in.

   Figure 2:
   $P = 36$ cm; $A = 80$ sq. cm

Tested Skills	Item Numbers	Every Day Counts Element(s)
Patterns	1, 2,	Calendar, Counting Tape
Number relationships	3, 28	Calendar, Counting Tape
Addition, subtraction, multiplication, division	4, 6, 7, 18, 24, 27	Daily Depositor, Counting Tape, Coin Counter
Place value and rounding	5, 10, 23	Daily Depositor
Fractions	8, 9, 25, 26	Coin Counter, Measurement, A Fraction A Day
Geometric shapes and their attributes	19, 20, 21, 22, 32	Calendar
Analyzing data and making predictions	30, 31	Calendar, Daily Depositor, Graph
Solving problems with time	17, 29	Clock
Solving problems with money	14, 15, 16	Daily Depositor, Coin Counter
Measuring length and weight	11, 12, 13	Measurement

© Great Source. Copying is prohibited.

NAME _____

Directions: Write your answer to each question.

1. What are the next three numbers in this pattern?

    7, 14, 21, 28, _____, _____, _____

2. Draw the next two shapes in this pattern.

    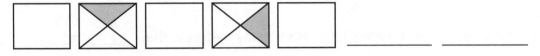 _____ _____

3. Write the numbers to complete the pattern in this table.

Week	1	2	3	4	5	6	7
Amount	$6	$12	$18	$24			

4. 10, 25, 40, and 65 are all multiples of what number? _____

5. What is 48 × 10? _____

6. What is 23 × 100? _____

7. What is 4,379 rounded to the nearest thousand? _____

8. Mr. Leonardo went bowling. He scored 235 in the first game and 188 in the second game. What was his total score for two games?

    _____

9. What is the greatest odd number you can make with the digits 0, 2, 3, 5?

    _____

© Great Source. Copying is permitted; see page ii.

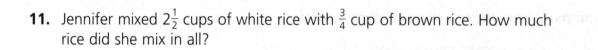

10. Write $\frac{17}{3}$ as a mixed number.

11. Jennifer mixed $2\frac{1}{2}$ cups of white rice with $\frac{3}{4}$ cup of brown rice. How much rice did she mix in all?

_____

12. Mrs. O'Connell's willow tree is 37 feet tall. How many yards is that? _____

13. Jeff's bike is 175 centimeters long. How many meters is that? _____

14. Suki's kitten weighs 24 ounces. How many pounds is that? _____

15. Melanie started playing the oboe at the time shown on the clock. She played for 35 minutes. At what time did she finish? _____

16. What is the value of these coins? _____

17. Using quarters, dimes, nickels, and pennies, how can you make $0.41 with the fewest possible coins?

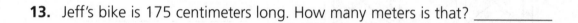
_____

18. Roman bought a bag of peanuts for $0.68. He paid for it with 3 quarters. How much should he get in change?

_____

© Great Source. Copying is permitted; see page ii.

Directions: Choose the best answer to each question. Mark your answer.

19. Which of these figures is a pentagon?

20. Which lines appear to be perpendicular?

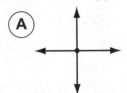 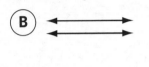 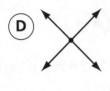

21. Which figure has exactly 12 edges?

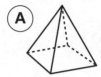 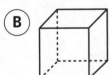 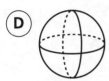

22. What is the area of this rectangle?

(A) 14 square units   (C) 40 square units

(B) 28 square units   (D) 45 square units

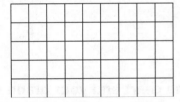

23. What is the value of the **4** in **4**3,925?

(A) 4 tens   (C) 4 thousands

(B) 4 hundreds   (D) 4 ten thousands

24. Of the 20 cars in a parking lot, 16 are blue. What fraction of the cars are blue?

(A) $\frac{4}{5}$ (B) $\frac{3}{4}$ (C) $\frac{2}{3}$ (D) $\frac{1}{2}$

25. Naureen bought 8 packs of women's soccer cards. Each pack has 5 cards. Which expression can be used to find how many cards she bought in all?

(A) $8 + 5$ (B) 8×5 (C) $8 \div 5$ (D) 8×8

© Great Source. Copying is permitted; see page ii.

26. Which picture shows $\frac{1}{2}$ shaded?

27. Camille rode her bike for 45 minutes. She finished at 12:10 P.M. At what time did she start riding?

  A 11:15 A.M.   **B** 11:25 A.M.   **C** 11:25 P.M.   **D** 12:55 P.M.

28. Which is the best estimate of 28×11?

  A $200   **B** $300   **C** $400   **D** $500

29. Which is the greatest common factor of 12 and 20?

  A 10   **B** 5   **C** 4   **D** 3

30. Frank plans to toss a coin 50 times and record the results. About how many times will he probably get tails?

  A 50   **B** 30   **C** 25   **D** 20

Use the chart and your graph to answer questions 31 and 32.

31. The chart shows the favorite school lunches of students in Ms. Charo's class. Use the grid to make a bar graph of the data. Label each part of your graph.

Favorite Lunches

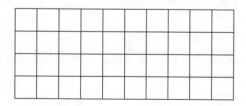

Lunch Item	Number of Students
Macaroni & Cheese	5
Sloppy Joe	3
Quesadilla	7
Pizza	9

32. What is the mean of the data shown on the graph?

  A 24   **B** 12   **C** 8   **D** 6

© Great Source. Copying is permitted; see page ii.

POST TEST ANSWER KEY

1. 35, 42, 49

2.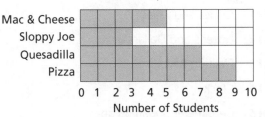

3. $30, $36, $42

4. 5

5. 480

6. 2,300

7. 4,000

8. 423

9. 5,203

10. $5\frac{2}{3}$

11. $3\frac{1}{4}$ cups

12. $12\frac{1}{3}$

13. 1.75

14. $1\frac{1}{2}$

15. 3:25

16. $0.77 or 77¢

17. 1 quarter, 1 dime, 1 nickel, 1 penny

18. 7¢ or $0.07

19. C

20. A

21. B

22. D

23. D

24. A

25. B

26. C

27. B

28. B

29. C

30. C

31. Example:

Mac & Cheese
Sloppy Joe
Quesadilla
Pizza

0 1 2 3 4 5 6 7 8 9 10
Number of Students

32. D

Tested Skills	Item Numbers	Every Day Counts Element(s)
Patterns	1, 2, 3	Calendar, Counting Tape
Number relationships	4, 29	Calendar, Counting Tape
Addition, subtraction, multiplication, division	5, 6, 8, 25, 28	Daily Depositor, Counting Tape, Coin Counter
Place value and rounding	7, 9, 23	Daily Depositors
Fractions	10, 11, 24, 26	Coin Counter, Measurement, A Fraction A Day
Geometric shapes and their attributes	19, 20, 21, 22	Calendar
Analyzing data and making predictions	30, 31, 32	Calendar, Daily Depositor, Graph
Solving problems with time	15, 27	Clock
Solving problems with money	16, 17, 18	Daily Depositor, Coin Counter
Measuring length, weight, and capacity	12, 13, 14	Measurement

© Great Source. Copying is prohibited.

TR1   Multiplication Facts Progress Record

TR2   Play Money: Bills

TR3   Inch Squared Paper

TR4   Hundred Chart

TR5   Equation Chart

TR6   Multiple Markers

TR7   Circular Array Paper

TR8   Play Money: Coins

TR9   100 Penny Grid

TR10   Measurement Record

TR11   Circles and Miles

TR12   Dozens and Dollars

TR13   Fraction Record

TR14   Clock

TR15   Centimeter Squared Paper

TR16   Quart/Liter Drawings

TR17   Shopper Cards

TR18   Shopping Record

TR19   Blank Hundred Chart

TR20   Calendar Cutouts

TR21   Calendar Cutouts

TR22   Calendar Cutouts

TR23   Sample Vocabulary A

TR24   Sample Vocabulary B

© Great Source. Copying is prohibited.

×	1	2	3	4	5	6	7	8	9	10
1	1 ×1	2 ×1	3 ×1	4 ×1	5 ×1	6 ×1	7 ×1	8 ×1	9 ×1	10 ×1
2	1 ×2	2 ×2	3 ×2	4 ×2	5 ×2	6 ×2	7 ×2	8 ×2	9 ×2	10 ×2
3	1 ×3	2 ×3	3 ×3	4 ×3	5 ×3	6 ×3	7 ×3	8 ×3	9 ×3	10 ×3
4	1 ×4	2 ×4	3 ×4	4 ×4	5 ×4	6 ×4	7 ×4	8 ×4	9 ×4	10 ×4
5	1 ×5	2 ×5	3 ×5	4 ×5	5 ×5	6 ×5	7 ×5	8 ×5	9 ×5	10 ×5
6	1 ×6	2 ×6	3 ×6	4 ×6	5 ×6	6 ×6	7 ×6	8 ×6	9 ×6	10 ×6
7	1 ×7	2 ×7	3 ×7	4 ×7	5 ×7	6 ×7	7 ×7	8 ×7	9 ×7	10 ×7
8	1 ×8	2 ×8	3 ×8	4 ×8	5 ×8	6 ×8	7 ×8	8 ×8	9 ×8	10 ×8
9	1 ×9	2 ×9	3 ×9	4 ×9	5 ×9	6 ×9	7 ×9	8 ×9	9 ×9	10 ×9
10	1 ×10	2 ×10	3 ×10	4 ×10	5 ×10	6 ×10	7 ×10	8 ×10	9 ×10	10 ×10

© Great Source. Copying is permitted; see page ii.

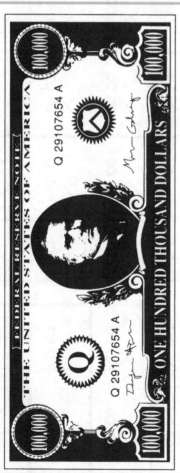

© Great Source. Copying is permitted; see page ii.

© Great Source. Copying is permitted; see page ii.

1	2	3	4	5	6	7	8	9	10
11	12	13	14	15	16	17	18	19	20
21	22	23	24	25	26	27	28	29	30
31	32	33	34	35	36	37	38	39	40
41	42	43	44	45	46	47	48	49	50
51	52	53	54	55	56	57	58	59	60
61	62	63	64	65	66	67	68	69	70
71	72	73	74	75	76	77	78	79	80
81	82	83	84	85	86	87	88	89	90
91	92	93	94	95	96	97	98	99	100

© Great Source. Copying is permitted; see page ii.

Day	Groups	Remainder	Equation

TR5 Equation Chart

© Great Source. Copying is permitted; see page ii.

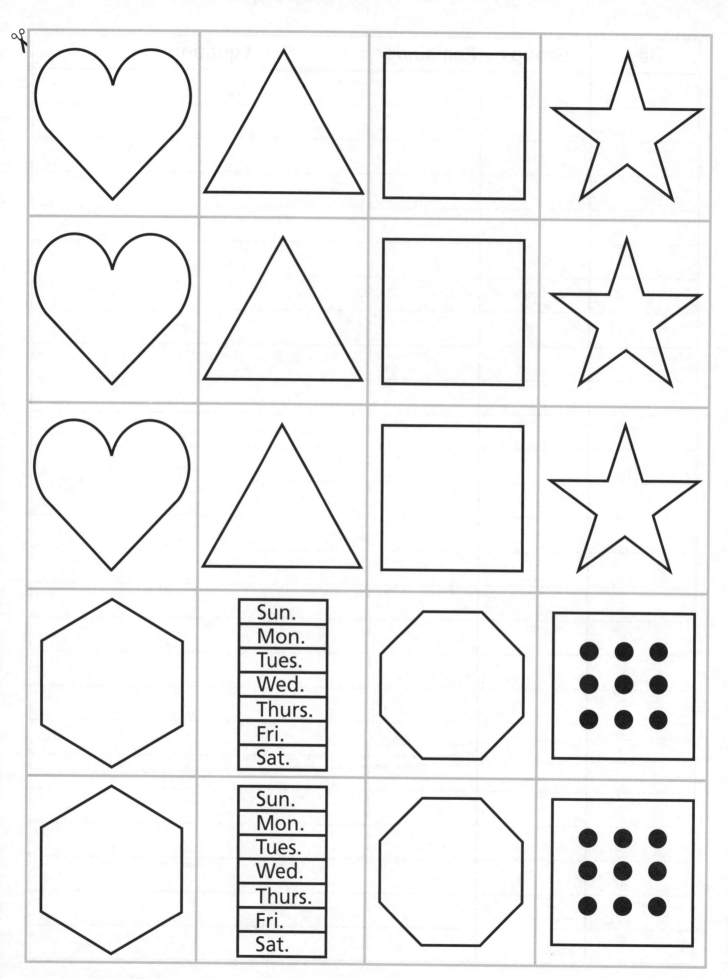

© Great Source. Copying is permitted; see page ii.

TR7   Circular Array Paper

© Great Source. Copying is permitted; see page ii.

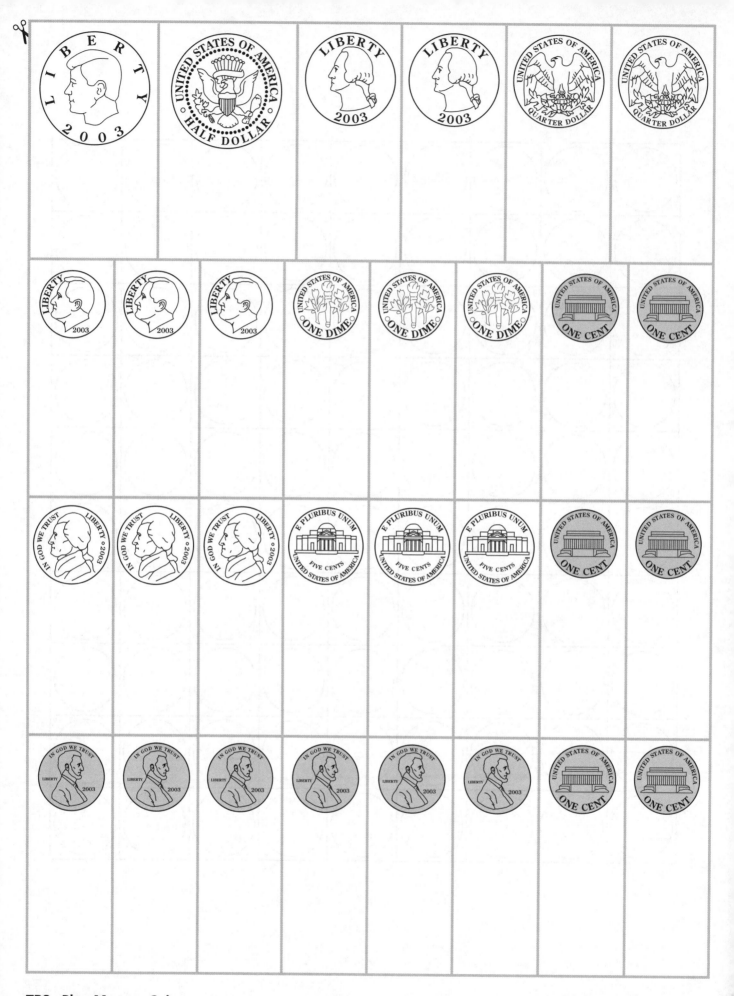

TR8 Play Money: Coins

© Great Source. Copying is permitted; see page ii.

Today we have

$ _____ . _____ _____

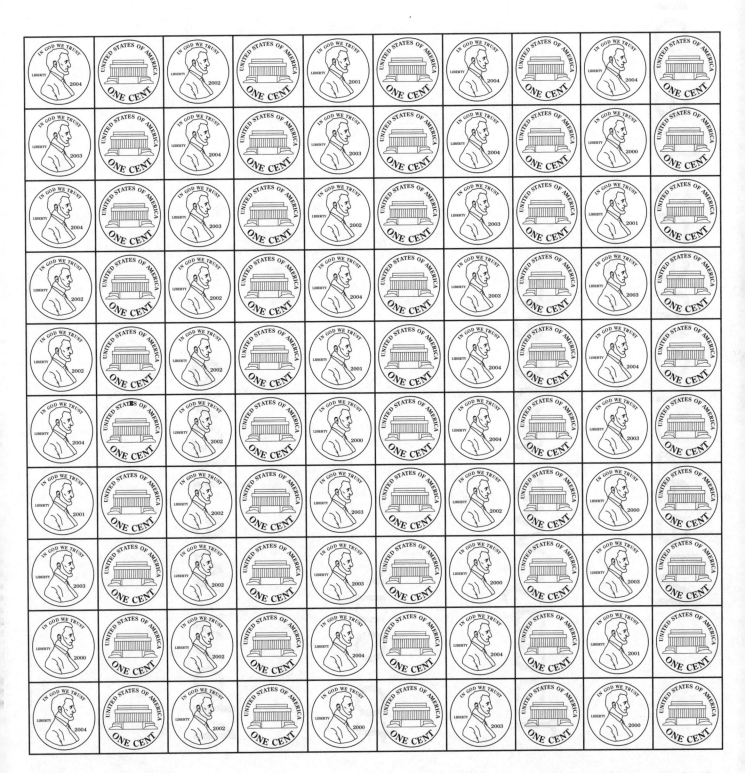

© Great Source. Copying is permitted; see page ii.

Measurement Record

Today we added _____

to our _____

Now we have _____

© Great Source. Copying is permitted; see page ii.

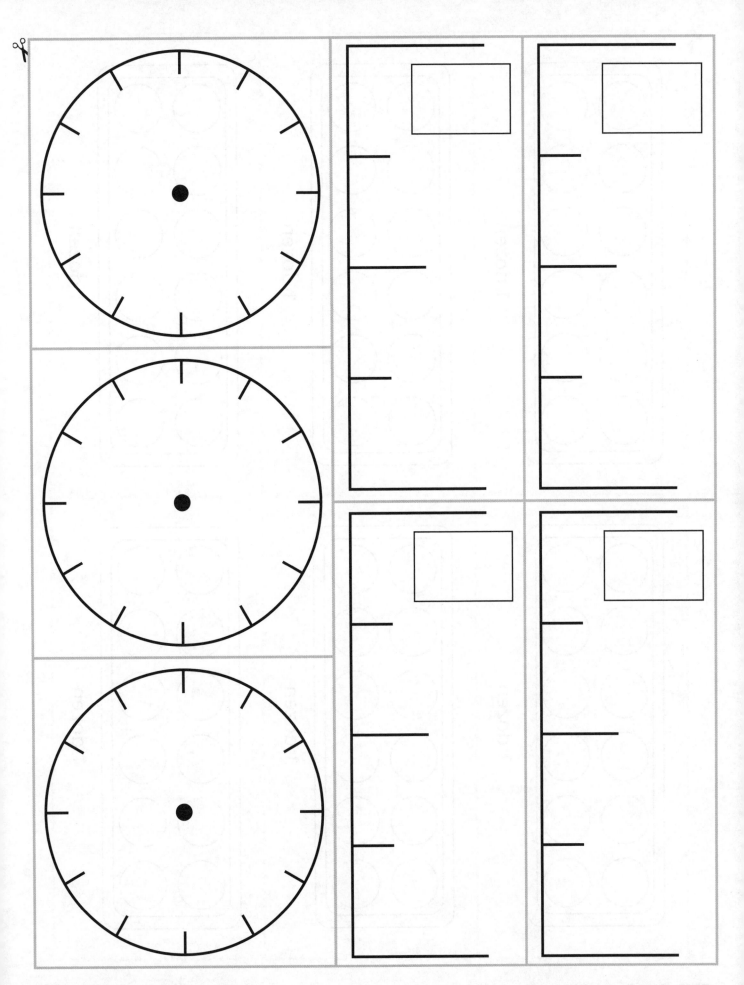

TR11 Circles and Giant Inches

© Great Source. Copying is permitted; see page ii.

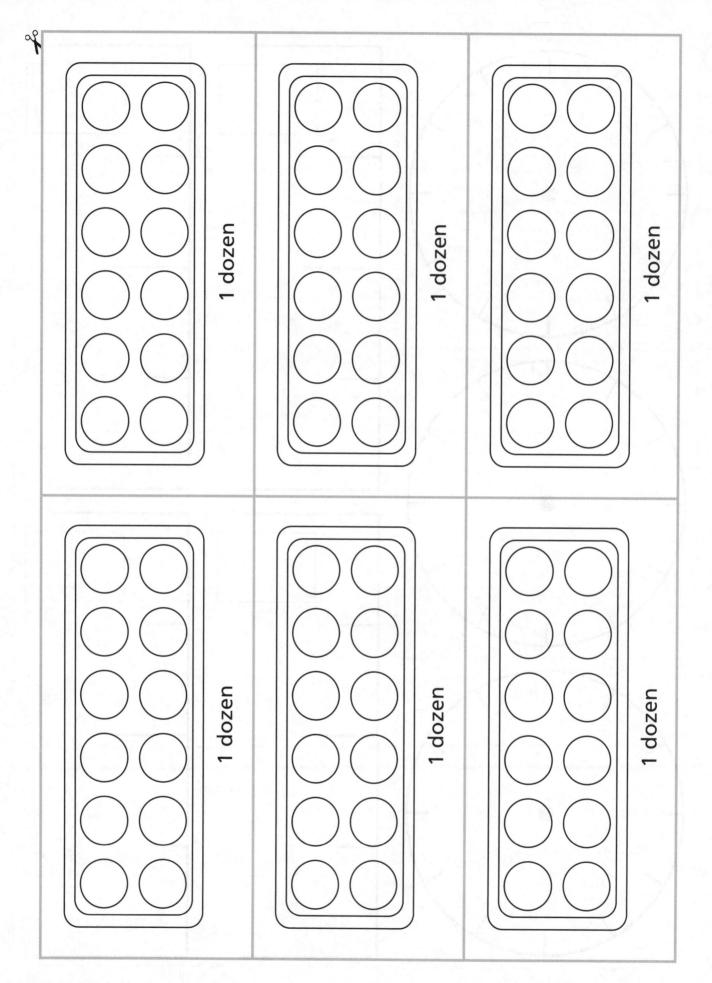

TR12 Egg Carton Dozens

© Great Source. Copying is permitted; see page ii.

Today we have _____

_____

_____

_____

Today we have _____

_____

_____

© Great Source. Copying is permitted; see page ii.

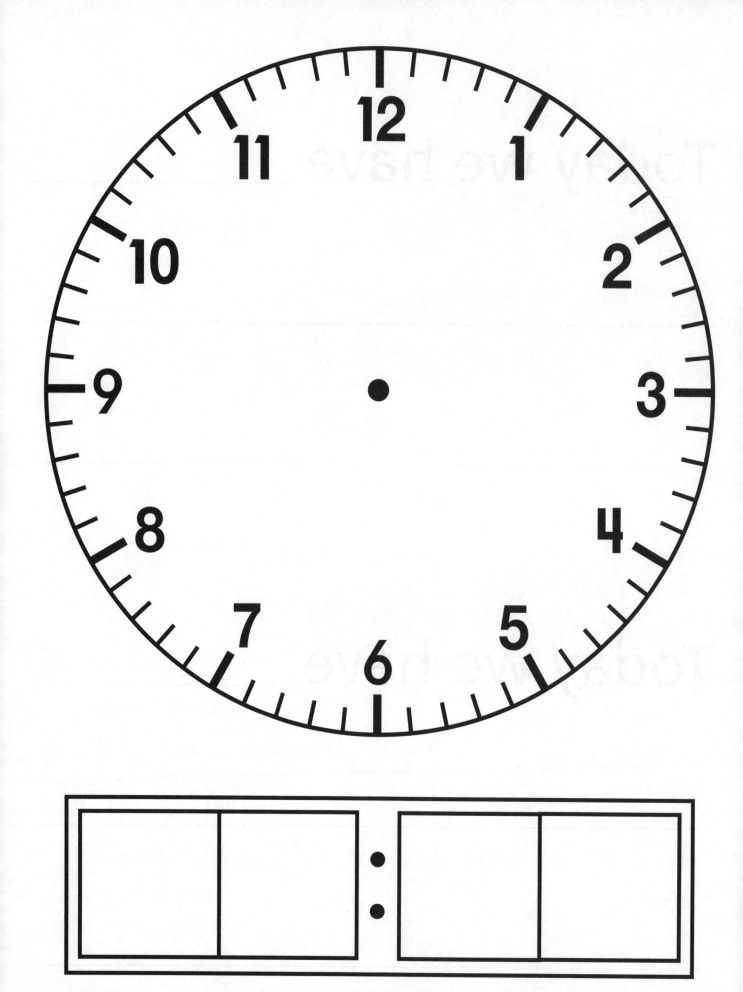

© Great Source. Copying is permitted; see page ii.

© Great Source. Copying is permitted; see page ii.

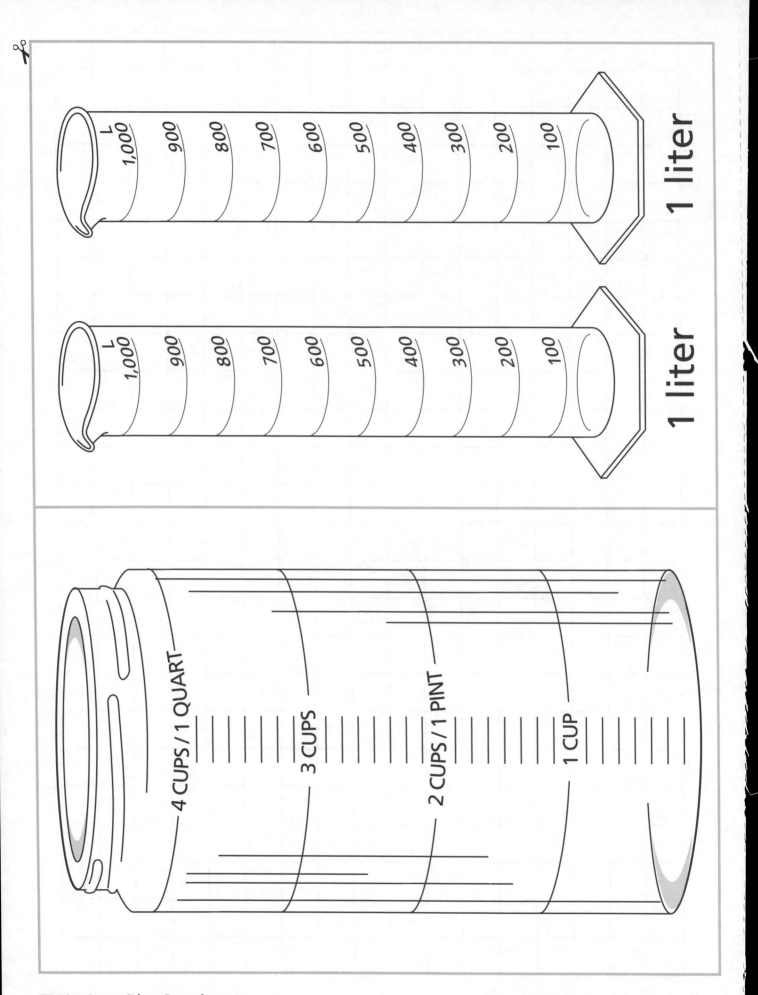

1 liter

1 liter

4 CUPS / 1 QUART

3 CUPS

2 CUPS / 1 PINT

1 CUP

© Great Source. Copying is permitted; see page ii.

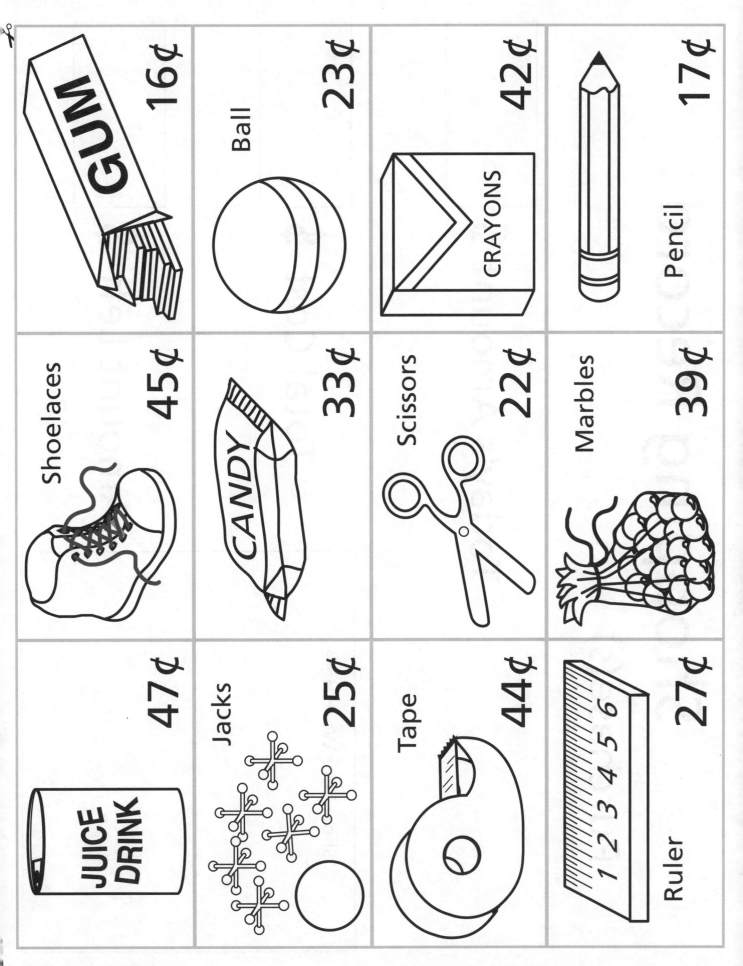

GUM 16¢

Ball 23¢

CRAYONS 42¢

Pencil 17¢

Shoelaces 45¢

CANDY 33¢

Scissors 22¢

Marbles 39¢

JUICE DRINK 47¢

Jacks 25¢

Tape 44¢

Ruler 27¢

© Great Source. Copying is permitted; see page ii.

Shopping Record

Purchase(s)

Today's Amount $

Total Cost $

Amount Left $

Show Your Work Here

© Great Source. Copying is permitted; see page ii.

© Great Source. Copying is permitted; see page ii.

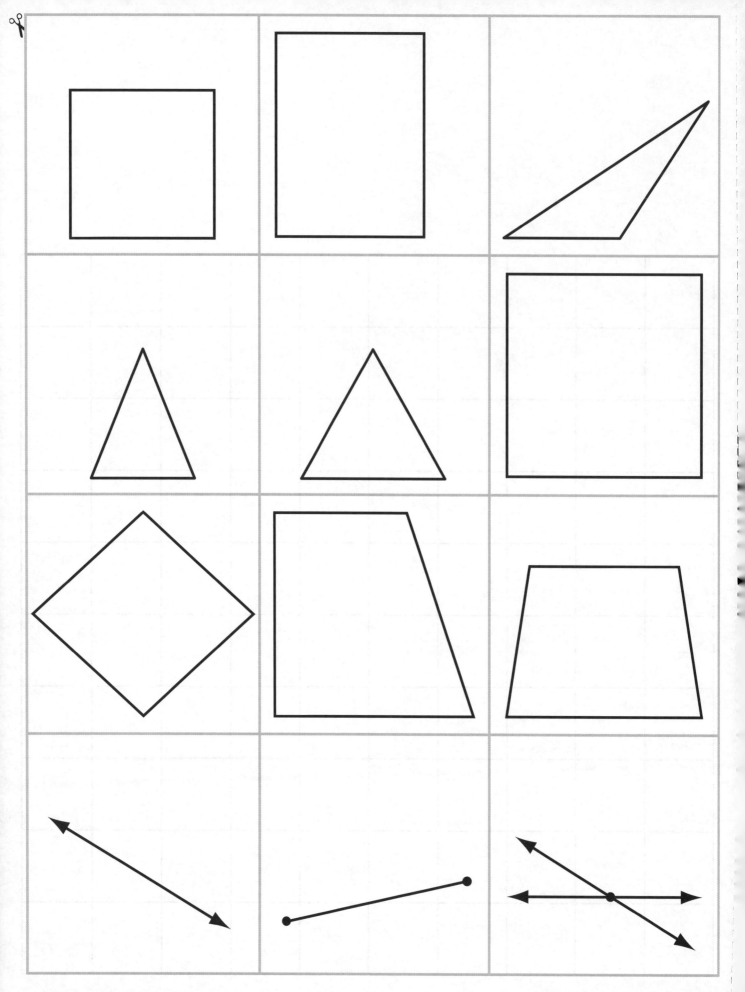

TR20   Calendar Cutouts

© Great Source. Copying is permitted; see page ii.

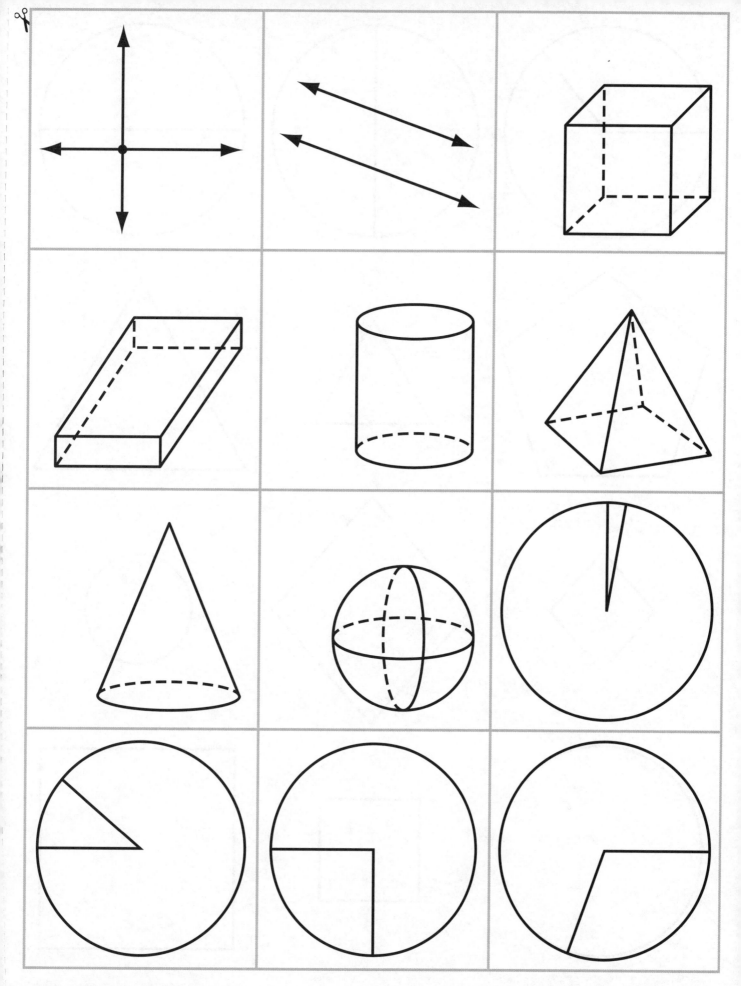

TR21   Calendar Cutouts

© Great Source. Copying is permitted; see page ii.

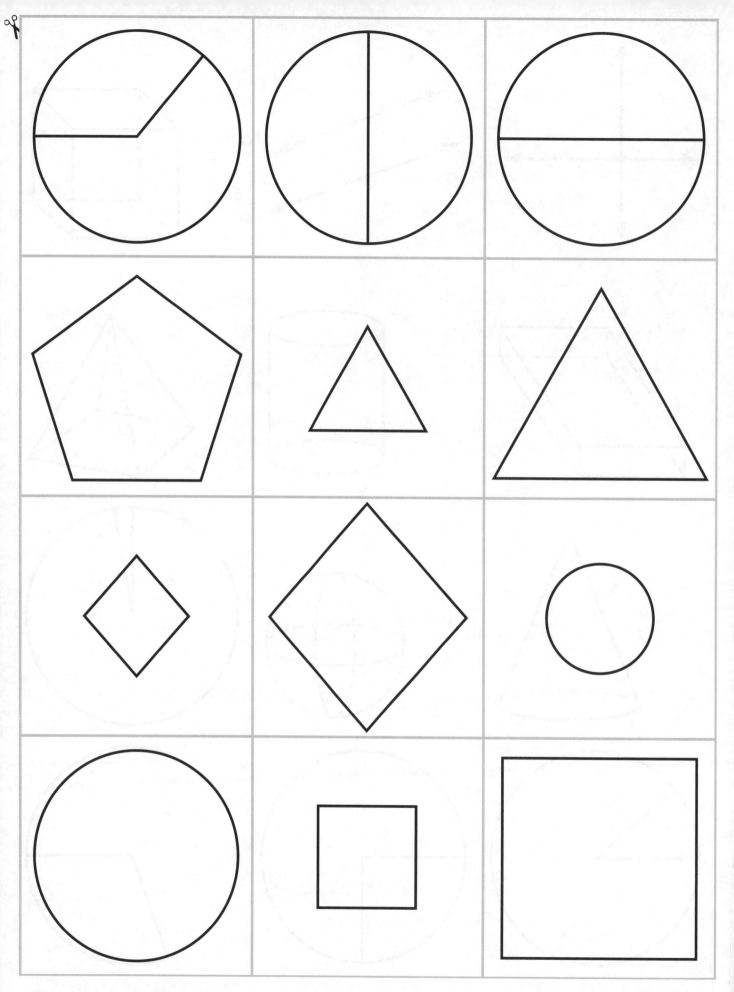

TR22   Calendar Cutouts

© Great Source. Copying is permitted; see page ii.

multiple The product of two whole numbers.	**polygon** A closed figure made with straight line segments.
$$4 \times 5 = 20$$ 20 is a multiple of both 4 and 5.	 This polygon has 5 sides.

line of symmetry A figure has a line of symmetry if you can fold it on that line and the two halves are exactly the same.	**mixed number** A number that has a whole number part that is one or greater and a fraction part.
 The two sides of this shape are exactly the same.	$4\frac{1}{5}$, $10\frac{1}{3}$, $7\frac{11}{12}$ These are mixed numbers.

denominator The bottom number in a fraction. It tells how many equal parts are in a whole.	**numerator** The top number in a fraction. It tells how many equal parts are being talked about.
$$\frac{3}{5}$$ In this fraction, 5 is the denominator.	$$\frac{7}{12}$$ In this fraction, 7 is the numerator.

common multiple A number that is a multiple of two or more numbers.	**quadrilateral** A figure with 4 straight sides.
12, 18, 24 These numbers are common multiples of 2, 3, and 6.	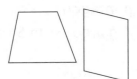 These are quadrilaterals.

trapezoid A quadrilateral with one set of parallel sides and one set of sides that are not parallel.	**right angle** An angle that measures exactly 90°, like a square corner.
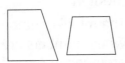 These are trapezoids.	 right angle

least common multiple The smallest common multiple of a set of two or more numbers.	**factor** Any whole number that divides evenly into any given number.
2, 3, 4 The least common multiple of these numbers is 12.	 5 is a factor of 10.

estimate To find a number close to an exact amount.	**angle** Two rays that share an endpoint.
311 + 593 To estimate this sum, round both numbers to the nearest hundred. Add the rounded numbers.	 The measure of an angle is the measure of how far one ray is turned from the other.

These might be used to accompany discussions, to build individual student word banks, or to enlarge for a Word Wall.

TR23 Sample Vocabulary A

© Great Source. Copying is permitted; see page ii.

acute angle

An angle that measures more than 0° and less than 90°.

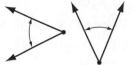

These are acute angles.

obtuse angle

An angle that measures more than 90° and less than 180°.

This is an obtuse angle.

rounding

Changing a number to one that is close and easier to compute with.

14,823

I can round that number to 15,000.

area

The measure of how much surface a figure covers.

4 in.

2 in.

The area of this figure is 8 square inches.

perimeter

A measure of the distance around a figure.

4 in.

2 in.

The perimeter of this figure is 12 inches.

prime number

A number that has only two factors, itself and 1.

2, 3, 5, 7 are prime numbers because they have only one factor other than 1.

pentagon

A polygon with 5 sides.

These are pentagons.

hexagon

A polygon with 6 sides.

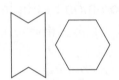

These are hexagons.

range

The difference between the greatest number and the least number in a set of numbers.

9 lb   12 lb   10 lb
8 lb   9 lb

The range of the weights of these boxes is 4 pounds.

median

The middle number when numbers are arranged in order from least to greatest.

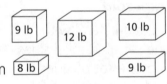
9 lb   12 lb   10 lb
8 lb   9 lb

The median weight of these boxes is 9 pounds.

mode

The number that appears most often in a set of numbers.

9 lb   12 lb   10 lb
8 lb   9 lb

The mode of the weights of these boxes is 9 pounds.

mean

The number found by dividing the sum of two or more numbers by how many numbers are being added.

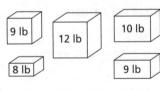
9 lb   12 lb   10 lb
8 lb   9 lb

The mean weight of these boxes is 9.6 pounds.

simplest form

A fraction whose numerator and denominator have no common factor greater than 1.

$$\frac{9}{12} = \frac{3}{4}$$

These are equivalent fractions. $\frac{3}{4}$ is the same as $\frac{9}{12}$ in simplest form.

greatest common factor

The largest number that is a common factor of two or more numbers.

15, 50, 100

The greatest common factor of these numbers is 5.

These might be used to accompany discussions, to build individual student word banks, or to enlarge for a Word Wall.

TR24   Sample Vocabulary B

© Great Source. Copying is permitted; see page ii.

INDEX

A

Addition

decimals, 26–28, 42, 57–59, 66–67, 72, 87–88, 99–100, 113

fractions, 36–37, 52–56, 68–70, 81–84, 109–111, 126–128

mixed numbers, 52–56, 81–84, 126–128

money, 21–23, 34–36, 50–52, 57–59, 63–66, 68–70, 79–80, 94–95, 108–109, 122–123

strategies, 34–36, 63–66, 79–80, 92, 108–109, 122–123, 136–137

whole numbers, 21–23, 34–36, 50–52, 57–59, 62, 63–66, 72–73, 79–80, 92, 94–95, 108–109, 122–124, 136–137

Algebra

algebraic notation, 23–26, 108, 111–112, 120–122

algebraic thinking, 23–26, 32–34, 48–50, 62, 68–70, 76–78, 85–86, 92, 108, 111–112, 120–122

equation, 23–26, 40–41, 62, 68–72, 84–86, 92, 97–98, 99–100, 108, 111–112, 120–122, 128–129

expression, 32–34, 70–71, 76–78, 97–98

functions, 32–34, 76–78, 108

order of operations, 23–26, 40–41, 62, 108, 111–112, 120–122

patterns. *See* Number patterns.

Angle

comparing, 32–34, 92–94, 106–108, 134–136

degrees, 92–94, 106–108

in a quadrilateral, 106–108, 134–136

in a triangle, 32–34, 106–108

Area, 95–97, 124–126

Array model, 26, 40–41, 56–57, 70–71, 84–86, 97–98, 111–112

Assessment

assessment materials, 141–161

ongoing assessment questions, 18, 21, 23, 26, 28, 32, 34, 36, 38, 40, 42, 44, 48, 50, 52, 54, 56, 57, 59, 62, 63, 66, 68, 70, 72, 73, 76, 79, 81, 83, 84, 87, 88, 92, 94, 95, 97, 99, 100, 101, 106, 108, 109, 111, 113, 115, 120, 122, 124, 126, 128, 130, 134, 136, 137, 139

B

Basic facts, 18–20, 23–26, 40–41, 56–57, 70–71, 79–80, 84–86, 97–98, 111–112, 128–130

C

Calculator, 21–23, 79–80

Calendar, 18–20, 32–34, 48–50, 62–63, 76–78, 92–94, 106–108, 120–122, 134–136

Capacity, 52–54, 109–111

Centimeter, 66–67

Circle, 92–94, 134–136

Classifying

angles, 92–94

lines, 62–63

polygons, 32–34, 106–108, 111–112, 128–130

quadrilaterals, 18–20, 48–50, 106–108

three-dimensional shapes, 76–78

triangles, 32–34, 106–108

two-dimensional shapes, 32–34, 48–50, 106–108, 134–136

Clock, 43–44, 59, 72–73, 100–101, 113–115, 130–131

Coins, 26–28, 42, 57–59, 72, 87–88, 99–100, 113

Congruence, 18–20, 48–50, 92–94, 134–136

Cube, 76–78

Cup, 52–54

Customary unit

capacity, 52–54

length, 36–37, 95–97, 115–117, 124–126

weight, 81–82

Cylinder, 52–54, 76–78, 109–110

© Great Source. Copying is prohibited.

Data analysis. *See also* Graph.
analyzing data, 23–26, 28–29, 44–45, 88–89, 92, 101–103, 115–117, 136–137, 139

collecting/recording data, 28–29, 44–45, 88–89, 101–103, 115–117, 136–137, 139

interpreting, 28–29, 44–45, 88–89, 92, 101–103, 115–117, 136–137, 139

making predictions with, 28–29, 34–36, 44–45, 50–52, 88–89, 92, 101–103, 115–117, 122–124, 136–137, 139

mean, 115–117

median, 115–117

mode, 115–117

organized list, 23–26, 44–45, 63–66, 92, 101–103, 115–117, 136–137, 139

range, 115–117

recording outcomes, 28–29, 101–103, 136–137

survey, 88–89, 139

table, 23–26, 34–36, 44–45, 50–52, 70–71, 88–89, 92, 101–103, 136–137

tally marks, 139

Decimal
compare and order, 26–28

fractions and, 26–28, 101–103, 109–111

notation, 57–59, 66–67

percents and, 57–59, 101–103

place value, 26–28, 42, 57–59, 66–67, 72, 87–88, 99–100, 101–103, 113

Decimeter, 66–67

Diagram
in problem solving, 63–66

Divisibility, 18–20, 23–26, 38–41, 54–56, 70–71, 92, 97–98, 111–112, 128–130, 137–139

Division
estimating quotients, 136–137

fractions, 38–40, 54–56, 68–70, 82–84

remainders, 23–26, 40–41, 54–56, 70–71, 82–86

whole numbers, 18–20, 23–26, 38–41, 54–57, 66–67, 70–71, 82–83, 85–86, 92–94, 97–98, 136–139

Edge, 76–78

Elapsed time, 43–44, 59, 72–73, 100–101, 113–115, 130–131

Equilateral triangle, 32–34, 106–108, 134–136

Equivalent
decimals, 99–100

fractions, 36–37, 38–40, 52–56, 66–70, 81–84, 109–111, 126–128

fractions, decimals, and percents, 66–70, 101–103

units, 36–37, 52–54, 66–67

Estimation, 21–23, 34–37, 50–53, 63–67, 72, 79–82, 94–95, 108–111, 113, 122–123, 136–137

Face, 76–78

Factor, 18–20, 23–26, 40–41, 56–57, 70–71, 84–86, 97–98, 111–112, 128–130, 137–139

Flip. *See* Reflection.

Foot, 36–37

Fraction
and percents, 57–59, 66–67, 101–103

as part of a region, 36–37, 66–67

as part of a set, 38–40, 52–56, 68–70, 81–84, 101–103, 109–110, 126–128

benchmarks, 36–37, 38–40, 52–59, 66–67, 72–73, 81–82, 81–84

comparing and ordering, 36–37, 54–59

decimals and, 42, 66–67

denominator, 38–40, 54–56, 68–70, 82–84, 126–128

equivalent, 36–37, 52–54, 66–70, 82–84, 126–128

improper, 36–37, 54–56, 68–70, 81–84, 126–128

mixed numbers and, 36–37, 52–56, 68–70, 81–84, 109–111, 126–128

numerator, 38–40, 54–56, 68–70, 82–84, 126–128

on a number line, 54–56

rename, 36–37, 38–40, 52–56, 68–70, 82–84, 109–111

simplest form, 36–37, 38–40, 52–56, 68–70, 82–84

Function, 32–34, 76–78, 108

© Great Source. Copying is prohibited.

Geometry

angle
   acute, 92–94
   central, 92–94
   obtuse, 92–94
   right, 18–20, 48–50, 62–63, 92–94, 134–136
   straight, 92–94
area, 95–97, 124–126
base, 76–78
circle
   center point, 92–94
   central angle, 92–94
congruence, 18–20, 48–50
corner, 18–20, 32–34, 48–50, 76–78
edge, 76–78
face, 76–78
hexagon, 84–86, 106–108
intersecting, 62–63
line, 48–50, 62–63
line segment, 62–63
opposite, 18–20, 32–34, 48–50
parallel, 18–20, 48–50
pattern, 40–41, 62–63, 106–108, 134–136
perimeter, 95–97, 124–126
perpendicular, 62–63
plane shape, 134–136
polygon, 32–34, 76–78, 106–108, 111–112, 128–130
prism, 76–78
pyramid, 76–78
quadrilateral. *See* Quadrilateral.
side, 18–20, 32–34, 48–50, 76–78, 106–108, 134–136
solid. *See* Three-dimensional shape.
symmetry, 32–34, 48–50, 106–108
transformation, 18–20
triangle, 32–34, 76–78, 106–108
vertex, 18–20, 32–34, 48–50, 76–78
volume, 52–54, 109–110

Graph

axis, 44–45
bar graph, 28–29, 44–45, 88–89, 139
create a graph, 28–29, 44–45, 88–89, 101–103, 115–117, 139
interpret a graph, 28–29, 88–89
line graph, 44–45
picture graph, 88–89, 115–117
stem-and-leaf plot, 44–45

Greatest Common Factor (GCF), 137–139

Hexagon, 84–86, 106–108

Home Involvement, 41, 101–103

Inch, 95–97, 115–117, 124–126

Isosceles triangle, 32–34, 106–108

Least Common Multiple (LCM), 56–57, 137–139

Length

customary units, 36–37, 95–97, 115–117, 124–126
metric units, 66–67

Liter, 109–111

Literature

bibliography, 140

Logical reasoning, 18–20, 40–41, 44–45, 48–50, 115–117, 134–136

Measurement

angle, 92–94
area, 94–95, 124–126
capacity, 52–54, 109–110
circle, 92–94, 134–136
customary, 36–37, 52–54, 81–82
estimating, 36–37, 52–54, 66–67, 81–82, 109–111

© Great Source. Copying is prohibited.

length, 36–37, 66–67, 115–117

metric, 66–67, 109–111

pan balance, 81–82

perimeter, 95–97, 124–126

square unit, 94–95, 124–126

temperature, 44–45

time, 43–44, 59, 72–73, 100–101, 113–115, 130–131

tool, 66–67, 81–82

volume, 52–54, 109–110

weight, 81–82

Mental math, 21–23, 34–36, 50–52, 57–59, 63–66, 72, 79–80, 94–95, 108–109, 113, 122–124, 136–137

Meter, 66–67

Metric unit

capacity, 109–110

length, 66–67

Milliliter, 109–110

Million, 21–23, 50–52, 136–137

Mixed number, 36–37, 52–56, 68–70, 81–82, 126–128

Money, 21–23, 34–36, 42, 50–52, 57–59, 63–66, 68–70, 72, 79–80, 87–88, 94–95, 99–100, 108–109, 113, 122–124, 136–137

Multiplication

common multiples, 40–41, 56–57, 70–71, 84–86, 97–98, 111–112, 128–130, 137–139

factors, 18–20, 23–26, 40–41, 56–57, 70–71, 84–86, 97–98

facts, 18–20, 23–26, 40–41, 50–52, 56–57, 70–71, 79–80, 84–86, 97–98, 111–112, 128–130

fractions, 38–40, 52–56, 68–70, 82–84

mixed numbers, 126–128

multiples, 18–20, 23–26, 32–34, 40–41, 43–44, 48–52, 56–57, 62–63, 70–71, 79–80, 84–86, 92–94, 97–98, 106–108, 111–112, 128–130, 137–139

percents, 57–59

power of ten, 63–66, 97–98, 122–124, 136–137

product, 18–20

whole numbers, 40–41, 56–57, 62–66, 72–73, 84–86, 92–94, 97–98, 111–112, 122–124, 136–139

Number(s)

comparing and ordering, 36–37

consecutive, 79–80, 120–122

even, 18–20, 23–26, 56–57, 62, 122–124, 124–126

expanded notation, 34–36, 50–52, 79–80, 108–109

greater, 122–124, 136–137

millions, 21–23, 50–52, 136–137

odd, 18–20, 23–26, 62, 122–124

patterns, 18–20, 32–34, 48–50, 62–63, 70–71, 76–78, 87–88, 92–94, 106–108, 111–112, 120–122, 134–136

prime, 97–98, 137–139

rounding, 50–52, 63–66, 94–95, 108–109

standard form, 108–109

triangular numbers, 120–122

word form, 108–109

Number line, 23–26, 40–41, 56–57, 70–71, 84–86, 97–98, 111–112, 128–130, 137–139

Number sense, 21–23, 34–36, 50–52, 62, 79–80

Operation. *See* Addition, Subtraction, Multiplication, *or* Division.

Ounce, 81–82

Pattern

extending, 18–20, 32–34, 48–50, 62–63, 76–78, 92–94, 106–108, 120–122, 134–136

identifying, 18–20, 32–34, 48–50, 62–63, 76–78, 92–94, 106–108, 120–122, 134–136

predicting, 18–20, 32–34, 44–45, 48–50, 62–63, 76–78, 92–94, 106–108, 120–122, 134–136

Percent, 57–59, 87–88

Perimeter, 94–95, 124–126

Perpendicular line, 62–63

Pint, 52–54

© Great Source. Copying is prohibited.

Place value

decimal, 42, 57–59, 66–70

understanding, 21–23, 34–36, 50–52, 63–67, 79–80, 94–95, 108–109, 113, 122–124, 128–130, 136–137

Plane shape. *See* Geometry.

Polygon. *See* Geometry.

Pound, 81–82

Prime, 97–98, 137–139

Probability

compound event, 101–103

event, 28–29, 101–103

likelihood of an event, 28–29, 101–103

organizing results of experiments, 28–29, 101–103

outcomes, 28–29, 101–103

performing simple experiments, 28–29, 101–103

prediction and, 28–29, 50–52, 101–103

theoretical probability, 101–103

Problem solving

act it out, 63–66, 87–88, 92–94

compare strategies, 36–37, 92–94, 111–112, 122–124

find a pattern, 63–66, 137–139

guess and check, 63–66, 92–94, 95–97, 122–124

logical reasoning, 18–20, 48–50, 87–88, 92–94, 122–124, 134–136

make a list, 40–41, 87–88, 92–94

number stories, 38–40, 122–124

use simpler numbers, 66

Product. *See* Multiplication.

Properties, 23–26, 40–41, 62, 84–86, 97–98, 120–122

Quadrilateral

classifying, 32–34, 134–136

interior angle, 32–34, 48–50, 106–108, 134–136

parallelogram, 32–34, 106–108, 134–136

rectangle, 18–20, 32–34, 48–50, 76–78, 106–108, 124–126, 134–136

rhombus, 32–34, 106–108, 134–136

square, 18–20, 32–34, 48–50, 76–78, 106–108, 134–136

trapezoid, 32–34, 106–108

Quart, 52–54

Reasoning

logical, 18–20, 40–41, 44–45, 48–50, 115–117, 134–136

observing patterns, 18–20, 40–41, 44–45, 48–50, 115–117, 134–136

recognizing relevant information, 40–41, 44–45, 48–50, 115–117, 134–136

Rectangle, 18–20, 48–50, 76–78, 124–126

Rectangular prism, 76–78

Reflection (flip), 32–34

Right angle, 18–20, 48–50, 62–63, 92–94, 134–136

Right triangle, 106–108

Rotation (turn), 18–20, 32–34, 48–50, 92–94

Rounding, 50–52, 63–66, 92–94, 108–109

Shape. *See* Geometry.

Simplest form, 36–40, 126–128

Slide. *See* Translation.

Solid. *See* Three-dimensional shape.

Square, 18–20, 48–50, 95–97, 106–108, 124–126, 134–136

Statistics. *See also* Graph *and* Probability.

mean (average), 79–80, 115–117

median, 115–117

mode, 115–117

range, 115–117

Stem-and-Leaf Plot, 45

Subtraction

estimating differences, 136–137

fractions, 70

money, 57–59, 108–109

whole numbers, 57–59, 62, 92–94, 108–109, 136–137

© Great Source. Copying is prohibited.

Table

organizing information, 23–26, 32–36, 50–52, 70–71, 76–78, 87–88, 136–137

tally table, 139

Three-dimensional shape

cone, 76–78

cube, 76–78

cylinder, 76–78, 109–111

prism, 76–78

pyramid, 76–78

rectangular solid, 76–78

sphere, 76–78

Time

calendar, 18–20, 32–34, 48–50, 62–63, 76–78, 92–94, 106–108, 120–122, 134–136

hour, 43–44, 59, 72–73, 100–101, 113–115, 130–131

minute, 43–44, 59, 72–73, 100–101, 113–115, 130–131

year, 18–20, 32–34, 48–50, 62–63, 76–78, 92–94, 106–108, 120–122, 134–136

Translation (slide), 32–34, 48–50, 76–78

Triangle

acute, 32–34, 106–108

classifying, 32–34, 106–108

equilateral, 32–34, 106–108, 134–136

isosceles, 32–34, 106–108

obtuse, 32–34, 106–108

right, 106–108

scalene, 32–34, 106–108

Turn. *See* Rotation.

Two-dimensional shape. *See* Geometry.

Visual learning, 23–28, 36–40, 42, 56–57, 82–84, 111–112, 115–117

Volume, 52–54, 109–111

Weight, 81–82

Yard, 36–37

Zero, 23–26, 62, 70–71, 92–94, 99–100

© Great Source. Copying is prohibited.